Human Resource Management in a Hospitality Environment

Human Resource Management in a Hospitality Environment

Jerald W. Chesser, EdD

*Professor, Collins College of Hospitality Management,
California State Polytechnic University,
Pomona, California, USA*

Apple Academic Press Inc. | Apple Academic Press Inc.
3333 Mistwell Crescent | 9 Spinnaker Way
Oakville, ON L6L 0A2 | Waretown, NJ 08758
Canada | USA

© 2016 by Apple Academic Press, Inc.
First issued in paperback 2021
Exclusive worldwide distribution by CRC Press, a member of Taylor & Francis Group
No claim to original U.S. Government works

ISBN-13: 978-1-77463-591-9 (pbk)
ISBN-13: 978-1-77188-300-9 (hbk)

Library and Archives Canada Cataloguing in Publication

Chesser, Jerald W., author
Human resource management in a hospitality environment / Jerald W. Chesser, EdD, Professor, Collins College of Hospitality Management, California State Polytechnic University, Pomona, California, USA.

Includes bibliographical references and index.
Issued in print and electronic formats.
ISBN 978-1-77188-300-9 (hardcover).--ISBN 978-1-77188-301-6 (pdf)
1. Hospitality industry--Personnel management--Textbooks. I. Title.

TX911.3.P4C44 2016   647.94068'3   C2016-901607-2   C2016-901608-0

Library of Congress Cataloging-in-Publication Data

Names: Chesser, Jerald W., author.
Title: Human resource management in a hospitality environment / Jerald W. Chesser, EdD.
Description: Toronto ; New Jersey : Apple Academic Press, 2015. | Includes bibliographical references and index.
Identifiers: LCCN 2016010354| ISBN 9781771883009 (hardcover : acid-free paper) |
ISBN 9781771883016 (eBook)
Subjects: LCSH: Hospitality industry--Personnel management.
Classification: LCC TX911.3.P4 C44 2015 | DDC 647.94068/3--dc23
LC record available at http://lccn.loc.gov/2016010354

Apple Academic Press also publishes its books in a variety of electronic formats. Some content that appears in print may not be available in electronic format. For information about Apple Academic Press products, visit our website at **www.appleacademic-press.com** and the CRC Press website at **www.crcpress.com**

Contents

Dedication

To Edison who makes the future bright.

List of Abbreviations

ACA	Affordable Care Act
ADA	American with Disabilities Act
ADEA	Age Discrimination in Employment Act
BFOQ	Bona Fide Occupational Qualification
CEO	Chief Executive Officer
DOL	U.S. Department of Labor
EAP	Employee Assistance Program
EEOC	Equal Employment Opportunity Commission
FLSA	Fair Labor Standards Act
FMLA	Family Medical Leave Act
FSLA	Fair Labor Standards Act
FTEE	Full-Time Equivalent Employees
GDP	Gross Domestic Production
HCS	Hazard Communication Standard
LMRA	Labor-Management Relations Act
LMRDA	Labor-Management Reporting and Disclosure Act
MBO	Management by Objective
MBWA	Management by walking-wandering around
MV	Minimum Value
NLRA	National Labor Relations Act
NLRB	National Labor Relations Board
OJT	On-the-Job Training
OLMS	Office of Labor-Management Standards
OLMS	The Office of Labor-Management Standards
OSH	Occupational Safety and Health Act
OSHA	Occupational Safety and Health Administration

PPACA	Patient Protection and Affordable Care Act
PPACA	The Patient Protection and Affordable Care Act
ROI	Return on Investment
TQM	Total Quality Management
UC	Unemployment Compensation Program
USCIS	The United States Citizenship and Immigration Services
WTTC	World Travel & Tourism Council

About the Author

Jerald Chesser is an internationally recognized author, speaker, and educator. He is a professor in the Collins College of Hospitality Management at California State Polytechnic University, Pomona. He has taught human resource management and leadership for the hospitality industry at the university level for over 20 years. He has taught culinary arts at the high school, community college, and university level. He has served as Dean of the Chef John Folse Culinary Institute at Nichols State University and Interim Dean of the Collins College of Hospitality Management and College of Extended University at California State Polytechnic University, Pomona. His areas of publication and research include human resource management, leadership, and culinary arts.

Dr. Chesser has earned certification from the National Restaurant Association as a Foodservice Management Professional and the American Culinary Federation as an Executive Chef and Culinary educator. He is a trustee of the National Restaurant Association Educational Foundation and was cocreator of and has served since its inception as lead judge for the National ProStart Invitational competition. He has received numerous honors including induction into the National Restaurant Association Educational Foundation's College of Diplomates and the American Academy of Chefs. He has received the Henry award from the American Culinary Federation and the Research Chef's Association's Lifetime Achievement award.

Prior to entering academe and consulting he spent more than a decade in restaurant operations, including ownership of a successful restaurant and off-premise catering company. His publications include *The Art and Science of Culinary Preparation* and *The World of Culinary Management: Leadership and Development of Human Resources*, 5th Edition.

Acknowledgments

I gratefully acknowledge the following individuals for their assistance and guidance in the development and completion of chapters of this textbook:

Gary Hamilton, Special Assistant to the President, California State Polytechnic University, Pomona; Jacqueline Bastawroos, future hospitality leader; the students of the Collins College of Hospitality Management, California State Polytechnic University Pomona; and last but not the least, Marla Chesser, my wife and greatest resource in all things.

Preface

Preparing individuals for the responsibilities associated with managing human resources in today's rapidly changing hospitality industry is critical to their success and the long-term success of the industry as a whole. Achieving this goal is not easy when teaching any subject today is challenging because the student is accustomed to information coming in compressed pieces accompanied by rapid feedback. I have developed this textbook to meet these challenges. The information it contains is current and also presents potential areas of change. The textbook addresses the processes, procedures, and laws, as well as, the impact of environment and attitudes on building the individual and the team to achieve desired outcomes. The content is presented in segments that allow the student to concentrate on one area of knowledge at a time. The support materials provided make it possible to constantly reinforce what the students read in the chapter and measure their comprehension with rapid feedback on their success.

This textbook and the supporting materials were piloted with over 600 students. The students provided a high level of comment on the materials that contributed greatly to the final materials provided in this work particularly in the area of clarity of information, test questions, and case content. The textbook is designed for use in a lecture, hybrid, or fully online course format. It has been successfully used with an online learning platform in a hybrid course format.

This textbook is designed for today's student. It is focused on the subject matter with no addition of ancillary material such as opinion or industry leader pieces. It is left to the teacher to enrich their course with those types of information. The students involved in the pilot found this format both functional and effective. The students who complete this textbook will have a solid knowledge of the management of human resources in the hospitality industry.

—*Jerald Chesser, EdD, CEC, FMP, CCE, AAC*

Management   1

CHAPTER OUTLINE

- ▶ Introduction
- ▶ The Hospitality Customer Defined
- ▶ Philosophies, Concepts, and Strategies of Management
- ▶ Scientific Management: A Historical Perspective
- ▶ Management by Objectives
- ▶ The Excellence Movement
- ▶ Reengineering
- ▶ Total Quality Management
- ▶ Contemporary Management Theories
- ▶ Change
- ▶ Conclusions
- ▶ Summary

LEARNING OBJECTIVES

When you complete reading this chapter, you will be able to:

- ▶ Define the customer within the wider context of the hospitality industry.
- ▶ Recall all the principles and philosophies of scientific management, management by objective (MBO), reengineering, the elements of the excellence movement, and total quality management (TQM).
- ▶ Identify contingency, systems, and chaos management theories.

- ▶ Recall the development, strengths, and weaknesses of different concepts of management.
- ▶ Recall information about Deming's 14 quality principles to hospitality management.
- ▶ Apply a basic knowledge of the principles of change.

Introduction

In this chapter, the term used for the professional and academic field that we discuss is "hospitality industry and hospitality management." Hospitality management is defined as the field of study of managing restaurants, other foodservice operations, hotels, destination attractions, and related business or government enterprises. These activities are sometimes grouped under the heading "travel and tourism industry or management."

The act of management is defined as (1) the conducting or supervising of something and (2) the judicious use of means to accomplish an end.[1] In many ways, supervision and management are the same. Further, in many ways they differ too. The difference is in the level of responsibility with special reference to planning, expenditure of resources, hiring, and firing. Supervision can be limited to just that, that is, supervising. By supervising, we mean watching to make certain the job is done correctly and on time. The term, "management," certainly implies an assumption of responsibility beyond just supervising. In this chapter, we specifically address theories of management and change.

Traditionally, the hospitality industry has been a follower rather than a leader in the area of management theories. Hence, most management models were developed with the manufacturing industry in mind. The hospitality industry is a people-oriented industry. It sells products and services to and makes a profit from people.

It has been said that a restaurant is a manufacturing plant directly attached to a distribution center and retail outlet. In the hotel business the management and staff are constantly recycling space for sale and immediate use by the consumer. In the theme park business, it is experiences that are being sold. The equipment and location make the experience possible and it is the experience the consumer buys. Hospitality management is the constant management of the production, distribution, and sale in tandem with the consumer experiencing the product immediately.

This is very different from manufacturing where production is removed from sales and consumption/use of the product.

In hospitality businesses, the consumer reacts immediately to the quality of the product, the service offered, and all other factors impacting their experience. The consumer's reaction is communicated through the chains of production and delivery often requiring analysis and possibly changes. At each point in that chain, the human factor impacts the process of analysis and change. Consequently, it is understandable that hospitality management professionals, the owners, operators, and managers, have been less inclined to embrace theories of management that focus on manufacturing without consideration of the distribution and interaction with the consumer. According to the World Travel and Tourism Council, the travel and tourism industry has outperformed the global economy in 2012 – growing faster than manufacturing, retail, financial services and communications. The industry has grown its total contribution to GDP by 3% and increased the number of jobs by five million to 260 million. It means that, for the first time, one in 11 of all jobs in the world is now supported by travel and tourism. More than 10% of all new jobs created in 2012 were from the industry.

According to the World Travel & Tourism Council's (WTTC) economic research, in 2012, travel and tourism's total economic contribution in 2012 prices, taking account of its direct, indirect and induced impacts, was US$6.6 trillion in gross domestic production (GDP) which was a rise of US$500 billion year-on-year, US$765 billion in investment and US$1.2 trillion in exports. This contribution represents 9% of total GDP, 5% of total investment and 5% of world exports.[2]

The growth of the hospitality industry shows no signs of slowing. The need for management to be well prepared for future challenges is great. The most successful company in the 21st century and beyond will require the highest quality management and leadership.

The Hospitality Customer Defined

A hospitality customer is any person of any demographic group frequenting any commercial hotel or resort, food service establishment, theme park, cruise ship, or transportation operation who is prepared to pay for services and products that are prepared by friendly, caring, and efficient professionals utilizing quality products and outstanding

Who is the customer?
Any of these at any age:
Casual restaurant diner
Hotel/motel restaurant guest
Cafeteria diner
Room-service guest
Hospital patient
Senior living home guest
School or college diner
Catered party guest
Airline, train, or cruise passenger
Fast-food diner
Theme and recreation park diner
Banquet diner
Office/factory diner
Upscale white tablecloth restaurant diner
Delicatessen and supermarket customer

FIGURE 1.1 Who is the Customer?

skills in a safe, sanitary environment and served by friendly, caring, and efficient professionals. Such a customer is more clearly defined in Figure 1.1.

Philosophies, Concepts, and Theories of Management

In recent years, there have been many theories, philosophies, strategies, and concepts developed and put forward to assist business organizations, managers, and supervisors to restructure, refocus, and plan for change. All of these contain within them the elements of change, customer focus, quality, and leadership. However, many of these theories have their roots in the manufacturing industries. The hospitality industry is not immune to the actions and effects of these business strategies and philosophies. The main thrust of this book is toward human resource management rather than business management; nevertheless, many of these philosophies, strategies, and theories contain elements that directly impact the management of both the business and the human resources related to the business.

Scientific Management

Discussion of this topic revolves around time-and-motion studies. The principles of scientific management were put forward by the industrial engineer Frederick Winslow Taylor around the turn of this century. Taylor held that human performance could be defined and controlled through work standards and rules. He advocated the use of time-and-motion studies to reduce jobs to simple, separate steps to be performed over and over again.

Scientific management evolved during an era of mass immigration. The workplace was being flooded with unskilled, uneducated workers, and it was efficient to employ them in large numbers. This was also a period of labor strife, and Taylor believed that his system would reduce conflict and eliminate the arbitrary use of power because so little discretion would be left to either the workers or the owners and managers. The methods used included careful selection of workers who were deemed to be competent, conforming, and obedient and a constant oversight of work. This system caused friction between workers and management. Consequently, unions were the outgrowth of such friction. It is during Taylor's period that the phrase, "a fair day's work" originated.

Scientific management provided employers a system that not only increased productivity but also reduced the number of workers. It was also rule bound, hierarchical, and top heavy with corporate structure. This began the era of standardization that many today believe contributed to the slow recognition of the changing nature of employees and the methods of managing them.

Management by Objectives

Peter Drucker in 1954 was the first to introduce MBO as a philosophy of management. It seeks to judge the performance of employees on the basis of their success in the achievement of set objectives established through consultation with managers and supervisors. Performance improvement efforts under MBO are focused upon goals to be achieved by employees rather than upon the activities performed or the methods by which employees achieve these goals.

MBO is part of a systemwide set of organizational goals that begins with setting the organization's common goals and objectives and returns to that point. The system acts as a goal-setting process whereby goals are set for the organization, individual departments, individual managers, supervisors, and employees. A distinct feature of an MBO is a broad statement of employee responsibilities prepared by the supervisor, reviewed, and jointly modified until both are satisfied with them. The goals are accompanied by a detailed account of the actions the employee proposes to take in order to realize the goals. Periodic review assesses the progress that the employee has made. At the end of the review period, the employee does a self-appraisal of whether the previously set goals have been achieved.

Further, MBO enabled managers and supervisors to plan and measure not only of their own performance but also that of the employees. It shifted the emphasis from appraisal to self-analysis. The major criticisms of MBO included the methods by which individuals achieved their goals. Factors such as cooperation, adaptability, and concern were not included as part of MBO rationale. Another criticism of MBO was that employee-rated success is tied to issues that ultimately are not directed toward customer satisfaction. Another problem with MBO is its link to employee evaluation and rewards, which causes conflict between the supervisor's roles as judge and leader.

Dr. Edward Deming was a contemporary of Drucker who was particularly critical of MBO. Deming considered MBO to be management by fear[3] because of its reliance on performance evaluations. He also believed that MBO discourages risk taking, builds fear, and undermines team work. In a team, it is difficult to tell who does what. Under MBO, people work for themselves, not the organization.

The Excellence Movement

If it "ain't" broke, fix it anyway.[4] The "excellence" movement began to emerge with Peters and Waterman with the publication of their book, *In Search of Excellence*, in 1982. This growth of the movement continued with the publication and broad-based acceptance of Peters and Austin's book in 1985, in *Passion for Excellence and Thriving on Chaos* by Peters published in 1988. These books and their strategies blended perfectly into what was happening in the world of business as the pace of change gathered momentum. The basic business and management philosophies put forward by these authors drove to make excellence in the management of product, people, and service a first priority. These works proposed many innovative approaches to management. They focused attention on the "customer revolution." This "revolution" was a customer who expected to be listened to and have products designed "for them" for "their wants and needs" and not those of the company. This drove a need to gain a competitive advantage, to become more effective. According to Peters, "We must end excuse making and look for new organizational models fit for the new world. New survivors will welcome change rather than resist it, and realize that people power, not robot power is our only choice.[5]" Figure 1.2 shows the primary factors at work in an organization if it focuses its survival and growth on the "excellence" and "thriving on chaos" philosophies.

The excellence movement considered people (personnel) as the organizations' prime source of "value addition" in customer interaction. Personnel could never be overtrained or involved too much. An outcome of this view of personnel is the flattening of the organizational structure. Layers of middle management and barriers to communication across the organization are reduced. Peters believes that "front-line supervisors as we know them give way to self-managed teams. Middle managers become facilitators rather than turf guardians. Leaders become levers of change and preachers of vision.[6]" Peters also states that strategies, ideas, and concepts come from the bottom-up approach. Staff functions support the line rather than the other way around. Each person has a valuable role in this management model.

Requirements

for the

Organization's Survival and Growth

* A bias toward action

* A simple form and a lean staff

* Continued contact with customers

* Productivity improvement via people

* Operational autonomy to encourage

entrepreneurship

* One key business value

* Emphasis on doing what they know best

* Simultaneous loose and tight controls

FIGURE 1.2   Requirements for the Organization's Survival and Growth.

Management by wandering around (MBWA) is an outgrowth of the excellence movement. Good manager's walk around and see what is happening in the operation. Ed Carlson, former chief executive officer (CEO) of the United Airlines, upon taking over the United Airlines, realized it was a service business that had lost sight of the customer. He introduced MBWA style of business management and instilled a hands-on customer focus. He said, "In a service business, you can't have a rigid set of rules. You can have some guidelines, but you must allow people the freedom to make a different interpretation.[7]"

Reengineering

Reengineering essentially calls for a radical rethinking of the ways in which organizations do business. Business reengineering involves putting aside much of what has been taught about industrial management for the past 200 years.[8] It has been described as "an approach to planning and controlling change.[9]"

In reengineering, work units change from functional departments to process teams. Jobs change from simple tasks to multidimensional work. The roles of people change from being controlled to being empowered. The focus of performance measures and compensation shifts from activity to results. Values change from protective to productive. Organizational structures change from hierarchical to flat. The role of executives changes from scorekeepers to leaders.[10] Part of the reengineering process is also about positioning within different markets. This planned positioning determines what should be reengineered.

Reengineering involves integrating tasks into processes and reorganizing the company around them. Often this reorganization results in collapsing or doing away with departments. The format becomes more collective with people united and with a common focus, such as a project. One of the outcomes can be a reduction in the need for continuous checking and controls. Conceivably, in this scenario, chefs could become restaurant or unit managers responsible not only for supervision and management of the kitchen but also for complete management of a foodservice operation. Additionally, titles and individual lines of demarcation can disappear.

Total Quality Management

The theory of total quality control was first espoused by Armand Feigeinbaum in his 1951 book *Quality Control: Principles, Practice and Administration*, released in 1961 as *Total Quality Control* by Joseph Juran. Philip B. Crosby and Kaoru Ishikawa laid the foundations of total quality management, a management theory that could be effectively applied to in the hospitality industry. At the heart of total quality control is the conviction that it is possible to achieve error-free quality product most of the time. This assertion is phrased in various ways as getting it right the first time, working smarter, or zero defects. When total quality control was introduced in the United States in 1981 by the United States Navy, the word "control" had been changed to "management."

TQM is not only about external customers, it is also about internal customers. In his book, *The Essence of Total Quality Management*, John Bank[11] discusses the internal customer. He defines this person as the person in a company who receives the work of another and then adds his or her contribution to the product or service before passing it on to someone else. In a restaurant, the chef has levels of internal customers in the culinary brigade and the service staff and the chef must meet their requirements if they are all to please the guest. In a hotel the director of engineering has internal customers in the manager of housekeeping, food and beverage manager, and the chef and must meet their requirements in order for them to please the guest.

In many previous managerial models, control was more of an issue than coaching and team building. The theory of quality management that came to be called TQM is about team building and investment in the development of people. The TQM movement peaked in the mid-1990s and the use of the terms total quality management and TQM have become marginal in the discussion of management theory. The concept of commitment by a company to total quality as defined by zero errors in all aspects of the operation through team building and investment in the development of people has not diminished in importance to the hospitality industry as a management design. The concept of developing a workplace culture that focuses on quality in every aspect of the operation continues to be central to a hospitality operation's success.

W. Edward Deming's 14 "quality" principles[12] are listed hereunder. It is upon these principles that much of the quality movement is based. Deming recommended that each company or organization work out its own interpretations and adapt them to their corporate culture. While Deming's quality principles were primarily directed toward the manufacturing industry, they have many applications to quality in the hospitality industry too.

1. Create constancy of purpose toward the improvement of product and service.
2. Management must take the leadership role in promoting change.
3. Stop dependence on inspection to achieve quality. Build quality into the product in the beginning.
4. Move to a single supplier for any one item. Create long-term relationships with suppliers.
5. Improve constantly the system of production and service and thus decrease costs. Institute training on the job.
6. Institute leadership. The aim of supervision should be to help people and machines do a better job.
7. Drive out fear, so that everyone may work effectively.
8. Break down barriers between departments. Promote team building as people from different departments work together to solve problems and improve quality.
9. Eliminate slogans, exhortations, and targets for the workforce, asking for zero defects and new levels of productivity.
10. Eliminate work quotas: substitute leadership.
11. Remove barriers that rob managers, engineers, and the hourly paid worker of their right to pride of workmanship.
12. Change the emphasis from numbers to quality.
13. Institute a vigorous program of education and self-improvement.
14. Put everyone in the company to work to accomplish the transformation. Make it an all-pervasive common goal and support it.[13]

The main aim of Deming's philosophy is empowerment of the individual. The lesson is that we have to empower all our people with dignity, knowledge, and skills so that they may contribute. They have to feel secure, be trained so that they can do the work properly, and be encouraged so that the organization can develop and grow.

Contemporary Management Theory

Contemporary theories of management[14] attempt to account for and interpret the rapidly changing nature of the business organization and business environment in today's world. Contingency theory might be called the "it depends" theory. Contingency theory calls on managers to take into account all aspects of the current situation and act on those aspects that are critical to the situation at hand when making decisions. Managers using this theory of management make decisions that "depend" on the current circumstances.

Systems theory proposes that a system is a collection of parts joined to accomplish a goal. Any action taken with one part of a system ultimately affects the total system. For example, removing a spark plug from an engine changes how the engine runs. In an organization, a change impacting one part of the organization affects the total organization. Systems theory requires supervisors and managers to have a broader perspective of the organization. Managers and supervisor are driven to address issues in relation to the total organization. This is an important change in management perspective. In the past, managers have generally taken one part of an organization and focused on it. The result was often actions that had a positive impact locally but a negative impact on the larger organization. Systems theory is particularly applicable to the hospitality industry. In a hotel, the actions of the housekeeping department directly impact the ability of the rooms' department to hire out rooms and accommodate guests. In a restaurant, the actions of the kitchen directly impact the dining room and the actions of the dining room, in turn, directly affect the kitchen. The more changes in these areas take into account both areas the greater the potential for changes to be positive both for team members and customers. Chaos theory is more of a scientific theory for the world and life in general. The concept of chaos theory may have some application to management as businesses continue to grow. Chaos theory implies that events are rarely controlled. In fact, it says that as the complexity of the system grows the more volatile it becomes and greater the energy required to maintain a semblance of stability. As more energy is expended, more structure is required to maintain the system. This pattern continues until the system splits, combines with another complex system, or falls apart entirely. Does this sound like a company that you are familiar with? Chaos theory may be used most frequently with reference to biological systems, but it appears that its application to management is not unreasonable.

Change

Change is a key component of management for continuous improvement. Studies have shown that people do not basically resist change; however, they resist being changed, and participation empowers change.[15] A major factor to be considered by managers when changing the hospitality operation is the people affected by the change. Resistance to change within any organization is as common as the need for change. After management decides on making changes, they typically meet with employee resistance, usually aimed at preventing the change from occurring. This resistance generally exists because team members fear some personal loss, such as a reduction in personal prestige, a disturbance of established social and working relationships, and personal failure due to an inability to carry out new job responsibilities as a result of the proposed change.

Since resistance accompanies proposed change, managers must be able to reduce the effects of this resistance so as to ensure the success of needed quality improvements. People need time to evaluate the proposed change before implementation. Elimination of time to evaluate how proposed changes may affect individual situations usually results in automatic opposition to change. Those team members who will be affected by change must be kept informed of the type of change being considered and the probability that the change will be adopted. When fear of personal loss related to a proposed change is reduced, opposition to the change is reduced. Individuals should receive information that will help them answer the change-related questions shown in Figure 1.3.

If the manager follows some simple guidelines, then implementing change will be less stressful for everyone. The following steps will assist in getting team members to "buy into" the change:

- Inform those concerned in advance so that they can think about the implications of the change and its effect on their position within the operation.
- Explain the overall objectives of the change, the reasons for it, and the sequence in which it will occur.
- Show people how the change will benefit them. Be honest with the team. If they are not to be part of the future plans, tell them and provide support and ample time for them to secure new positions.

Change:

Questions Team Members Will Ask

* Will I lose my job?

* Will my old skills become obsolete?

* Will I be capable of being effective under the new system?

* Will my power and prestige decline?

* Will I receive more responsibility than I want?

* Will I have to work longer hours?

FIGURE 1.3   Change: Questions Team Members will Ask.

- Invite those affected by the change to participate at all stages of the process.
- Allow time and demonstrate patience as the team adapts to new work or quality-driven changes.
- Provide for constant communication and feedback during the changes.
- Demonstrate constant commitment and loyalty to the change. Indicate confidence in the team and each individual's ability to implement the change.

The most powerful tool for reducing resistance to change is a positive attitude toward the change and the anticipated outcome of the change by the manager. As with all change, time should be taken for evaluation, to examine what needs to be modified, and what can be added to increase the effectiveness of operation. Evaluation of change often involves watching for symptoms that further change is necessary, particularly if team members are more oriented toward the past than the future or if they are more concerned with their own "pecking order" than with meeting the challenges of quality. A challenge for the manager is the immediate and constant negative responders. These are the individuals that react negatively to change of any type. Examples of statements that "kill-off" creative ideas and change are shown in Figure 1.4. Managers should listen carefully for these types of remarks

---

Statements that Kill Change

* Don't be ridiculous.
* We tried that before.
* It costs too much.
* You must be crazy.
* That's beyond our responsibility.
* It's too radical a change.
* We don't have the time.
* We've never done it before.
* Let's get back to reality.
* We're not ready for that.
* We'd be laughed at.
* We did all right without it.
* Let's shelve it for the time being.
* It's not practical for an organization like ours.
* It's too hard to get accepted.

FIGURE 1.4   Statements that Kill Change.

and monitor the dissent within the group. This dissent should be met with a positive approach and the benefits of the new ideas pointed out.

Conclusions

This brief overview of management theory is intended only to give a glimpse of what has shaped different directions in human resource management. Each theory has had its own champions at various times. A noteworthy change is the subtle yet vitally important shift of designation from "personnel managers" to "human resources managers" and the greater emphasis placed on the development of people. This shift clearly underlines the philosophy that people must be led, not managed. This overview provides insight and understanding of change. It also shows that workers have changed; they can be more than mindless, uninterested employees who need constant control and supervision. Supervision, management, and leadership in the business is evolving and changing. Managers who realize that not all change is bad will succeed in the future hospitality industry.

Summary

The theories of management have evolved from scientific management, TQM, and MBO to the contemporary systems theory. The theories shape the operation of the business. Change is a constant and in business has moved toward development of people. Understanding the elements of change and the fear with which people approach change is critical to moving toward implementation of change and success of the business.

Study Questions

1. Define management.
2. How is the customer defined in the hospitality industry?
3. For each of the following management theories state how it developed, its philosophy and principles, and strengths and weaknesses:

    i. Scientific management

    ii. Management by objective

    iii. Reengineering

    iv. Excellence movement

    v. TQM

    vi. Contingency

    vii. Systems

    viii. Chaos

4. List Deming's 14 quality principles.

5. Discuss the application of Deming's quality principles to hospitality management.

6. State three principles of change.

Case Studies

The case studies listed below relate to the information presented in this chapter and reading, answering the case study questions and participating in discussion of a case will reinforce and expand what you have learned in this chapter. All case studies are provided in this text after the last chapter.

    Bill & Jean Restaurant

    Naples by the Sea

    Prairie View Country Club

    Shady Lane Inn

    Shandong House Restaurant

    Shepherd Mountain Hotel

    Stone Lion Hotel and Conference Center

    Summit Resort

Notes

1. Merriam-Webster. Retrieved July 14, 2014, from http://www.merriam-webster.com/dictionary/management.

2. World Travel and Tourism Council. Global Travel & Tourism industry defies economic uncertainty by outperforming the global economy in 2012—and

predicted to do it again in 2013, February, 2013. Retrieved February 12, 2014, from http://www.hospitalitynet.org/news/4059643.html

3. Aguay, R. (1991). *Dr. Deming* (p. 243). New York: Carol.

4. Peters, P. (1988). *Thriving on chaos: Handbook for a management revolution* (p. 3). New York: Harper & Row.

5. Ibid., p. 357.

6. Ibid., p. 358.

7. Peters, T. (1983). *Putting excellence into management: Managing behavior in organizations* (p. 603). New York: McGraw-Hill.

8. Hammer, M., & Champy, J. (1993). *Reengineering the corporation: A manifesto for business revolution* (p. 2). New York: Harper Collins.

9. Morris, D., & Brandon, J. (1993). *Re-engineering your business* (p. 13). New York: McGraw-Hill.

10. Hammer, M., & Champy, J. (1993). *Reengineering the corporation: A manifesto for business revolution* (p. 79). New York: Harper Collins.

11. Walton, M. (1986). *The Deming management method* (p. 34). New York: Putnam.

12. Deming, E. (1989). *Out of crisis* (p. 111). Cambridge, MA: MIT Center for Advanced Engineering Study.

13. Walton, M. (1986). *The Deming management method* (p. 34). New York: Putnam.

14. Mcnamara, C. *Brief overview of contemporary theories in management.* Retrieved June 12, 2007, from http://www.managementhelp.org/mgmnt/cntmpory.htm

15. Belasco, J. (1990). *Teaching the elephant to dance* (p. 49). New York: Crown.

Supervision 2

CHAPTER OUTLINE

LEARNING OBJECTIVES

When you complete reading this chapter, you should be able to:

- ▶ Define the term supervisor
- ▶ Identify and discuss the attributes a successful supervisor
- ▶ Identify elements of ethics and professionalism in supervision
- ▶ Identify and apply the elements of supervision
- ▶ Define and apply the concept of authority
- ▶ Identify elements of the evolution of supervision

Introduction

The first step to becoming a supervisor is work ethic. The individual selected to be a supervisor is at first a good worker. Beyond the first step, qualifications for the supervisor's job are impressive. Whatever position a supervisor holds in an organization, he/she must be technically competent. They need to know all aspects of the positions they hold and the positions they supervise. These include the processes, equipment, and quality standards. The supervisor needs to know the company policies and procedures and applicable laws and regulations for the tasks being done. However, in general, supervisors fail because they are unable to get others to work effectively. They fail principally because they lack good people-management skills.

In the hospitality industry, the supervisor's ultimate goal is guest satisfaction. The supervisor is constantly working with others to satisfy guests. They work to establish an atmosphere of trust and a workplace in which the golden rule is the standard against which all conduct is validated. By providing the direction, assistance, and encouragement required for the staff to give their best, the prime objective of guest satisfaction will be realized.

Defining Supervision

Simply put, a supervisor is anyone in the position of directing the work of others and who has the authority that goes with this responsibility. The legal status is defined by the federal Taft–Hartley Act (1947). The act states that a supervisor is:

> . . . any individual having authority, in the interest of the employer, to hire, transfer, suspend, lay off, recall, promote, discharge, assign, reward or discipline other employees, or responsibility to direct them, or to adjust their grievances, or effectively to recommend such action, if in connection with the foregoing the exercise of such authority is not merely routine or clerical in nature, but requires the use of independent judgment.

The knowledge and skills required to be a successful supervisor fall into four broad skill categories: (1) personal, (2) interpersonal, (3) technical, and (4) administrative. To be a supervisor, the individual needs the vision to know what to do. They need the necessary skills to know how to do it. The supervisor must have the ability to get it done by empowering other people to carry out quality standards of performance. The supervisor plans, organizes, communicates, trains, coaches, evaluates, and leads. The supervisor must motivate the team members to meet the company's goals and objectives. The goals and objectives are realized by supervising people in an effective and caring way. The supervisor accepts responsibility for providing a positive work place.

Philip Crosby, a leading management expert, states that "in the final equation, the supervisor is the person the employee sees as the company. The type of work accomplished and the attendance maintained by employees are very much indications of their relationship with the supervisor.[1]" Crosby suggests that the good supervisor can overcome, at least to some extent, the poor management practices of a weak company. At the other extreme, the weak supervisor can offset the good management practices of a good company.

Supervision is not the act of controlling; on the contrary, it is directing, coaching, and supporting the staff member. The quality of the supervisor's performance is judged by looking at a variety of factors. These factors include customer satisfaction and customer retention. The factors also include the ability of the staff to carry out the workload to meet and exceed set standards of quality. Poor supervisory skills negatively affect the quality of the guests' experience because they affect the work climate and the performance of the team member. The undesired outcome of poor supervision is unhappy staff and high attrition levels, which result in customer dissatisfaction.

Attributes of a Successful Supervisor

Nowadays, supervisors—in addition to being excellent at their job whether that is in front desk, lead cook, or some other position—must have developed a strong inventory of personal and professional qualities. An example of the supervisor's inventory of personal and professional qualities is shown in Figure 2.1. Today's supervisor is a take-charge individual but approachable. The management style that works best for the supervisor is that of coaching. According to Bill Marvin, a respected restaurant consultant and author, "Coaches help bring out natural talent and measure their own success by the success achieved by their players.[2]" As in all good coaching, the coach—working in tandem with his or her support staff—tries to get the best possible performance from the team. The coach motivates the team members. Communication and training are also critical components of coaching.

```
┌─────────────────────────────────────────────────────────────┐
│                Inventory of a Supervisor's                   │
│             Personal and Professional Qualities              │
│                                                              │
│   * Positive Personal Attitude                               │
│   * Innovativeness in dealing with problems                  │
│   * Honesty and sincerity                                    │
│   * Awareness of employee problems                           │
│   * Respect and courtesy in communicating with employees     │
│   * Impeccable personal hygiene and grooming                 │
│   * Technical competence                                     │
│   * High motivation with the ability to motivate others      │
│   * Consistency                                              │
│   * Assertive and action oriented                            │
│   * Acceptance of diversity                                  │
│   * Ability to trust others                                  │
│   * Constant search for new ways to enhance skills           │
│   * Ability to praise others when deserved                   │
│   * Leadership by example                                    │
│   * Team-building skills                                     │
│   * Loyalty to organizational goals and employees            │
│   * Ability to maintain control                              │
│   * Good listening skills                                    │
│   * Desire to please customer                                │
│   * Good persuasive skills and interest in imparting         │
│   knowledge                                                  │
└─────────────────────────────────────────────────────────────┘
```

FIGURE 2.1   Inventory of a Supervisor's Personal and Professional Qualities

The coach demonstrates respect for each team member. The coach not only manages but also leads the team. A good coach maintains an acute awareness of each staff member's strengths and weaknesses.

Supervisors need to be able to bring all these qualities to the work place. The individual must be able to coach and supervise under pressure. The supervisor should have the ability to understand the feelings, attitudes, and motives of others. The supervisor must communicate effectively. Good relations with the team members and all other departments in the company are critical. These attributes apply whether the supervisor is employed in a restaurant, hotel, institution, club, the military, education, or any other hospitality organization.

Ethics and Professionalism in Supervision

Professionalism and ethics are essential for a very effective supervisor. Ethics refers to the moral principles of individuals and society. Professionalism is the conduct or actions that characterize a profession positively. Together with professionalism, ethics is concerned with the determination of right and wrong in human behavior. The actions of the supervisor impact the staff being supervised and the management of the property. Equally important, the supervisor's actions can impact the health and safety of the public being served. The effect of the supervisor's actions can be positive or negative. "Ethical behavior is recognized as resulting in good business with increased profits and reduced turnover.[3]"

An ethical code of professional practice is necessary for both employees and supervisor. According to Jernigan, "It serves as a framework in which various other standards can be evaluated.[4]" Professional practices drive policy content. A policy is a statement of how the individual is expected to handle specific matters. Policies are devised by companies to address a number of issues. The issues include the areas of hiring or firing and confidentiality. Policies are also devised to address the evils of stealing and lying. A major concern in policy making is any action that dishonors human dignity. Actions in this area can include malicious gossip, harassment and racial, gender, or ethnic slurs.

The company should establish a code of professional practice and the supervisor should religiously follow that code in its entirety. A code must be applied fairly and without bias to all employees regardless of their position, gender, and ethnic or religious backgrounds.

To be a leader in any profession, it is necessary to model a high standard of ethics and professional practice. Workers who lack ethics and professionalism are certainly a threat. They are an obvious threat to the image of the hospitality industry. More importantly, they are a threat to the health and safety of the public. Therefore, it is understood that true hospitality professionalism will always embrace high ethical standards.

Elements of Supervision

Supervision is the most effective use of personnel and materials to realize the set goals. The goals of the supervisor focus on customer satisfaction and retention. These goals are achieved by maintaining a highly motivated, well-trained team. A major responsibility of being a supervisor is clearing away obstacles and providing the resources needed to allow the team to accomplish the declared goals and objectives. The goals and objectives must be clear and well defined.

Planning

Following the successful invasion of Europe by Allied forces during the World War II, it was suggested to the supreme commander of the successful invading forces, General Dwight D. Eisenhower that he must have had an outstanding plan to have carried out such a massive operation. The operation involved moving thousands of men and equipment with all the ancillary support of materials and men. His response to this suggestion was most enlightening: "The plan is nothing, but planning is everything.[5]"

A plan can be defined as a carefully considered and detailed program of action to achieve the desired objective. The development of a plan that can be communicated and then executed requires three steps: (1) information gathering, (2) analysis of the information, and (3) development of the program of action. The process requires the supervisor to stop, look, and listen. This allows a broader and more long-term view of the current situation and potential future situation. Planning is very different from "firefighting." Firefighting is the solving of problems as they arise without consideration of the root cause of the problems. Obviously, firefighting does not achieve long-term goals. To plan effectively, the supervisor must take time to plan.

Extensive planning is required to run a smooth, efficient hospitality operation. The major areas of planning for the supervisor are listed hereunder:

- setting and communicating standards of performance
- communicating clear job expectations
- determining training needs
- planning and forecasting workloads
- preparing employee work schedules
- ascertaining guest satisfaction levels
- planning equipment repair and replacements
- determining supply inventories
- developing employee-empowerment programs
- planning future personnel levels

- providing effective communication with team members and other departments
- conducting employee performance appraisals.

The supervisor's execution of each of these areas of planning will impact the success of the team and the operation.

Organizing

A quality plan is the basis for a good organization. A good organization effectively brings together all of the necessary elements in a manner that will allow achievement of a plan's goal. A key role of the supervisor is the organization of people and materials to succeed in completing the plan. This happens through good organizational ability on the part of the supervisor. Carrying out the plan requires using the available resources and being prepared to adapt as circumstances and conditions warrant. Typical organizational goals of a department are listed hereunder:

- Organizing the staff to:
  - serve guests in the most efficient, economical, and effective fashion
  - utilize each team member within a limited time period and within criteria of effort and productivity
- Defining job tasks, analyses, and descriptions
- Preparing task lists to accomplish the planned goals
- Determining relationships with each member of the team together with management, other departments, and customers
- Organizing support areas
- Organizing training sessions
- Organizing and implementing employee empowerment and reward systems

Coaching

Coaching means guiding, supporting, and empowering staff to perform their jobs in a way that is compatible with the goals and objectives of an organization. It means creating a work place in which staff members feel comfortable enough to give their best. Good coaching requires excellent communication and leadership skills.

More importantly, coaching requires supervisors who trust people. To succeed as a coach, the supervisor needs to be consistent, objective, and fair in performance evaluation. An effective coach is firm when addressing the need for changes and improvement in performance. At the same time, the coach communicates that he or she care about the individual staff member and the team's success and growth. The supervisor needs to believe in the "team" concept. They are the link between management and team members. A good coaching style involves:

- a positive people attitude
- an interest in helping people attain personal goals
- respect for the dignity of every individual in the team
- sincerity, honesty, fairness, and impartiality
- sensitivity and respect for different cultures
- strong ethical and moral values
- an emphasis on the future rather than the past
- praise where praise is due
- mistake correction without apportioning blame.

Effective supervision requires adaptability combined with quality coaching. This combination will allow the team to succeed and consistently achieve the objective of guest satisfaction.

Team Building

A team exists when members of a group integrate their skills to build on strengths and minimize weaknesses to increase their ability to achieve objectives. Teams are developed by committed supervisors. A group that is poorly led and in which the members work as individuals will often fail and will coalesce into a team. The supervisor must recognize their role as a team builder and transform individual staff into teams. The natural outcome of this transformation is productive teams.

Effective teamwork has no level to compare. It is just as important among top executives as among line employees. If the supervisor does not place high value on teamwork, it will not occur. Teamwork takes conscious effort to develop and continuous effort to maintain. Part of that maintenance is recognition of team performance through celebration of positive performance. There must also be acknowledgment of and assistance in correcting negative performance. A team that is properly trained and is working in a positive environment will require less direct supervision. The team will not need to be micromanaged. Central to team building is investment in both the individual and the team. The supervisor who ensures that the team has the training, equipment, and guidance to succeed will inevitably spell success.

Communication

This is the art or process of optimizing information both internally and externally. Communication is a basic and essential element of the supervision process. Supervision often breaks down or fails because of poor communication. All elements of supervision and management require effective communication. The challenge that must be addressed is the difference that often exists between what is said and what is heard. The communication process involves a sender and a receiver. The goal is an exchange of information in which what the sender *sent* is what the receiver *received*. The communication is only successful if the receiver gains a clear understanding of the information, not just their impression or interpretation of the information.

Communication is the foundation for understanding, cooperation, and action. A good communication system maintains a two-way flow of ideas, opinions, information, and decisions. The first step in any effort to open communication is to establish and maintain a climate that encourages the free exchange of ideas. It is the umbrella under which all effective supervision lies.

Delegation

Delegation means granting a team member the authority to oversee specific tasks and responsibilities. This must include letting other team members know that these responsibilities have been delegated to the team member. Telling a team member to perform a task is not delegation; on the contrary, it is assigning work. Assigning work may be sufficient for simple, short-term jobs, but more complex tasks that require a sustained effort should be delegated.

Before delegating, the supervisor should determine the following parameters:

- Does the team member understand the purpose of the task?
- Is the value of the task recognized by the team member?

- Is the workload too much for just one person?
- Has the employee been provided with detailed, step-by-step instructions?
- Has the employee been given the resources needed to accomplish the task?
- How will satisfactory completion of the tasks be evaluated and measured?

Supervisors should not "delegate" work just because they consider that work unpleasant, unimportant, or risky. Team members are seldom deceived by the supervisor's efforts to hand-off a less desirable task. What usually results from such practice is resentment. The team member's motivation to do the task will decrease. The end result is often a team member trying to avoid or off-load the task. Effective delegation is grounded in an environment in which staff works *with* not simply *for* the supervisor. In addition, before delegating, it is useful to consider the following points:

- Is there acceptance and understanding of the task?
- Has a reason for delegation been given?
- Is the task being delegated a worthwhile and whole task?
- Can the team member be trusted and encouraged to do the job correctly?
- Have checkpoints been built in to check progress?
- Has knowledge been shared by pinpointing possible problems?
- Has information been withheld that could have simplified and speeded up the task?
- Have sufficient training, encouragement, coaching, and leadership been provided to make the team member look good and succeed?

Delegation by the supervisor encourages cooperation among team members. It demonstrates trust in both the individual team members and the team as a whole while boosting morale. The advantage of delegating is that the workload is distributed in a planned, orderly way. The supervisor has more time at his or her disposal for planning. The supervisor who tries to personally do everything will hardly succeed. This is primarily because support of the team members is essential. It is impossible for a supervisor to personally do all that needs to be done. The supervisor who fails to delegate to other team members will be frustrated, unproductive, and viewed as a weak leader by the entire team.

Empowerment and Ownership

Empowerment is the process of enabling people to do what they have been trained for and are qualified to do. Hence, empowerment per se leads to a feeling of ownership. A team member who has a feeling of ownership and a personal stake in the operation will work harder to make the operation a grand success. Empowering team members to take more initiative is an important part of team building. It is a basic tenet of supervision and management in any industry. There is no better way to create a shared vision and generate commitment and loyalty than through empowerment and the feeling of ownership.

The goal is to have a team member who has "buy-in." This is possible only when the team members feel that they have had a part in creating the vision of the company. They believe that there is respect for their ideas. The team members feel that the supervisor recognizes their contribution to the company's success. The "buy-in" will therefore naturally lead to continuous improvement and innovation.

Both in 1992 and in 1999, the Ritz-Carlton Hotel Company won the Malcolm Baldrige National Quality Award. The Ritz-Carlton is the only hotel company to date (2016) to have been awarded the Malcolm Baldridge. Part of their winning strategy in 1992 was called "applied employee empowerment." According to Horst Shulze, the Ritz-Carlton's chief operating officer, "all our employees are empowered to do whatever it takes to provide instant pacification. No matter what their normal duties are, other employees must assist if aid is requested by a fellow worker responding to a guest's complaint or wish.[6]" When the Ritz-Carlton won the award in 1999 also, as part of the company's employee empowerment program, every employee was empowered to spend up to $2,000 to immediately correct a problem or handle a complaint.[7]

The biggest challenge to the concept of empowerment and ownership is its acceptance by supervisors. Supervisors and managers often feel threatened by the concept of empowering staff. The supervisors and managers who embrace empowerment as part of their supervision and management tool chest find it is a very positive addition.

Technology

The supervisor must stay ahead of technological advances in all aspects of the operation in order to be competitive and focused. Innovation in communication and labor-saving devices is ongoing. The supervisor must be a life-long learner to stay updated. Information technology has changed the nature of many positions in the hospitality industry and will continue to do so in the future.

The Concept of Authority

The supervisor is the person in charge of the group because of the authority of position. Authority is the right and power to command and it rests in the position but not with the individual. A supervisor's success, however, depends on more than this source of authority. A supervisor's success depends on many skills. A high level of team-building skill is critical to the success of the supervisor. It is this skill that makes it possible to enhance the overall team productivity in addition to instilling the invaluable feel of job satisfaction in the individual team members. When team-building skills are applied rather than just the authority of position, employees naturally cooperate more with each other and other departments. Consequent to this, they develop better interpersonal relationships. Team spirit is well and truly generated. As stated by John Maxwell in his book on leadership, "The only thing a title can buy is a little time either to increase your level of influence with others or erase it.[8]" The requisites of proper and effective use of authority are to:

- require an obedience in which employees retain their freedom
- strike a balance between authority and individual freedom
- lead individuals toward growth
- possess practical judgment skills
- act as a uniting element of a group's common goals
- enhance cooperative efforts
- reserve the right and power to make decisions

For authority to be genuine, supervisors exercising their authority must know what they are requesting of team members and why they are making those requests. Authority for the sake of power is useless. The supervisor must seek to inspire desired outcomes from each person. Requests or demands made on employees without good reason often lead to anger and frustration on the part of both the employee and the supervisor. While the supervisor's request is generally an order a team member will still respond more freely to a request than they will to an order.

The Evolution of Supervision

Supervision has evolved over the past century. This evolution was based to a great extent on knowledge gained initially from two studies: (1) the Hawthorne studies and (2) the Likert studies.

The Hawthorne Studies

Begun in the 1920s, the Hawthorne studies represented an effort to determine what effect hours of work, periods of rest, and lighting might have on worker fatigue and productivity. These experiments were conducted by university professors Elton Mayo, Fritz Roethlisberger, and J. W. Dickson. The studies took place at the Western Electric Company's Hawthorne Works near Chicago, Illinois, USA. These studies represented one of the first endeavors to evaluate employee productivity. The Hawthorne studies revealed that the attitudes employees had toward management, their work group, and the work itself significantly affected their productivity. Initially, the results of the research on the small study group baffled the researchers. Despite altering the work environment and measuring productivity against this changing environment (reducing rest periods and eliminating rest time), the productivity of the study group increased continuously. The group had fewer sick days than other workers who were not in the research group.

The leaders of the research group concluded that productivity increased, not as a result of any of their contrived stimuli, but rather as a result of the absence of any authoritarian supervision and the interest shown in employees by the researchers. The fact that they were being studied was sufficient for the workers to improve their productivity. This phenomenon is still referred to by researchers as the Hawthorne effect: change will occur simply because people know they are being studied, rather than as a result of some form of treatment. However, the most important result of the Hawthorne studies was that people respond better when they have a sense of belonging.

The findings of the Hawthorne studies provided a new direction for "people management." As a result of these studies, greater emphasis was placed on managing employees, with concern for them as individuals. The studies also focused attention on the need for managers and supervisors to improve their communication skills and become more sensitive to employee needs and feelings. This new movement also emphasized the need to develop more participative, employee-centered supervision.

Likert Studies

In the 1940s, Renis Likert conducted research regarding the creation of a productive and desirable work climate. He observed four approaches to supervision and leadership.[9] The first type was an authoritative approach that was potentially explosive. It involved high pressure on subordinates through work standards. It obtained compliance through fear techniques. This approach resulted in high productivity over short periods but low productivity and high absenteeism over longer periods. The second approach was authoritarian but benevolent in nature. The third approach was a consultative supervisor/employee approach. The fourth approach was group participation in which the supervisor was supportive and used group methods of supervision, including group decision making. The last three approaches yielded high productivity, low waste, and low costs, along with low absenteeism and low attrition rates of the employee.

Likert also developed the "linking pin" concept that focused on coordinating efforts through layers of middle management. It provided a formal, structured approach. Central to its philosophy was the idea that each level of management is a member of a multifunctional team that includes the next upward level.

The Hawthorne and Likert research make it clear that the authoritarian style of leadership and supervision are not the most effective for long-term productivity. Authoritarian conduct by the supervisor may be necessary and effective when the goal is a rapid change in performance or short-term production is needed but it does not deliver long-term productivity. It does not create the positive work place that results in high productivity of quality products and great guest service in the long term. Today's supervisor must be what Merritt calls a Theory Z[10] manager. This is a manager who believes not only that people want to do a good job but also thrive when supported and encouraged to grow.

Conclusions

The end of the twentieth century was a very exciting time for the US hospitality industry. The economy was strong, with rapid job growth.

These good times brought about a change in American dining, travel, and lodging habits. People were eating out and traveling more and consequently gained more exposure to different cultures, cuisines, and business models. The net result was a more sophisticated consumer. Today, economic uncertainty has been added to the mix. The result is a consumer who is more sophisticated, seeking change, and always looking for the best price. This consumer has little loyalty to any brand expect based on the quality of service and product they experience. In such an environment, the effectiveness of supervision is critical to business success.

Today's supervisor must value training, education, diversity, individual initiative, and team cohesiveness. As the hospitality industry changes, the role of the supervisor will continue to evolve. Those who constantly pursue knowledge will help to shape the changes rather than just reacting to the changes that are always part of the progress.

Supervisors have responsibilities to senior management, customers, and other team members. By understanding the different elements that are part of a supervisor's role, it will be easier to refocus efforts toward creating a motivational environment in the operation. The attributes a successful supervisor demonstrates are shown in Figure 2.2.

Experience has shown that the establishment of a team culture results in a feeling of ownership by the team members which is the foundation for a quality-conscious staff. The modern supervisor's skill sets include the abilities to coach and lead a team by creating a motivational environment. Successful supervisors see themselves as facilitators and enablers whose primary responsibility it is to develop the team members and the team. This means demonstrating attributes that

---

Attributes of the Successful Supervisor

* Practices a code of ethics and administer this code fairly and without bias to all team members

* Customer satisfaction driven professionals

* Knows, understands, and applies the elements of supervision

 * Knows how the elements interrelate with the organization's goals, other departments, and team

* Knows and understands the various steps in planning, organizing, coaching, team building, communicating, delegating, empowering and technology

* Realizes the limitations of authority

FIGURE 2.2   Attributes of the Successful Supervisor

include an understanding of feelings and attitudes that motivate the entire team.

Study Questions

1. Define the term supervisor.
2. Identify and discuss the attributes a successful supervisor.
3. Identify elements of ethics and professionalism in supervision.
4. Identify and apply the elements of supervision.
5. Define and apply the concept of authority.
6. Identify elements of the evolution of supervision.

Case Studies

The case studies listed below relate to the information presented in this chapter and reading, answering the case study questions and participating in discussion of a case will reinforce and expand what you have learned in this chapter. All case studies are provided in this text after the last chapter.

Good Night Inn

Naples by the Sea

Prairie View Country Club

Shady Lane Inn

Shandong House Restaurant

Shepherd Mountain Hotel

Stone Lion Hotel and Conference Center

Summit Resort

Notes

1. Crosby, P. (1978). *Quality is free* (p. 111). New York: McGraw-Hill.
2. Marvin, B. *Coaching skills*. Retrieved July 24, 2014, from www.restaurant-doctor.com/articles/coaching.html#ixzz1HMhqtqWr
3. Lynn, C. (November, 2007). *Teaching ethics*. Retrieved July 24, 2014, from www2.nau.edu/~clj5/Ethics/Teaching%20Ethics.doc

4. Jernigan, A. K. (1989). *The effective foodservice supervisor* (p. 213). Rockville, MD: Aspen.

5. Anderson, P. (Ed.) (1989). *Great quotes from great leaders* (p. 52). Lombard, IL: Carrier Press.

6. (1993). *Ritz Carlton publicity pamphlet*. Boston, MA: The Ritz Carlton Co.

7. National Institute of Standards and Technology. *Baldridge performance excellence program: Baldridge award recipient information*. Retrieved July 24, 2014, from http://patapsco.nist.gov/Award_Recipients/index.cfm

8. Maxwell, J. C. (1998). *The 21 irrefutable laws of leadership: Follow them and people will follow* you (p. 14). Nashville, TN: Thomas Nelson Publishers.

9. Sherman, A., Bohlander, G., & Crudden, H. (1988). *Managing human resources* (8th ed., p. 352). Cincinnati: South-Western.

10. Merritt, E. (2008). *Strategic leadership: Essential concepts* [United States]: Day Press.

Human Resource Management and the Law   3

LEARNING OBJECTIVES

When you complete reading this chapter, you should be able to:

- ▶ Identify and compare and contrast laws relative to the relationship between employers and unions.
- ▶ Identify laws related to fair labor standards.
- ▶ Identify and discuss the laws administered by the Equal Employment Opportunity Commission (EEOC).
- ▶ Identify and discuss the Occupational Safety and Health (OSH) Act.
- ▶ Discuss and describe laws related to immigration.

Introduction

The supervisor/manager has responsibilities to senior management, customers, and other team members. By understanding the different elements that are part of a supervisor/manager's role, it will be easier to refocus efforts toward creating a positive work environment. An element of great importance is the law. While a supervisor/manager is not a lawyer she/he must be sufficiently familiar with the law to insure that the rights of the employee and the employer are protected. What is commonly referred to as *labor law* has existed in the United States right from the establishment of the country. In 1791, carpenters in Philadelphia successfully went on strike for a 10-hour-work day and overtime pay. Then, almost 50 years later, in 1840, President Van Buren declared a 10-hour-work day for federal employees on public works. This is just one example of how movements in society can become reflected in government policy and law. It is in the last few decades, however, that the number of labor laws has drastically increased. Today's supervisor/manager must understand and have a solid knowledge of the multiple laws that govern employee and employer in the United States today. The laws discussed here are the most prominent today. These are not all the laws relative to labor and employer and new laws are constantly being enacted. The supervisor/manager must stay updated in this regard to be effective.

The Laws

National Labor Relations Act (Wagner Act) (1935)

The National Labor Relations Act (NLRA) was created to establish a national policy of encouraging collective bargaining, guaranteeing certain employee rights, and detailing specific employer unfair labor practices. The act established the *National Labor Relations Board (NLRB)* to enforce these provisions. The NLRB has the power to investigate, dismiss charges or hold hearings, issue "cease and desist" orders, or pursue cases via Circuit Courts of Appeals or the U.S. Supreme Court. The NLRA applies to private employers, their employees, and unions.

Labor-Management Relations Act (Taft–Hartley Act) (1947)

The Labor-Management Relations Act (LMRA) is an expansion and refinement of the NLRA. The act established control of labor disputes on a new basis by enlarging the NLRB and providing that the union or the employer must, before terminating a collective-bargaining agreement, serve notice on the other party and on a government mediation service. The government was empowered to obtain an 80-day injunction against any strike that it deemed a peril to national health or safety. The act also prohibited jurisdictional strikes and secondary boycotts. A jurisdictional strike is a strike called by a union because of a dispute with another union over which of the two unions should act as the bargaining agent for the employees. The secondary boycott is a boycott against a unionized company doing business with another company that a union is trying to organize. The LMRA clarified that the protections provided union members in the NLRA and by the NLRB did not extend to union members involved in a wildcat strike. A wildcat strike is a strike not organized or declared by union officials. The LMRA allowed the creation of union shops but only when approved by a vote of the majority of the employees. In a union shop, a nonunion worker can be hired but is required to become a member of the union within a specific period of time. Most of the collective-bargaining provisions of the NLRA were preserved in the LMRA with the addition that before using the facilities of the NLRB a union must file with the U.S. Department of Labor (DOL) financial reports and affidavits that union officers are not Communists.

Labor-Management Reporting and Disclosure Act (Landrum–Griffin) (1959)

The Labor-Management Reporting and Disclosure Act (LMRDA) provided additional regulations for unions. It also guaranteed certain rights to all union members. Referred to as the union members' "Bill of Rights," these rights are as listed hereunder:

- equal rights to participate in union activities
- freedom of speech and assembly
- voice in setting rates of dues, fees, and assessments

- protection of the right to sue
- safeguards against improper discipline.

The Office of Labor-Management Standards (OLMS) of the U.S. Department of Labor (DOL) administers and enforces most provisions of the LMRDA.

Fair Labor Standards Act (1938) – as amended by 29 United States Code (USC) β201 et seq.; 29 Code of Federal Regulations (CFR) Parts 510–794

The Fair Labor Standards Act (FLSA) establishes minimum wage, overtime pay, recordkeeping, and child labor standards affecting full-time and part-time workers in the private sector and in federal, state, and local governments. The FLSA is administered by the Employment Standards Administration's Wage and Hour Division within the U.S. Department of Labor. The act contains numerous sections and specifications. We now discuss some of the most common and broadly applied sections and specifications of this act.

- Covered, nonexempt workers are entitled to a minimum wage currently of $7.25 per hour effective July 24, 2009.

  Nonexempt workers (generally defined as hourly personnel) must be paid overtime pay at a rate of not less than one and one-half (1.5) times their regular rates of pay after 40 hours of work in a workweek.

- Tipped employees are individuals engaged in occupations in which they customarily and regularly receive more than $30 a month in tips. The employer may pay a minimum wage of $2.13 an hour if the combination of the $2.13 an hour plus the tips the employee receive equal or exceed the federal minimum wage. The employer must be able to verify that the combination of direct wages and tips meets or exceeds the minimum wage. If it does not, then the employer is required to make up the difference.

- A minimum wage of less than $4.25 (as of 2010) is permitted for employees <20 years of age during their first 90 consecutive calendar days of employment. This is termed the youth wage. A youth wage employee cannot be hired to replace a regular minimum wage employee.

- According to the FSLA, the workweek is a period of 168 hours during 7 consecutive 24-hour periods. It may begin on any day of the week and at any hour of the day established by the employer. Generally, for purposes of minimum wage and overtime payment, each workweek stands alone; however, there can be no averaging of 2 or more workweeks. Employee coverage, compliance with wage payment requirements, and the application of most exemptions are determined on a workweek basis.
- According to the FSLA, covered employees must be paid for all hours worked in a workweek. In general, *hours worked* includes all time an employee must be on duty, or on the employer's premises, or at any other prescribed place of work, from the beginning of the first principal activity of the work day to the end of the last principal work activity of the workday. Also included is any additional time the employee is allowed (i.e., suffered or permitted) to work.
- The FLSA child labor provisions are designed to protect the educational opportunities of minors and prohibit their employment in jobs and under conditions detrimental to their health or well-being. The provisions include restrictions on hours of work for minors <16 years of age and lists of hazardous occupations with orders for both farm and nonfarm jobs declared by the Secretary of Labor to be too dangerous for minors to perform.
- Some employees are exempt from both the minimum wage and overtime pay provisions. Those exempted include executive, administrative, and professional employees (including teachers and academic administrative personnel in elementary and secondary schools), outside sales employees, and employees in certain computer-related occupations (as defined in the DOL regulations), and employees of certain seasonal amusement or recreational establishments.

Patient Protection and Affordable Care Act

The Patient Protection and Affordable Care Act (PPACA), signed into law on March 23, 2010 (P.L. 111-148), amended Section 7 of the FLSA, to provide a break time requirement for nursing mothers. This act is better known as the Affordable Care Act (ACA). This act also established nationwide health care coverage. The intent of the health care coverage provisions of the act took effect from January 2014.

The intent of the act is to expand health care coverage to all the Americans. The salient features of this law are listed hereunder:

- Individual mandate: Mandates all Americans, with some exceptions, to maintain a minimum level of health coverage or face a tax.
- Insurance exchanges: Creates health insurance exchanges and provides premium tax credits to assist eligible individuals with the purchase of coverage.
- Medicaid expansion: Allows states to expand Medicaid up to 133% of the federal poverty level.
- Employer mandate: Mandates employers with 50 or more full-time equivalents to offer coverage to full-time employees and their dependents or pay taxes if an employee obtains exchange coverage and a premium tax credit.

The large employer (50 or more full-time equivalent employees [FTEE]) who does not provide insurance coverage will pay an excise tax (penalty) for each FTEE. Depending on the circumstances of the failure to provide coverage, the fine can vary from $2,000 to $3,000 per FTEE. The ACA defines a full-time employee as one that works 30 hour per week or 130 hour per calendar month. Large employers are not required to offer health coverage to part-time employees, that is, employees working for less than 30 hour per week.

The small employer, a company with <50 FTEE, does not face tax penalties if they do not offer coverage to full-time employees. The ACA does provide tax credits to the small employers to assist them in offering coverage.

Insurance offered by any employer should meet the standards set in the ACA. These standards address the coverage's minimum value (MV) and affordability. The standard for affordability is that an employee's share of the self-only premium for the employer's lowest cost plan that provides MV cannot exceed 9.5% of the employee's household income. A plan fails to provide an MV if the plan's share of the total allowed costs of benefits provided under the plan is less than 60% of such costs.

Equal Pay Act

The Equal Pay Act (1963) is part of the FLSA. It prohibits differential wages paid to men and women doing substantially the same work.

If both sexes are doing the same work with similar skills, responsibility, working conditions, and effort, then the pay must be equal.

Laws administered by the EEOC

Title VII of the Civil Rights Act

Title VII of the Civil Rights Act (1964) (Title VII) is the principal federal law relating to most types of employment discrimination. The purpose of Title VII is to give everyone an equal chance to obtain employment. The law has a number of objectives, specifically those listed hereunder:

- outlaws certain discriminatory employment practices
- creates a federal agency to enforce the law and give it regulatory powers
- sets penalties for violators of the law
- requires state laws to uphold title VII
- requires that certain records be maintained by designated persons or agencies
- does not alter state or federal veterans' preference laws.

Title VII prohibits employment discrimination based on race, religion, sex, color, or national origin. Employers are also prohibited from discriminatory practices regarding:

- recruiting and hiring
- job advertising
- ability and experience
- occupational qualification
- testing
- prehire inquiries
- employment status
- compensation
- merit, incentive, or seniority plans
- insurance, retirement, and welfare plans
- promotion and seniority
- dress and appearance
- leave of absence benefits
- discharge
- retirement
- union membership

- persons opposed to discriminatory practices or exercising their rights under Title VII.

Title VII applies to all employers who have more than 15 employees. Employers who do not comply with the law are subject to court-decreed affirmative action programs and can be required to pay back pay. The act is administered by the EEOC.

Age Discrimination in Employment Act

The Age Discrimination in Employment Act (1967, 1978, 1986) (ADEA) promotes the employment of older persons based on ability rather than age. The act prohibits arbitrary age discrimination in employment of workers 40 years or older and it helps employers and workers resolve age-related employment problems. The ADEA applies to private employers with 20 or more workers and all government agencies regardless of the number of employees. Federal employment has no upper age limit. The act also applies to employment agencies and unions with 25 or more members. Failing to comply with the ADEA can lead to court-decreed affirmative action programs, awards of back pay, fines up to $10,000, and possible imprisonment of the employer. The act is administered by the EEOC.

American with Disabilities Act (1990) with amendments (2008)

The American with Disabilities Act (1990) with amendments (2008) (ADA) provides broad nondiscrimination protection for individuals in employment, public services, public accommodations, and services operated by private entities, transportation, and telecommunications. Title I states that no entity covered by this act shall discriminate against a qualified individual because of a disability with regard to a job application procedure or in the hiring, advancement, or discharge of employees, employee compensation, job training, and other terms, conditions, and privileges of employment.

The ADA defines a *disability* as listed hereunder:

- a physical or mental impairment that substantially limits one or more major life activities of such individual;
- a record of such an impairment; or

- being regarded as having such an impairment (An individual meets the requirement of *being regarded as having such an impairment* if the individual establishes that he or she has been subjected to an action prohibited under this chapter because of an actual or perceived physical or mental impairment whether or not the impairment limits or is perceived to limit a major life activity.)

It is important to note that the act of the Congress specifically states "The definition of disability in this chapter shall be construed in favor of broad coverage of individuals under this chapter, to the maximum extent permitted by the terms of this chapter."

Failure to comply with the ADA can result in injunctive relief and back pay but not compensatory and punitive damages. The ADA is administered by the EEOC.

Civil Rights Act of 1991

The Civil Rights Act of 1991 extends punitive damages and jury trials to victims of employment discrimination based on the employee's sex, religion, disability, as well as race. Under previous acts, employees could only seek back pay. The result of not complying with this act can be punitive damages at the rate of $50,000 for businesses with 101 or fewer employees; $100,000 for firms 101–200; and $200,000 for firms with 201–500 workers; and a maximum limit of $300,000 for business with over 500 employees. This act is administered by the EEOC.

Family Medical Leave Act

The Family Medical Leave Act (1993) (FMLA) permits employees to take up to 12 weeks of unpaid leave per year from work for the birth or adoption of a child; for the case of a seriously ill child, spouse, or parent; or for a serious illness afflicting the worker. Employers must guarantee the worker can return to the same or a comparable job. Employers must also continue health care coverage during the leave period. During the leave time workers are not eligible for unemployment or other government compensation. This law applies to employers that have 50 or more employees within a 75-mile radius. Employees who have not worked for at least one year and have not worked 1,250 hours or 25 hours a week in the previous 12 months are not covered by this law. The act is administered by the EEOC.

Occupational Safety and Health Act (1970)

The Occupational Safety and Health Act (OSH Act) created regulations and enforcement practices to render the work environment safe and healthy for workers. Most employees in the nation come under the OSH Act's jurisdiction. Further, OSH Act covers private sector employers and employees in all the 50 states, the District of Columbia, and other US jurisdictions either directly through the Federal OSH Act or through an approved state program. State run health and safety programs must be at least as effective as the Federal OSH Act program. Moreover, the OSH Act standards are rules that describe the methods that employers must use to protect their employees from hazards. There are OSH Act standards for construction work, maritime operations, and general industry, which is the set that applies to most worksites, including hospitality operations. These standards limit the amount of hazardous chemicals to which workers can be exposed, require the use of certain safe practices and equipment, and require employers to monitor hazards and keep records of workplace injuries and illnesses. Failure to comply with the act can result in fines up to $100,000 per violation. The OSH Act is administered by the Occupational Safety and Health Administration (OSHA) in the Department of Labor.

Immigration Reform and Control Act (1986)

The Immigration Reform and Control Act (IRCA) prohibits employers from knowingly hiring, recruiting, or referring for a fee any alien who is unauthorized to work in the United States. As a result of this law, all employers are required to verify both the identity and employment eligibility of all regular, temporary, casual, and student employees hired after November 6, 1986. Employers must have all employees complete the *INS Form I-9* documenting this verification. However, this one-page form must be retained as part of the employee's personal record. Failure to comply with these requirements may result in both civil and criminal liability with the imposition of substantial fines ranging from $100 to $1,000 per hire. If it is not possible to verify an individual's identity and employment eligibility, then that person cannot be hired or if already hired must be terminated. Determination by the government of a pattern or practice of noncompliance can lead to imprisonment of the employer. The United States Citizenship and Immigration Services (USCIS) is responsible for implementing this law.

Conclusions

There are few things that evolve as rapidly as the law. There are also few things that can have as devastating an effect on a business. Today is the age of transparency. This transparency may be initiated by an individual or a company. The transparency may also be initiated by others. It is easy today to quickly achieve wide distribution of personal and company information. Therefore, we advise you to have this in mind when considering your actions as a supervisor/manager.

As a supervisor/manager you must be familiar with the law in order to balance your actions with the law. In the past the question was "How will this action look in the headlines (newspaper) tomorrow morning?" Today the question is "How will this action look as a tweet within the next few minutes?"

Laws are generally created in response to a demonstrated need for reinforcement of a society's standard of behavior. This means that the first "law" that should be put into force as a supervisor/manager is not actually a "law." The golden rule is better termed a formula for creating a positive environment that leads to success for all. Always remember, first and foremost: "Do unto others as you would have them do unto you."

Summary

The supervisor/manager's skill sets must include knowledge of laws relative to the employee and employer. These laws include those related to the relations between the employer and unions. The employees have the right to decide if they want a group such as a union to represent them. These decisions, that is, the formation of a representative group such as a union; the manner in which the representative group takes action; and the actions of the employer in relation to the representative group are all subject to the federal law. The laws addressing fair labor standards address minimum wage, overtime pay, employment records, and child labor. Equal employment opportunity is safeguarded by numerous laws and these laws are administered by the US Equal Opportunity Employment Commission. The rights of disabled individuals are the focus of the ADA. The safety and health of the worker is the focus of the OSH Act. Both these laws are constantly changing. The role of the supervisor/manager is to protect the rights of both the employee and the employer. To meet this responsibility constant updating of the supervisor/manager's knowledge of the law is required.

Study Questions

1. Define the term, "labor law."
2. List the laws that address the relationship between the employer and unions.
3. State three specific directives pertaining to the formation and function of a union in the work place.
4. List the laws administered by the EEOC.
5. Discuss the features of the FMLA.
6. What was the purpose of the Civil Rights Act of 1964 (Title VII) and the Civil Rights Act of 1991?
7. Discuss the features of the OSH Act.
8. Discuss the specifics of three laws related to fair labor standards.
9. Discuss the features of the IRCA.

Case Studies

The case studies listed below relate to the information presented in this chapter and reading, answering the case study questions and participating in discussion of a case will reinforce and expand what you have learned in this chapter. All case studies are provided in this text after the last chapter.

Good Night Inn

Shepherd Mountain Hotel

Stone Lion Hotel and Conference Center

Notes

1. United States Department of Labor. Employment Law Guide. Retrieved July 15, 2014, from http://www.dol.gov/elaws/elg/
2. United States Government Printing Office. United States Code. Retrieved July 15, 2014, from http://uscode.house.gov/
3. Washington Council Ernest and Young. The Affordable Care Act: Summary of Employer Requirements. Retrieved February 2013, from http://www.nahu.org/meetings/capitol/2013/attendees/jumpdrive/Employer_ACA_Reference_Deck_02_14_2013.pdf

Recruiting and Hiring Personnel 4

CHAPTER OUTLINE

LEARNING OBJECTIVES

When you complete reading this chapter, you should be able to:

- ▶ identify the methods and steps for completion of a job analysis
- ▶ analyze a job description for correct content
- ▶ differentiate between a job description and a job specification
- ▶ define various recruitment techniques employed to attract a pool of qualified job candidates
- ▶ interpret the legal issues associated with recruiting and selecting job applicants
- ▶ apply the steps in screening potential new team members
- ▶ classify different types of interviews used to screen applicants

- ▶ list the steps to be considered when interviewing potential team members
- ▶ recognize appropriate and inappropriate questioning techniques
- ▶ differentiate elements associated with the hiring decision-making process.

Introduction

A key part of management is finding and hiring the best people for the job. Recruiting and hiring decisions must reflect the vision and values of the company. Hiring the right people builds the culture of the company. When the right people are hired, the result is quality in performance and operations. People make the difference between success and failure.

The process of recruiting and hiring staff begins with job analysis. To hire the right person the activities, responsibilities, and working conditions of the position must be clear. It is the match between the individual and the position that determines the quality of performance on the job. A good match is not possible without a job description that clearly states the specifics for the position. The specifics of the position are determined through a job analysis.

There are a number of laws and regulations that protect the job seeker and the company. These laws and regulations directly impact the recruiting and hiring process. Recruiting and hiring varies from company to company. In some companies, the manager is directly responsible for this process. In other companies, the recruiting and hiring processes are done by the human resource/personnel department. In both the situations, the role of a manager is critical. Staff recruitment and selection is a responsibility shared by all members of the management. All members of management are responsible for knowing and complying with labor laws and regulations.

The recruiting and hiring process may be managed by a human resource or personnel department. This does not mean that the manager is not part of the process. The final decision to hire should be made by the manager. The manager has the best understanding of the needs of the operation. The manager is in the process of building a team. A new hire—who knows—if were personally selected by the manager will be more committed to the team.

Job Analysis

Job analysis is the determination of the activities, responsibilities, and working conditions of a position. The job analysis is also used to determine the skills and knowledge required to do the job. The first step in job analysis is information gathering. This can be done in a number of ways. These include a position audit, self-analysis, survey, and observation.

An audit-of-position output is conducted by the human resource or personnel department. The information about the product produced or jobs completed is compiled over a period of time. Self-analysis is completed by a current position holder. The individual is asked to keep a log of all their activities and responsibilities over a period of time. It can also be valuable to conduct a survey of individual's holding similar positions in other locations or companies. This would be done by developing a questionnaire directed to gaining information about what they do on the job. Another method of information gathering is direct observation. The observer monitors the activities of an individual or individuals in the position over a period of time. In all cases where the information gathering is over a period of time the length of time needs to be sufficient to extract enough information to accurately reflect the position.

The most effective information gathering is realized via a combination of various methods. Each method has weaknesses. An audit-of-position outcome provides a narrow picture of the position. It does not indicate activities such as coaching and training. It also provides little information about working conditions. The activities, skills, and knowledge may not be directly reflected in the individual's product output. The job analysis is intended to capture all aspects of the position. This is best done by using multiple methods of information gathering.

Once the information has been gathered, then the next step is to analyze such information. The information gathered is analyzed to answer the following questions:

- What does the individual in the current position actually do?
- What are the responsibilities of the individual in the current position?
- What specific skills are needed to carry out the activities and responsibilities of the current position?
- What type of knowledge is needed to carry out the activities and responsibilities of the position?
- What are the working conditions for the position?
- If there is an existing job description and specification, are the answers to the above questions a match with their content?
- What is currently done by the position and still what is needed from the position?

Once these questions have been answered an accurate job description and specification can be written.

Job Description and Specification

Job descriptions are used to clearly state the activities, responsibilities, and working conditions of a position. The job description also specifies the knowledge and skills desired and required of the person in the position. It is a key tool in selecting the right person. A well-developed job description is the foundation of the recruiting, selection, and performance appraisal sequence. As shown in Figure 4.1, the sequence begins with job analysis.

Working from the information in the job analysis, the job description is developed. The job description must be carefully developed.

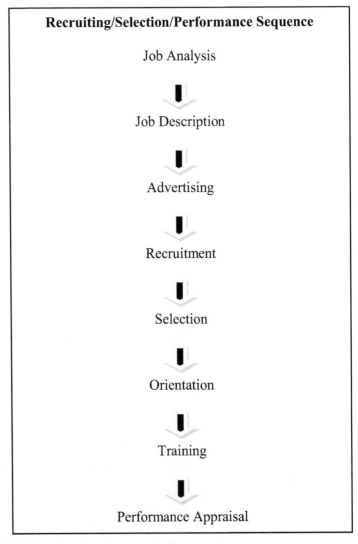

Recruiting/Selection/Performance Sequence

Job Analysis

Job Description

Advertising

Recruitment

Selection

Orientation

Training

Performance Appraisal

FIGURE 4.1   Recruiting/Selection/Performance Sequence

It is considered a legal document in disputes between the employee and the employer pertaining to the performance of job duties. The job description for a position should be reviewed and updated regularly to ensure that it correctly reflects the requirements for the position. A clear job description is the foundation of quality performance by the employee. The employee must have a clear understanding of what he or she is expected to do in order to do a job well. An up-to-date job description is also critical to performance evaluation. In order for performance evaluation to be meaningful it must be based on what the staff member was told to do. The job description is the primary means of clear communication for everyone and hence signifies what responsibilities a position is entrusted with.

A job description states clearly the skills, knowledge, and physical requirements of the position. In addition to this information, it includes the following information about the position: title; classification, if applicable; wage category; duties and responsibilities; subordinate staff, if applicable; reporting structure; and working conditions. The skills, knowledge, and physical requirements of a position are collectively called job specification. This is part of the job description but can also be used as a separate document. The clarity and accuracy of the job specification will determine the quality of the match of the person to the position. In a job specification, two types of qualifications can be stated. The first type of qualification is termed "required." A required qualification is something that the individual must possess to carry out the activities and responsibilities of the position. The second type of qualification is termed "desired." This type of qualification that can be termed "nice to have" but the individual does not have to possess it to do the job. Many desired qualifications are those that make the individual a candidate for greater growth in the position and the company. An example of a qualification that is often required in the restaurant business is ServSafe® certification. An example of a qualification that is often desired is a degree in hospitality management. The details of a job description are provided in Figure 4.2.

Recruiting

Recruiting involves seeking and attracting a diverse pool of qualified candidates for a position. The more applicants there are for a position, the better chance the manager has of selecting the right person. The key to successful recruiting is to begin the process well in advance of any

```
                                    Job Description
Title:                      Line Cook
Department:                 Culinary
Job Analyst:                Chef Ortega
Date of Job Analysis:       6/21/11
Wage Category:              Hourly
Reports to:                 Evening Sous Chef
Subordinate Staff:      Not Applicable
Other Internal Contacts:    Kitchen personnel and service staff
External Contacts:      Not Applicable
Job Summary:    Perform food preparation and presentation to specification and to order, set-up and maintain work station, prep food as directed
Job Duties:
```

- Prep food
  - Inventory station stock levels and equipment
  - Gather supplies as need to return station to par for service period
  - Process food to level necessary to meet requirements of the station for quality and timely preparation and presentation of food
  - Prepare sauces according to recipe, properly cool, and store
- Station set
  - Inspect station for sanitation and safety issues
  - Correct sanitation and safety issues
  - Test operational condition of major equipment
  - Gather equipment required to return station to ready-state for service period
  - Store and position prepped supplies
  - Organize station for efficient work flow
- Food preparation to order
  - Mastery of standards for all menu items assigned to station
  - Quality preparation and presentation of all items ordered
    - To specification
    - In a prescribed time for each item
  - Minimal waste (maintain waste report)
  - Maintenance of sanitary and organized station at all times
- Station changeover and sanitation
  - Return station to order
  - Stock station according to standard
  - Correct sanitation and safety issues
  - Submit waste report to Line Supervisor
  - Report equipment issues to Line Supervisor
- Other duties as assigned

Working Conditions:
Kitchen setting, exposure to cleaning materials (protective equipment and MSD sheets provided)
Job Specifications:

- Required
  - High School graduate
  - Minimum of 2 years experience working in a restaurant food preparation
  - Demonstrated knowledge of basic knife cuts
  - Demonstrated knowledge of classical sauce preparation
  - ServSafe® certified
  - US Citizen
  - Ability to stand for extended periods with minimal breaks
  - Ability to lift 25 lbs unassisted
- Preferred
  - Certificate or degree in culinary arts or ACF certification
  - English/French speaker

FIGURE 4.2   Job Description

openings occurring in the team. Part of this process is building a positive company reputation and culture. This process is part of building a foundation for attracting the best individuals to be part of the team. It has often been said that an organization's reputation precedes it. The reputation of the company, the manager/management team, and the work place are factors impacting the quality of job applicants.

There are many ways to begin actively searching for new team members. Recruiting can be either formal or informal. It can be done internally or externally. Some of the most reliable methods of recruiting are listed hereunder:

- advertising using electronic media
- asking friends, customers, or suppliers
- seeking candidates at colleges and professional associations
- reviewing past applicants
- attending job fairs
- networking.

In some areas of the United States, the public employment service is also a good source for recruiting. Private employment agencies provide another source. When using private employment agencies, the new team member sometimes pays the agency, but in most cases it is the employer who pays. Employment company fees can range from 10% to 50% of the employee's first month's or first year's salary.

Networking is generally a positive recruiting source. Networking is interacting with people who can be helpful in getting the word of the job opening in the right places or possibly refer a good potential employee. Current staff is a potential source for new staff members. A staff recommendation can yield good results because they know your business and the needs. There can also be problems associated with staff recommendations because if the result is a bad hire and the individual is fired, then the staff member who made the recommendation may be unhappy or angry about the outcome. Whatever method is used to recruit potential staff members, it must always be in compliance with the law.

Obviously, the best recruiting philosophy is to seek out quality people. Active recruiting is the basis on which good managers acquire the best team members. They work on attracting talented individuals rather than hoping that qualified people will report for an interview. This process of recruiting therefore involves saying to a potential team member, "You are someone special and I want you on my team."

Recruiting people who are a good match to the culture of the company is the basis for success. Esprit de Corps, the spirit of the team members that inspires dedication and devotion to the goal of the company/team, is critical to building a strong team. The baseline goal of recruiting is to build a strong team that will achieve synergy. Team synergy is achieved when the sum of the parts—the individuals—is greater than the whole—the group. This synergy, this increased effectiveness of the team, requires the best possible "neatness of fit" between people and company/team. Hiring an individual that fits well is the hiring of an asset to the company, not just a "warm body."

Turnover of staff costs the company the cost of recruiting, training, and lost productivity during training and ramp-up of the new staff member. These costs amount to ~20% of the staff member's salary.[1] Turnover of a staff position that is paid $10.00 per hour and makes $20,800 per year costs the company ~$4,160 in turnover cost. Recruiting that brings qualified people that are a good match to the company's culture reduces turnover. The hire that is a good match stays the longer. Whatever the recruiting method, the goal is to achieve the best match of individual, company/team, and position.

Legal Impact

It is important that managers consider the legal impact of recruiting and hiring. Title VII of the Civil Rights Act (1964) is the principal federal law relating to most types of employment discrimination. Title VII prohibits employment discrimination based on race, religion, sex, color, or national origin. In recruiting and selection, the employer must insure that no action taken in the process was discriminatory.

The ad shown hereunder could easily lead to charges of discrimination.

- Wanted cook, female, 18–22 years old, unmarried, must have a working car, non-Christian preferred. Apply in person at the Not Bright Restaurant.

The correctly worded ad would be as shown hereunder:

- Wanted cook, must be able to demonstrate basic food preparation skills; must be able to walk and stand for extended periods of time; and lift 20 pounds unassisted. Apply in person at the Smart Way Restaurant.

The first ad contained numerous requirements but none were bona fide occupational qualifications (BFOQ). The gender, age, marital status, personal information, and religion do not determine the individual's ability to do the job. There are times that factors such as gender may be considered a BFOQ. An example of gender as a BFOQ is requiring that the attendant for the women's locker room at the golf club is considered reasonable. In the second ad the employer has declared walking, standing, and lifting as BFOQs. The employer must be prepared to prove that these are BFOQs.

Screening

The recruiting process yields applicants whose qualifications must be assessed against the requirements of the job and the culture of the company. Initial screening is the first step in selecting the new staff member. It is based on a comparison of the application materials and the requirements of the job stated in the job description. Screening also includes an initial impression of the applicant's potential fit with the company's culture. All levels of screening need to be done carefully. The selection of new staff members has long-term impact on team performance. Careful screening results in better hiring. The staff and the guest benefit from a careful selection process. One of the manager's most important responsibilities is staff selection. They should fully understand the objectives and policies relative to evaluating and selecting new staff members.

The goal of initial screening is to generate an initial pool of potential staff members. These are the best fit with the job requirements and the rate of pay available.

Screening and selection in some instances may also be affected by union contracts. Union contracts often require that all in-house applicants for a position be interviewed. Additionally, a union contract may require that consideration be given to seniority with the company. In a unionized workplace, the manager must know the terms of the union contract. Failure to comply with the provisions of the union contract can lead to the union disputing the hiring decision. This can delay the filling of the position and also creates ill will between the union and management.

Complete, clear, and unambiguous job descriptions and specifications reduce the influence of ethnic and gender stereotypes in the screening process. These tools help the manager differentiate between qualified and unqualified individuals based on proper criteria. There are other steps that can be taken to reduce the influence of ethnic and gender stereotypes. Job seekers are generally required to complete application forms because they provide a variety of information about the potential staff member. As with interviews, the Equal Employment Opportunity Commission(EEOC) and the courts have found that many questions asked on application forms disproportionately reject females and minorities and often are not job related. To keep in line with this legal requirement, application forms should be developed with great care and revised as necessary.

The information on the application form is generally used as a basis for further exploration of the applicant's background. It should be designed to provide as much information as possible that will help predict job success. The application should always require the signature of the applicant indicating that all information provided is accurate. In the screening process, an incomplete application should be a matter of concern. In most situations an incomplete application should mean the individual is not eligible for an interview. Even if an applicant has provided a resume it is still important that application forms are completed early in the application process.

The resume is a standard means for an applicant to initially present his or her information to the potential employer. A resume does not replace an application. The strength and the weakness of the resume is that a well-written resume will always present the individual in the most positive manner. The straight forward questions of the application provide the information in a more basic fashion. The value of the resume is in the broader information about the applicant that may not be requested on the application.

A company is responsible for the actions of an employee when they are representing the company. This dictates that the company needs to carefully check the background of potential staff members. For the hiring of nonexecutive and staff not in high security areas staff the most common background check is contacting references and previous employers. Contract foodservice or other types of companies that are serving high security facilities such as government installations or prisons may require more in-depth background checks.

Conducting a background check is often reserved for those applicants who have been selected for the interview pool. The initial step is verification of the applicant's employment history. Permission to contact previous employers should be requested on the application. Failure by an applicant to give permission to contact a previous employer should not automatically be considered a cause to remove them from the applicant pool. If the applicant is a good match in all other ways it may be worth asking them why. When contacting previous employers the majority of companies will only provide verification of employment. Companies will generally not comment on job performance.

This situation is the result of lawsuits by former employees who disputed the comments made by the company.

The primary sources for information on the applicant's previous job performance are references. The applicant should be asked to provide references that can and will comment on their job performance. On the application the applicant should be asked to grant permission for the references to be contacted.

When doing background checks, remember that the information should be job related. The information requested and received about the applicant should be documented. Individuals have a legal right to examine letters of reference about themselves (unless they have waived the right to do so or were protected by the Privacy Act of 1974 or by state laws). Written documentation should exist outlining that the employment decision was based on relevant information.[2]

Interviewing

The most crucial step in selecting potential staff members is the face-to-face interview. An interview is a conversation or verbal interaction between two people (in this case, the manager and the applicant). The goal is to evaluate compatibility for a particular reason. It is a process for choosing the applicant who is most suited for the staff position to be filled. The interview has three main purposes as listed hereunder:

- to validate previously submitted information;
- to discover those skills and attitudes necessary to achieve right fit for the position; and
- to predict the successful integration of the applicant into the company's culture.

When meeting somebody for the first time, it is natural to react to him or her in some way. Sometimes this is taken further and some definite judgments are made based only on the first impression. If this is done, the interviewer will usually tend, often without realizing it, to listen to and observe the person selectively. This means, the interviewer sees and hears only what confirms the first impression. The interviewer filters out anything that contradicts that initial impression.

Research indicates that first impressions are based to a large extent on nonverbal cues: 55% on what is seen, 9% on what is said, and 36% on how it is said. Nonverbal cues are based almost entirely on reliving old memories. They are therefore based not on the person, but on others in the past. The interviewer must work to overcome these tendencies. The goal is to see the person as they are not based on other memory-based perception.

There is no best way to an interview. Interviews can be structured or unstructured, or they may be conducted in groups. Three interview types are most commonly used in the hospitality industry as listed hereunder:

1. Structured interviews consist of a series of carefully designed and structured questions that are asked by the interviewer of each job applicant. This type of interview is based on a clear set of job specifications. Through this type of interview, the interviewer maintains control of the interview by systematically asking prepared questions. An advantage of using a structured interview is that it provides the same criteria for all interviews.

2. Unstructured interviews require very little preparation on the part of the interviewer. These types of interviews are conducted without a predetermined checklist of questions. Open-ended questions are used. This type of interview may pose problems of subjectivity and bias on the part of the interviewer. However, unstructured interviews can provide a more relaxed atmosphere for interviewees.

3. Group interviews are interviews in which several applicants are questioned together in a group discussion. They typically involve a structured and unstructured question format. This format may be used as an initial interview format to screen large numbers of applicants. Those selected from the group interview are then interviewed individually at a later date.

Additional types of interviews are shown in Figure 4.3.

Although interviews are the most widely used method to select staff members, they can create a host of problems. One of the most significant in this regard is that interviews are subject to the same legal

Additional interview types
* Board interviews
* Stress interviews
* Counseling interviews
* Evaluation or job appraisal interviews
* Exit interviews

FIGURE 4.3   Additional Types of Interviews

requirements of validity and reliability as other steps in the recruitment and selection process. The interview should also follow EEOC guidelines. The basic thrust of equal employment legislation is straightforward: do not discriminate against people on the basis of their race, color, sex, religion, national origin, or age. However, subtle interpretations of the laws make this area one of the most actively pursued in the courts. Interview questions should be tied to job descriptions. These should detail only the characteristics of the position. If the interview questions stick to job-related items, are objective, and are applied consistently to all applicants then the interviewer will most certainly stay within the law.

Conducting the Interview

By putting the potential staff member at ease, the interviewer is more likely to get a true picture of the applicant's skills, abilities, and attitudes. The interview should take place in a pleasant and nonthreatening environment. Begin the interview by welcoming the applicant warmly. An applicant who is at ease will be more likely to answer questions spontaneously. Introduce yourself by name and title. Ask the applicant his or her preferred name and use it throughout the interview. Prepare the atmosphere by initiating a brief conversation on issues unrelated to the interview. Establish and maintain rapport with applicants by displaying sincere interest in them and by listening carefully. Indicate the intention to take notes or complete an evaluation form; and be sure to extend this opportunity to the applicant. Strive to understand what is only suggested or implied.

A good listener's mind is alert, and his or her face and posture reflect this. Some interviewers tend to talk too much. According to Bill Marvin, in his book, *The Foolproof Foodservice Selection System,* "Most interviewers talk half of the time or more during an interview, but it is the candidate who should be talking 80 or 90 percent of the time. After all, how can you learn about an applicant if you do all the talking?"[3]

Focus on the questions and the applicant's responses to questions. Listen for observations beyond the content required to answer the question. Watch the body language of the applicant. All of these provide clues to that person's attitude and feelings. Answer fully and frankly the applicant's questions. Use questions effectively to elicit truthful answers. Questions should be phrased as objectively as possible, without an indication of the desired response. During the interview, separate facts from inferences. Use open-ended questions that give the applicant an opportunity to talk and share information about past work experiences, training, or lifestyle. A number of things to avoid doing in an interview is shown in Figure 4.4.

When an interviewer is not getting honest answers to carefully prepared questions, it is possible to hire the wrong person. To become an effective interviewer, the dynamics of verbal and nonverbal communication must be mastered so that dishonest applicants can be identified. It has been reported that 80% of communication is nonverbal rather than verbal, and that 80% of that communication is manifest in a person's face, particularly in the eyes. Previously it was stated that your ability to interpret nonverbal signs is based on memory. When speaking of first impressions, this can be a liability. Once you move forward in the interview you want to draw on those memories, experiences, which assist you in recognizing the subtle nonverbal cues that indicate an attempt to deceive. Few applicants can lie without feeling tightness in the stomach, along with some involuntary change in facial expression or diverting of the eyes from the interviewer.[4] Verbal clues that sometimes can indicate deception include remarks such as "to tell the truth," "to be perfectly honest," or "I wouldn't tell most people this." Sometimes verbal and nonverbal cues are combined, for example, an "honest to God" remark accompanied by a major break in eye contact, a shift in body orientation, or a movement of a hand to the face.

Things to avoid during an interview

* Biases and traps including favoring people who have interests, backgrounds, or experiences similar to the interviewer.

* Allowing an exciting attitude overshadow the need to ask essential questions about skills and knowledge.

* Allowing beautyism A universal and reoccurring discrimination against unattractive individuals

* The "halo effect," judging persons favorably or unfavorably on the basis of one strong point (or weak point) on which high (or low) value has been placed.

* Permitting first impressions (good or bad) to overrule the information gathered from the interview.

* Basing decisions on pre-interview material and either spending the entire time trying to verify the material or simply rendering the interview pointless.

* Making a pre-mature decision.

* Talking too much.

FIGURE 4.4 Things to Avoid During an Interview

Be sure that all of the information needed is obtained before ending the interview. Always keep in mind the qualities needed for the job. Cover all major skills that are needed on the job. As a final step in the interview process, ask the applicant if there are further questions or more information to be discussed before closing the interview. Guidelines for effective interviewing are shown in Figure 4.5.

Interview Questions

To evaluate the qualifications of potential staff members, the manager must ask a series of questions. However, certain types of questions violate the EEOC guidelines. Other types of questions are inappropriate, but inexperienced interviewers may ask them unwittingly. Following are some examples of appropriate and inappropriate questions.

Name

- Inappropriate: Inquiries about name that would indicate applicant's lineage, ancestry, national origin, or descent. Inquiries about preferred courtesy title: Mr., Mrs., and Ms.
- Permissible inquiries: "Have you worked for this organization under a different name?" "Is any additional information relative to change of name, use of an assumed name, or nickname necessary to enable a check on your work and educational record? If yes, please explain."

Guidelines for effective interviewing

* Put the applicant at ease.

* Focus attention on the applicant's responses to questions.

* Use open-ended questions.

* Avoid biases that may affect judgment.

* Avoid the halo effect.

* Don't allow first impressions to overrule information gathered from the interview.

* Know what questions are inappropriate and those that are permissible.

FIGURE 4.5 Guidelines for Effective Interviewing

Marital Status

- Inappropriate: "Are you married, divorced, or separated?"
- Permissible inquiries: Whether applicant can meet specific work schedules or has activities, commitments, or responsibilities that may hinder the meeting of work attendance requirements.

Age

- Inappropriate: "How old are you?"
- Permissible inquiries: Requiring proof of age in the form of a work permit or a certificate of age if a minor. If it is necessary to know that someone is over a certain age for legal reasons, this question could better be stated, "Are you 21 or over?"

National Origin

- Inappropriate: "Are you native born or naturalized?" "Have you proof of your citizenship?" "What was your birthplace?" "Where were your parents born?"
- Permissible inquiries: If it is necessary to know if someone is a US citizen for a job, this question could be asked directly, without asking anything that might reveal national origin. If it is necessary to require proof of citizenship or immigrant status, employment can be offered on the condition that proof is supplied.

Mental or Physical Handicap

- Inappropriate: "Do you have or have you ever had a life-threatening disease?" "Questions regarding treatment for alcohol or drug abuse or on-the-job injury." "Have you ever been treated for a mental condition?"
- Permissible inquiries: For employers, subject to the provisions of the Rehabilitation Act of 1973 and the Americans with Disabilities Act of 1990, applicants may be invited to indicate how and to what extent they are handicapped. All applicants can be asked if they are able to carry out all necessary job assignments and perform them in a safe manner. The employer must indicate that

compliance with the invitation is voluntary or that the information is being sought only to remedy discrimination or provide opportunities for the handicapped.

Religion

- Inappropriate: "What is your religious affiliation?" "What clubs/associations are you a member of?" "Can you work on Saturdays or Sundays?"
- Permissible inquiries: None. However, an applicant may be advised concerning normal hours and days of work required by the job, to avoid possible conflict with religious or other personal convictions.

Conviction, Arrest, and Court Records

- Inappropriate: Any inquiries relating to arrests. Any inquiry into or a request for a person's arrest, court, or conviction record if not substantially related to functions and responsibilities of the particular job in question.
- Permissible inquiries: Inquiry into actual *convictions* that relate reasonably to fitness to perform an actual job.

Military Record

- Inappropriate: The type of discharge.
- Permissible inquiries: Type of education and experience in the service as it relates to a particular job.

Credit Rating

- Inappropriate: Any questions concerning credit rating, charge accounts, ownership of car, etc.
- Permissible inquiries: None.

Questions are also asked in the interview to gain insight into the character of the applicant. We now provide examples of character insight questions that can be asked in an interview.

Motivation

The following questions can provoke responses that help determine a person's motivation, initiative, insight, and planning abilities.

- "How will this job help you get what you want?"
- "What have you done to prepare yourself for a better job?"

The underlying intent of these types of questions is to determine the applicant's priorities and how motivated he or she may be.

- "How did you get into this line of work?"
- "When have you felt like giving up on a task? Tell me about it."

The intention here is to determine if the person is a self-starter or can complete an unpleasant assignment.

- "What is the most useful criticism you have received?"
- "From whom? Tell me about it."
- "What is the most useless?"

Criticism

From answers to these questions, it is possible to develop an understanding of the applicant's ability to take constructive action on weakness and determine how the applicant can take criticism.

- "Tell me how you spend a typical day."
- "If you were the boss, how would you run your present job?"

Right Fit

One of the goals of the interview process is to determine the quality of fit. This concept is best is expressed as the right fit. How well a new hire fits into the culture of the team, property, and company is one of the major factors which will determine if the individual becomes a long-term employee. When seeking insight to determine fit there are two areas that are the focus of the interview questions: personal aspects and company.

Personal Aspects

These questions are general in nature. The answers to these questions provide insight into the individual's nature.

- "Tell me about yourself."
- "What practical experience have you had in this area?"
- "What is your major strength? Weakness?"
- "What types of people annoy you?"
- "What have you done that shows initiative and action?"
- "How do you spend your spare time?"
- "What personal characteristics do you feel are necessary for success in the hospitality industry?"
- "Where would you like to be in one year?"
- "Why do you want to work for us?"
- "Why do you want to leave your present job?"

Company

The answers to this type of question provide an indication of the individual's view of the company, job, and possible future with the company.

- "What do you know about our organization?"
- "Why do you want to work for us?"
- "Why would you like this particular job?"
- "How can you benefit our company?"
- "What experience(s) have you had that makes you a good fit with our company?"
- "What position would you like to hold with us in five years? In ten years?"
- "What interests you about our company?"
- "What kind of manager do you prefer to work with?"
- "What do you feel determines a person's progress in a good company?"

In addition to verbal and nonverbal responses during the interview, much can be learned from the actions and appearance of the applicant. These positive actions are listed hereunder:

- arriving early for the interview
- being alert and responsive
- being dressed appropriately
- being well groomed, with clean hair and nails
- making good eye contact
- listening carefully
- speaking well of other people
- sticking to the point.

Obviously, the person who arrives late for an interview, is inappropriately dressed and unclean, looks away, complains about other people, or exhibits inappropriate responses presents a negative image. The interview session provides the manager with the opportunity to form an impression about the applicant's abilities and general disposition and to make a reasoned judgment as to his or her suitability for the company.

The Hiring Decision

In reviewing all the information from the screening, background check, and interview the manager must ask: Is this the person I want for my team? Is he or she qualified for the position? Is the individual the right fit for the team, property, and company?

Checking references is an important part of the process leading to the hiring decision. References are checked to indicate accuracy of presented application and resume materials and seeking insight into job performance. The assumption in checking references is the past will indicate the future, and that performance in one job has some continuity with the next. While this is not always the case, a reference check can provide insight that is beneficial. In this process it should be remembered that while the reference contacted praises highly or criticizes greatly the applicant will never look or behave better than they have throughout the evaluation process.

The character of the applicant will impact the individual's job performance and fit in the position and as a member of the team. There are a number of questions the manager needs to strive to answer when considering the character of the individual. We list a few of these hereunder:

- How well will this person fit into the team?
- Can this person be trained and developed?
- What is his or her energy level?
- Is the applicant a team player?
- Is this an ethical individual?

Factors that should be noted in the interview process will provide answers for these questions. These factors are good listener, flexible, adaptable, accepts responsibility, considers others in their actions, willing to speak/contribute in a group, and is willing to be both a follower and a leader.

Compensation is important to both the individual and the company. Compensation will be discussed in detail in Chapter 5. It is important to point out here that factors that must be considered in the hiring decision are the fit of the compensation to both the individual and the company. The compensation must be competitive in the market place or the individual will decline and go to another company, but the company can only hire what it can afford. If the position being filled pays less than the potential staff member has been making or has indicated is their desired wage and there are no immediate promotional opportunities for the individual, then the fit is probably not good for either the individual or company. The overriding factor in compensation is that it must provide a fair salary for the work and that the salary is a fit to the company.

Hiring for skills-based positions such as housekeeper or cook and positions requiring specific knowledge such as math ability or computer skills should include basic testing. Requiring applicants for a housekeeping position to perform some basic functions of the position, such as making a bed or having the applicant for the front desk complete a basic math test will provide a clearer picture of their actual abilities.

A critical factor in hiring an individual is attitude which includes willingness to learn. It is possible to train an individual to do a job. However, rarely is it possible to make major adjustments in an individual's attitude. In the hospitality industry, attitude is of paramount importance. The individual who is unwilling to learn, does not like to work with others, assist people, step up when things become difficult, and cannot keep a positive approach to the guest even in adversity is not a good fit in the hospitality industry. There is a saying that is very appropriate for the recruiting and selection of hospitality staff: "hire for attitude first." Attitude must be balanced in many hiring decisions with the individual's knowledge and skill. This balance is clear when hiring, for example, a server. The individual under consideration has little or no experience as a server but in the interview exhibits an excellent attitude. This is an individual that should be given careful consideration. The chances for successfully training the person in the skills and knowledge of the position are much better than the chances for changing the person's attitude. While an element of risk is involved when knowledge and skills are not entirely fulfilled the manager needs to remember that training and development can fix the knowledge and skills if the attitude is strong. Other critical factors involved in the hiring decision are shown in Figure 4.6.

Other factors in the hiring decision

* Compensation: The rate of pay available affects the degree of selectivity.

* Labor relations: Unions may influence who is selected.

* Training and development: Training costs in terms of time and expense may be reduced or increased

FIGURE 4.6   Other Factors in the Hiring Decision

Summary

Recruiting and selection procedures that are well developed and applied assist in hiring the best possible candidates for the company. Managers must be aware of the legal issues involved in hiring a team member. Well-developed hiring procedures aid the manager in observing all of the laws pertaining to hiring personnel. Additionally, the managers must always remember that they can only hire what the organization can afford.

Ultimately, recruiting and hiring decisions should be based on the presence of the following characteristics:

- right fit to the team, property, and company and
- balance of attitude and knowledge and skills.

The right fit and the balance of attitude with knowledge and skills determines future turnover. The reduction in turnover achieved with a good fit effectively decreases training costs. Knowing the sources and methods of recruiting is critical to succeeding in the right fit in the hiring process.

Job descriptions should be used to format the essential and desirable skills of new team members. The EEOC criteria with regard to employment applicants must be followed strictly so that all applicants are afforded the same employment opportunities. Discrimination in employment opportunity is illegal and ignorance of the various laws is not a defense in this regard. Careful and effective screening of applicants will reduce the risk of selecting unsuitable team members. Screening requires the manager to actively check references. Interviewing permits face-to-face evaluation of potential new team members. Knowledge of interviewing techniques and processes, along with an understanding of the various types of interviews and appropriate use of skills and knowledge testing is foundational to quality personnel selection.

The hiring decision is based on analysis of all the information gathered. Key to the decision is the balancing of attitude with knowledge and skills with the desired outcome being hiring the right person for the job.

Study Questions

1. Identify the methods and steps used for completion of a job analysis.
2. Analyze a job description for correct content.
3. Differentiate between a job description and a job specification.
4. Define various recruitment techniques employed to attract a pool of qualified job candidates.
5. Interpret the legal issues associated with recruiting and selecting job applicants.
6. Apply the steps in screening potential new team members.
7. Classify different types of interviews used to screen applicants.
8. List the steps to be considered when interviewing potential team members.
9. State two examples of inappropriate and appropriate questions.
10. Differentiate elements associated with the hiring decision-making process.

Case Studies

The case studies listed below relate to the information presented in this chapter and reading, answering the case study questions and participating in discussion of a case will reinforce and expand what you have learned in this chapter. All case studies are provided in this text after the last chapter.

Shandong House Restaurant

Shepherd Mountain Hotel

Stone Lion Hotel and Conference Center

Notes

1. Bousley, H., & Glynn, S. J. (2012). There are Significant Business Costs to Replacing Employees. Center for American Progress. Retrieved

November 16, 2012, from http://www.americanprogress.org/issues/labor/report/2012/11/16/44464/there-are-significant-business-costs-to-replacing-employees/

2. Worthington, E., & Worthington, A. (1993). *People investment* (p. 108). Grant's Pass, OR: Oasis Press.

3. Marvin, B. (1993). *The foolproof foodservice selection system.* New York: John Wiley.

4. Wilson, R. (1997). *Conducting better job interviews* (p. 1). New York: Barron's.

Compensation, Benefits, and Staff Scheduling 5

CHAPTER OUTLINE

- ▶ Introduction
- ▶ Compensation Structure
- ▶ Compensation Classification and Overtime Pay
- ▶ Determining Job Worth
- ▶ Benefits
- ▶ Incentive Programs
- ▶ Employee Assistance Programs
- ▶ Scheduling
- ▶ Summary
- ▶ Notes

LEARNING OBJECTIVES

When you complete reading this chapter, you should be able to:

- ▶ summarize the principles of compensation structure
- ▶ define hourly, salaried, and exempt and nonexempt personnel
- ▶ apply the regulations governing overtime pay
- ▶ recall the principles of determining job worth
- ▶ identify the benefits common in hospitality operations
- ▶ differentiate components of government mandated benefits
- ▶ relate the value and types of incentives

- ▶ identify the purpose and components of an employee assistance program (EAP)
- ▶ state the steps in scheduling employees
- ▶ apply the principles of scheduling.

Introduction

The elements of compensation, benefits, incentives, employee assistance, and scheduling are keys in the success of any business. The management of all of these elements is central to an effective human resource management.

Compensation is not considered a motivational factor but it is central to an employee's morale. Management has to balance the level of compensation for the employees with the operation's ability to meet its bottom line. Being the highest paying employer will make it easier to find staff but it may also put the company out of business.

Benefits are part of a total compensation package. Employee meals in the restaurant industry, "friends and family" rates in the lodging industry, and complimentary entry of staff and their family to the amusement park are all examples of nonmonetary benefits common in the hospitality industry. Benefits with a direct monetary value, such as paid vacation or sick leave and health insurance are also offered to hospitality employees.

The hospitality industry is not normally thought of as an incentive-based employer. This is actually a misleading perception. In the restaurant industry wait staff and in the lodging industry front desk staff may be asked to upsell. To encourage upselling, the staff member is often given an incentive.

Employee wellness and morale are fundamental to the success of a hospitality enterprise. Employees that are experiencing personal distress diminish team synergy and generally deliver less than excellent interaction with guests. The team member or team that is demoralized is destined for failure in achieving team and company goals. EPAs provide a means for the employee to seek help. Management has the ability to create a positive work environment and generate a high level of staff and team morale.

A critical factor in a well-run hospitality operation is having the right number of staff on hand at the right time. Poor scheduling impacts the quality of product and service delivered to the guest. It also impacts the morale of the staff. Trying to do too much with too little can be as costly as overstaffing.

The manager must be prepared to deal with all aspects of human resource management. This includes the elements of compensation, benefits, incentives, employee assistance, and scheduling.

Compensation

Compensation is the pay an individual receives for doing a job. Compensation can take many forms. This includes barter such as when an individual does a job and receives some type of good in return. Individuals can also work for food and lodging. The most common form of payment in the hospitality industry is money. The individual performs assigned duties for a set length of time and receives money, commonly termed pay, wages, or salary in return.

The amount of compensation, however, will vary with the type of job. Jobs requiring little to no experience, knowledge, or skill receive the lowest pay. In contrast, jobs requiring the highest levels of experience, knowledge, and skill receive the highest pay. The position's level of pay is also impacted by the position's level of responsibilities and decision making.

Minimum Wage

In the United States there is level of wage below which the employer is not allowed to pay except for rare exemptions. This level is termed the minimum wage. The Federal minimum wage is currently $7.25 per hour for the first 40 hours worked in a seven consecutive day period. The minimum for a state can also be set by the state through state law. The state law must be adhered to if the state minimum wage exceeds the Federal Minimum wage. Currently there is movement across the United States to raise the minimum wage in both states and municipalities. An example of a state minimum wage that is higher than the Federal minimum wage are California with $10.00per hour, Rhode Island $9.60 per hour, and Colorado at $8.31 per hour.

Compensation Classifications and Overtime

Compensation is further divided into hourly wage and salary. An employee receiving an hourly wage is paid only for the number of hours worked. An example is Josef and Bill who both are paid $11.00 per hour. Last week Josef worked 25 hours and he was paid before deductions $275. Bill worked 40 hours last week and he was paid before deductions $484. On the other hand Yen Li and Yolanda are managers and paid a salary of $750 per week before deductions. Managers may take turns working "long" and "short" schedules each week. Last week Yen Li worked the "long" schedule of 52 hours while Yolanda worked the "short" schedule of 44 hours. Each manager was paid $750 for the week.

Under the Fair Labor Standards Act (FSLA), there are two compensation classifications: exempt and nonexempt. The exempt classification refers to those employees that do not receive additional pay for overtime. Both salaried and hourly can be classified as exempt employees but it is most often salaried employees that have this classification. The current standards for exempt status that apply to the restaurant and foodservice industry are shown in Figures 5.1, 5.2, and 5.3, respectively as excerpts from the US Department of Labor Wage and Hour Division Fact Sheet 17A.[1]

Exempt Status Standards

The FLSA requires that most employees in the United States be paid at least the federal minimum wage for all hours worked and overtime pay at time and one-half the regular rate of pay for all hours worked over 40 hours in a workweek.

However, Section 13(a)(1) of the FLSA provides an exemption from both minimum wage and overtime pay for employees employed as bona fide executive, administrative, professional and outside sales employees. Section 13(a)(1) and Section 13(a)(17) also exempt certain computer employees. To qualify for exemption, employees generally must meet certain tests regarding their job duties and be paid on a salary basis at not less than $455 per week. Job titles do not determine exempt status. In order for an exemption to apply, an employee's specific job duties and salary must meet all the requirements of the Department's regulations. See other fact sheets in this series for more information on the exemptions for executive, administrative, professional, computer and outside sales employees, and for more information on the salary basis requirement.[1]

FIGURE 5.1 Exempt Status Standards.

```
Executive Exemption

To qualify for the executive employee exemption, all of the following tests must be met:

* The employee must be compensated on a salary basis (as defined in the regulations) at a rate
not less than $455 per week;

* The employee's primary duty must be managing the enterprise, or managing a customarily
recognized department or subdivision of the enterprise;

* The employee must customarily and regularly direct the work of at least two or more other
full-time employees or their equivalent; and

* The employee must have the authority to hire or fire other employees, or the employee's
suggestions and recommendations as to the hiring, firing, advancement, promotion or any other
change of status of other employees must be given particular weight.[1]
```

FIGURE 5.2 Executive Exemption.

```
Administrative Exemptions

To qualify for the administrative employee exemption, all of the following tests must be met:

* The employee must be compensated on a salary or fee basis (as defined in the regulations) at
a rate not less than $455 per week;

* The employee's primary duty must be the performance of office or non-manual work
directly related to the management or general business operations of the employer or the
employer's customers; and

* The employee's primary duty includes the exercise of discretion and independent judgment
with respect to matters of significance.[1]
```

FIGURE 5.3 Administrative Exemptions.

The current standards for overtime pay and nonexempt personnel that apply to the restaurant and foodservice industry are shown
in Figure 5.4 as an excerpt from the US Department of Labor Wage
and Hour Division Fact Sheet 14.[2] These standards are revised often
so it best to check the current law at www.wagehour.dol.gov/. It is
important to note that individual states generally have their own regulations relating to overtime pay. The manager must be up-to-date
on all of the regulations. Failure to pay overtime when it should be
paid can result in major fines costing the company far more than the
overtime pay.

Non-Exempt Status Standards

Fact Sheet #14: Coverage Under the Fair Labor Standards Act (FLSA)

This fact sheet provides general information concerning coverage under the FLSA.

The FLSA is the Federal law which sets minimum wage, overtime, recordkeeping, and youth employment standards.

The minimum wage for covered nonexempt workers is not less than $7.25 per hour effective July 24, 2009. With only some exceptions, overtime ("time and one-half") must be paid for work over forty hours a week. Child labor regulations prohibit persons younger than eighteen years old from working in certain jobs and additionally sets rules concerning the hours and times employees under sixteen years of age may work.

More than 130 million American workers are protected (or "covered") by the FLSA, which is enforced by the Wage and Hour Division of the U.S. Department of Labor.

There are two ways in which an employee can be covered by the law: "enterprise coverage" and "individual coverage."

Enterprise Coverage

Employees who work for certain businesses or organizations (or "enterprises") are covered by the FLSA. These enterprises, which must have at least two employees, are:

(1) those that have an annual dollar volume of sales or business done of at least $500,000

(2) hospitals, businesses providing medical or nursing care for residents, schools and preschools, and government agencies

Individual Coverage

Even when there is no enterprise coverage, employees are protected by the FLSA if their work regularly involves them in commerce between States ("interstate commerce"). The FLSA covers individual workers who are "engaged in commerce or in the production of goods for commerce."

Examples of employees who are involved in interstate commerce include those who: produce goods (such as a worker assembling components in a factory or a secretary typing letters in an office) that will be sent out of state, regularly make telephone calls to persons located in other States, handle records of interstate transactions, travel to other States on their jobs, and do janitorial work in buildings where goods are produced for shipment outside the State.

Also, domestic service workers (such as housekeepers, full-time babysitters, and cooks) are normally covered by the law.[2]

FIGURE 5.4 Non-Exempt Status Standards.

States often have labor laws pertaining to overtime compensation. The state is law is superseded by the federal law if the federal law is more stringent. If the state is more stringent and imposes greater requirements than the federal law, then the state supersedes the federal law. An example of a state law that supersedes federal law is the law in the state of California which states:

California Overtime Regulations

"Eight hours of labor constitutes a day's work, and employment beyond eight hours in any workday or more than six days in any workweek is permissible provided the employee is compensated for the overtime at not less than:

One and one-half times the employee's regular rate of pay for all hours worked in excess of eight hours up to and including 12 hours in any workday, and for the first eight hours worked on the seventh consecutive day of work in a workweek; and

Double the employee's regular rate of pay for all hours worked in excess of 12 hours in any workday and for all hours worked in excess of eight on the seventh consecutive day of work in a workweek. (http://www.dir.ca.gov/dlse/faq_overtime.htm)"

Compensation Structure

Job Worth

The first step in determining a compensation structure is establishing job worth. Job worth is the value placed on the work and responsibilities assigned to a position and the experience, knowledge, and skills required to carry out the work and responsibilities. Establishing job worth begins with the job analysis which leads to the job description. Once it is clear what the position does and what is needed to succeed in the position there are two primary ways to determine the value: (1) external and (2) internal equity. The desired outcome is a pay structure that is reflective of the market value of positions and creates equity across positions in the company.

The establishment of job worth is a complex undertaking. The ability of companies to conduct the research and analysis needed to properly carry out the work is limited. In most cases, an outside consultant is used. Methods used to establish job worth include the ranking method, classification method, point method, and factor comparison method. Each method involves an in-depth analysis of what is termed compensable factors.

A compensable factor is one the company values and is willing to pay for. Examples of a compensable factor include education, skills, experience, and position responsibilities. The company will probably be willing to pay for a college degree for a management position but not for a dishwasher position.

The ranking method is typically the ranking of positions by a group of managers based on difficulty of the work, skill required, or possibly importance to organization. For example, positions would be ranked from least difficult to most difficult. The classification method is also called "job grading." This method is often used by government agencies. Positions are classified at set levels which have established pay ranges. Classifications for federal employees the GS (general scale) ratings include the following:

- clerical and nonsupervisory personnel (GS1 to GS4)
- management trainees (GS5 to GS10)
- general management and highly specialized jobs (GS11 to GS15).

The point method assigns a point value to each position based on set criteria. The development of the criteria is a complex process but once done the method is easy to use. The factor comparison method is based on identifying key jobs in the company. Once the key jobs are identified the wage for these positions becomes the benchmark for all other positions.

Compensation Package

The establishment of the worth of a position is part of creating a compensation structure for the company. A company's compensation structure is a reflection of the mission, values, and goals of the company. A well-structured compensation structure encourages high morale, loyalty, and quality performance. The compensation structure is not just pay it is a package. That package includes pay, benefits, and incentives.

Benefits

Benefits are part of a comprehensive compensation structure. Benefits can generally be classified in four broad categories: mandatory, optional/voluntary, retirement, and miscellaneous. Mandatory benefits are those mandated by the state or federal government. There four primary mandatory benefits that most nongovernmental employers must provide. These include social security, workers compensation, unemployment compensation, and health insurance.

"The Social Security Act of 1935 (Public Law 74-271) created the Federal-State Unemployment Compensation (UC) Program. The program has two main objectives: (1) to provide temporary and partial wage replacement to involuntarily unemployed workers who were recently employed; and (2) to help stabilize the economy during recessions. The U.S. Department of Labor oversees the system, but each State administers its own program.[9]"

Social security was established in 1935 by the Federal Insurance Contribution Act. The purpose of social security is to provide financial security for all employers, employees, and their dependents through retirement and disability income and survivor benefits. In 2013 the employer contributed 6.2% and the employee contributed 6.2% of the employees pay per year to the taxable maximum.[3]

The taxable maximum is the contribution and benefits base set by the federal government.[4] The contribution and benefits base for social security in 2013 was $117,000. However, the taxable maximum can change. Changes in the taxable maximum are generally tied to increases in the "average wage index." For example, the taxable maximum was $102,000 in 2008 and was adjusted to $106,800 in 2009 and $106,800 in 2010 or 2011.[5]

Related to social security is the Medicare hospital insurance program which is intended to provide the same type of security for health care. The employer also contributes 1.45% of the employees' pay to Medicare but there is no contribution base limit for this contribution.[6]

Both social security and Medicare benefits are available to the employees at retirement if they have met the age requirement. The eligible age for retirement and benefit amount based on birth year for 2013[7] is shown in Figure 5.5. These benefits are also available to employees who have become disabled and the survivors of employers that have passed away.

Workers' compensation provides for the medical care and disability pay for individuals injured in the work place. The amount the employer pays for this benefit will vary with the claims rate of the employer. The fewer the claims the employer has the lower the rate for the insurance. Workers' compensation insurance may be provided by the state, private insurance companies, or associations. Many states allow companies to self-insure. This means that the company creates a fund that is available to pay in case of injury. Companies that self-insure generally have to have their funding certified by someone in the state government and submit to audit by the state.[8]

Age To Receive Full Social Security Benefits	
Year of Birth	**Full Retirement Age**
1937 or earlier	65
1938	65 and 2 months
1939	65 and 4 months
1940	65 and 6 months
1941	65 and 8 months
1942	65 and 10 months
1943--1954	66
1955	66 and 2 months
1956	66 and 4 months
1957	66 and 6 months
1958	66 and 8 months
1959	66 and 10 months
1960 and later	67

The earliest a person can start receiving Social Security retirement benefits will remain age 62.[6]

FIGURE 5.5   Age To Receive Full Social Security Benefits.

This benefit is generally paid by the state to qualified individuals. The overall purpose of the federal–state unemployment compensation is to provide minimal support to the unemployed individuals till they find new employment. The unemployment insurance fund in a state is generally at least partially funded by a tax on employers based on their number of employees and claim rate. Again, as with workers compensation, the fewer the claims the lower the rate paid by the employer.

The Patient Protection and Affordable Care Act (PPACA), commonly called the Affordable Care Act (ACA) is intended is to expand health care coverage to all Americans.[10] The ACA mandates employers with 50 or more full-time equivalents to offer coverage to full-time employees and their dependents or pay taxes if an employee obtains exchange coverage and a premium tax credit.

The large employer (50 or more full-time equivalent employees [FTEE]) who does not provide insurance coverage will pay an excise tax (penalty) for each FTEE (Figure 5.6). Depending on the circumstances of the failure to provide coverage, the fine can vary from $2,000 to $3,000 per FTEE. The ACA defines a full-time employee as one that works 30 hours per week or 130 hours per calendar month. Large employers are not required to offer health coverage to part-time employees.

The small employer, with <50 FTEE, do not face tax penalties if they do not offer coverage to full-time employees. The ACA does provide tax credits to the small employer to assist them in offering coverage.

Insurance offered by any employer should meet the standards set in the ACA. These standards address the coverage's minimum value (MV) and affordability. The standard for affordability is that an employee's share of the self-only premium for the employer's lowest cost plan that provides MV cannot exceed 9.5% of the employee's household income. A plan fails to provide MV if "the plan's share of the total allowed costs of benefits provided under the plan is less than 60 percent of such costs.[11]"

Common optional benefits include what are considered monetary benefits such as paid sick days, paid vacation days, life insurance, dental insurance, and paid holidays and nonmonetary benefits

---

For 2015 and after, employers employing at least a certain number of employees (generally 50 full-time employees or a combination of full-time and part-time employees that is equivalent to 50 full-time employees) will be subject to the Employer Shared Responsibility provisions under section 4980H of the Internal Revenue Code (added to the Code by the Affordable Care Act). As defined by the statute, a full-time employee is an individual employed on average at least 30 hours of service per week. An employer that meets the 50 full-time employee threshold is referred to as an applicable large employer.

Under the Employer Shared Responsibility provisions, if these employers do not offer affordable health coverage that provides a minimum level of coverage to their full-time employees (and their dependents), the employer may be subject to an Employer Shared Responsibility payment if at least one of its full-time employees receives a premium tax credit for purchasing individual coverage on one of the new Affordable Insurance Exchanges, also called a Health Insurance Marketplace (Marketplace).[11]

FIGURE 5.6 Affordable Care Act.

(often called "perks") such as employee meals and "family and friends" lodging rates. The cost associated with each of these benefits, whether monetary or nonmonetary, can be significant. According to the US Department of Labor as of December 2010 on average total employee compensation broke down to 70.8% for wages and 29.2% for benefits.[12] This means that for every dollar spent on wages an additional 41 cents were spent for benefits. This means the employee who was being paid the federal minimum wage of $7.25 per hour is actually receiving $10.23 in compensation. Benefits are costly but generate positive outcomes. "Results indicate that among the industry groupings examined, firms that offer more benefits have lower employee turnover.[13]" The cost of turnover is high. Turnover involves training cost and impacts quality of service. Providing these types of benefits can increase employee loyalty.[14] The monetary benefits can be funded 100% by the employer or provided on a cost share basis. A cost share program is one in which the employer pays a portion of the cost of the benefit and the employee also pays a portion of the cost.

Paid sick leave is moving closer to becoming a mandatory benefit. The state of California has passed the Healthy Workplace Healthy Family Act of 2014 (AB 1522). This act states that "An employee who, on or after July 1, 2015, works in California for 30 or more days within a year from the beginning of employment, is entitled to paid sick leave. Employees, including part-time and temporary employees, will earn at least one hour of paid leave for every 30 hours worked. Accrual begins on the first day of employment or July 1, 2015, whichever is later."[15] Employers may limit the usage of sick leave to 24 hours or 3 days per year and the sick leave can accrue but the accrual is capped at 48 hours or 6 work days. The potential for paid sick leave legislation at the federal level is high.

Retirement benefits can add to the stability of the company's workforce. "Benefits continue to attract and retain employees, and the importance of benefits to employees across all generations will only increase over the coming years, Leopold predicted. Employees and employers acknowledge the importance of salaries and health benefits to employee loyalty. But other benefits are important drivers of loyalty as well, Leopold (Ronald Leopold, vice president MetLife) said, especially retirement benefits and nonmedical benefits, including life, dental and disability insurance. Yet only about 37 percent of employers recognize this.[16]" There are two primary types of retirement plans: (1) contributory and (2) noncontributory. A contributory retirement plan is one in which the employer and employee contribute to the plan.

An example would be the employer matching every $1.00 contributed by the employee with $2.00. This is the most popular type of retirement plan today. A noncontributory plan is one in which only the employer contributes to the plan. In both types of plans, the funds invested in the plan are tax-deferred income. Tax-deferred income is income which will be taxed when the funds are taken out of the plan. Generally this is done at retirement and the tax rate for the individual is lower than at the time of investment. There are specific guidelines for the handling and withdrawing of funds from a retirement plan. The Employee Retirement Income Security Act of 1974 established guidelines that must be adhered to by the employer (Figure 5.7).

The terms "vested" or "vesting" are of importance when discussing retirement plans. Vesting is a provision generally applied to retirement plans to encourage employees to stay with a company for an extended period of time. The act of becoming "vested" in a retirement plan means that the individual is contributing to the plan (and working for the company) for a specific length of time. If the employee leaves the company and stops contributing to the plan before the specified length of time they will receive back what they have put into the plan but they will not

---

Employee Retirement Income Security Act

The Employee Retirement Income Security Act of 1974 (ERISA) is a federal law that sets minimum standards for most voluntarily established pension and health plans in private industry to provide protection for individuals in these plans.

ERISA requires plans to provide participants with plan information including important information about plan features and funding; provides fiduciary responsibilities for those who manage and control plan assets; requires plans to establish a grievance and appeals process for participants to get benefits from their plans; and gives participants the right to sue for benefits and breaches of fiduciary duty.

There have been a number of amendments to ERISA, expanding the protections available to health benefit plan participants and beneficiaries. One important amendment, the Consolidated Omnibus Budget Reconciliation Act (COBRA), provides some workers and their families with the right to continue their health coverage for a limited time after certain events, such as the loss of a job. Another amendment to ERISA is the Health Insurance Portability and Accountability Act (HIPAA) which provides important new protections for working Americans and their families who have preexisting medical conditions or might otherwise suffer discrimination in health coverage based on factors that relate to an individual's health. Other important amendments include the Newborns' and Mothers' Health Protection Act, the Mental Health Parity Act, and the Women's Health and Cancer Rights Act.

FIGURE 5.7 Employee Retirement Income Security Act.

receive any funds contributed by the company. The length of time to achieve "vesting" varies from company to company and plan to plan.

Miscellaneous benefits often include educational scholarships, and flexible work schedules. It is becoming more common for employers to offer assistance to employees that are pursuing education or training. This assistance may be a scholarship that is awarded based on work performance. The assistance may also be in the form of a reimbursement plan. The employee successfully completes course work and submits to the company for reimbursement of the cost of the course or training. These types of programs generate employee loyalty. They also can be a cornerstone of a program to develop a pool of employees in house suitable for advancement. "Education benefits have long been associated with full-time workers who want to move up within their companies with advanced degrees. But, eager to recruit and retain employees, local businesses such as Bill Miller Bar-B-Q are beefing up their investment in higher education and training even for young, part-time employees.[17]"

In the hospitality industry flexible work schedules are not as easily provided as in some other types of businesses. In general a flexible work schedule means that a company allows employees to adapt their work schedule to their other life responsibilities. This might include the parent who works from home to allow them to take care of children or elderly parent. This is probably not realistic for most hotel or restaurant positions but may be for some administrative support positions such as a social media manager. What is realistic is asking employees what hours are best for them to work and taking this into consideration when creating a work schedule.

Incentive Programs

Incentive programs can be an important part of a compensation package or can simply be a moral builder depending on the type of program. An incentive is something that encourages the employee to take action. An incentive program is a program that encourages employees to achieve specific goals set by the company. The program is built on rewards for achieving those goals. This type of program is a common part of a management compensation package. Generally the program is structured around the achievement of a specific performance, sales, or profit level for the operation. The reward for achieving the goal set may be a bonus or profit sharing. The level of bonus or profit sharing is generally scaled according to the level of the employee. A manager would receive more than an assistant manager but less than the general manager. Programs of this type may also extend to the other staff in the property or company. If a property achieves a specified goal, then there may be a bonus for all team members.

Another common type of incentive program in the restaurant and hotel part of the hospitality industry is sales based. An example is creating a reward for the server who sells the most wine or desserts. Generally, these types of programs are intended to accomplish two goals. The incentive is designed to increase overall sales. The incentive is also designed to drive sales of a particular part of the menu or menu item.

Employee Assistance Programs

Generally, EAPs are considered to be a benefit but they benefit both the employee and the employer. An EAP is intended to help employees deal with personal problems that could adversely impact the employees' work performance, health, and well-being. EAPs focus on issues such as a personal crisis. This type of situation could include a death in the family, abuse of the employee by someone either in or outside the company, or financial hardship. Drug and alcohol abuse are also a major focus of the EAPs. The EAP provides short-term counseling and refers the employee to professionals and agencies that can assist them on a long-term basis.

The EAP is part of the company but must have the ability to deal with issues confidentially. In light of the ability of the EAP to deal with issues confidentially it may also be the go-to place with regard to what is termed "whistle blowing." "Whistle blowing" is when an employee feels there is an activity taking place that is inappropriate or unsafe and that it should be reported but fears he or she could lose his or her job for being the one that reports the activity.

The number of companies providing EAPs is increasing. These programs allow companies to assist long-term employees through difficult times so that they continue to be an asset to the company.

Staff Scheduling

Scheduling is the action of establishing the flow of staff over a set period of time for a property based on the projected need for personnel at a specific time. A staff schedule can contribute to the company's profit or loss. Scheduling more staff than are needed to provide the level of service and production output for a period of time increases labor expense unnecessarily.

Developing a schedule requires information such as sales projections and output standards. Sales projections are based on sales histories. A sales history is the result of keeping track of sales. To develop a schedule the previous sales for the same or similar time of year, month, day, and even hour should be reviewed. This information is considered along with weather predictions, the current economic climate, and any special circumstances.

For example when building a staff schedule for the week of June 23–29, the scheduler looked at the sales for the period in the previous three years. A single year can be used but it is more accurate to look at multiple years to predict sales for the coming year at that time. The sales looked at are not just dollar sales. An example is in a hotel, the scheduler is considering the number of guests in house, rooms sold, in-house foodservice guest counts, banquet event numbers, and times of day for the sales. The scheduler also considers that overall sales have been down for the past 12 months on average by about 5% from the previous year. The downward trend of sales it looks like will be balanced for the week being scheduled because a special festival is scheduled that is expected to bring a 15% temporary increase in room sales but because of food outlets at the festival a 20% decrease in sales at in-house food outlets. Based on all of this information it is possible for the scheduler to make an educated estimate of sales for the period in question.

The sales are now predicted but how many staff will be needed to take care of that level of business must still be determined. This is decided based on the standards of the operation for production and service, which can also be called output standards. The standard will vary depending on the type of property but the question is always the same. How many guests can a service staff member serve and still deliver the standard of service established for the hotel? How many housekeepers, line cooks, valet attendants, front desk staff, security, and other staff will be needed to deliver all aspects of product and service at the level of quality established for the hotel?

Companies apply a variety of methods for scheduling in an effort to control both quality and costs. One of the more common methods is called sales-per-labor-hour. Sales-per-labor-hour when applied to scheduling is the dollar amount of sales 1 hour of labor is

Chef Bert's Food Emporium
Store 8
Charlotte, NC
Week of: January 25-31, 2018

	Monday January 25	Tuesday January 26	Wednesday January 27	Thursday January 28	Friday January 29	Saturday January 30	Sunday January 31		Hours per Week
Kitchen Supervisor 1*	8am-6pm	8am-6pm	8am-6pm	Off	Off	8am-6pm	8am-6pm	=	50
Kitchen Supervisor 2*	Off	Off	2pm-12am	2pm-12am	2pm-12am	2pm-12am	2pm-12am	=	50
Kitchen Supervisor 3*	2pm-12am	2pm-12am	Off	8am-6pm	8am-6pm	Off	11am-10pm	=	50
Line Cook 1	8:30am-4:30pm	Off	8:30am-4:30pm	Off	8am-4pm	8am-4pm	8am-4pm	=	40
Line Cook 2	Off	8:30am-4:30pm	Off	8:30am-4:30pm	10am-6pm	10am-6pm	10am-6pm	=	40
Line Cook 3	4pm-12am	Off	4pm-12am	Off	4pm-12am	4pm-12am	4pm-12am	=	40
Line Cook 4	Off	4pm-12am	Off	4pm-12am	3pm-11pm	3pm-11pm	12pm-8pm	=	40
Cooks Assistant 1	8am-4pm	Off	8am-4pm	Off	8am-4pm	8am-4pm	8am-4pm	=	40
Cooks Assistant 2	Off	8am-4pm	Off	8am-4pm	10am-6pm	10am-6pm	10am-6pm	=	40
Cooks Assistant 3	4pm-12am	Off	4pm-12am	Off	3pm-11pm	3pm-11pm	11am-7pm	=	40
Cooks Assistant 4	Off	4pm-12am	Off	4pm-12am	4pm-12am	4pm-12am	4pm-12am	=	40
Cooks Assistant 5	Off	Off	Off	10am-6pm	3pm-11pm	3pm-11pm	3pm-11pm	=	32
Prep Cook 1	8am-4pm	8am-4pm	Off	8am-4pm	8am-4pm	8am-4pm	8am-4pm	=	40
Prep Cook 2	Off	Off	Off	8am-4pm	11am-7pm	11am-7pm	10am-6pm	=	40
Prep Cook 3	Off	Off	8am-4pm	Off	1pm-6pm	1pm-6pm	5pm-12pm	=	25
Dishwasher 1	11:30am-3:30pm	Off	11:30am-3:30pm	Off	11:30am-3:30pm	11:00-7pm	11:00am-7pm	=	28
Dishwasher 2	5:30pm-12:00am	Off	5:30pm-12:00am	Off	5:30pm-12:00am	12pm-8pm	12pm-8pm	=	35.5
Dishwasher 3	11:30am-3:30pm	11:30am-3:30pm	Off	11:30am-3:30pm	6:00pm-11:00pm	7:00pm-12:00pm	7:00pm-12:00pm	=	23
Dishwasher 4	Off	5:30pm-12:00am	Off	5:30pm-12:00am	Off	Off	Off	=	13
Pot & Pan Cleaner 1	9:30am-5:30pm	9:30am-5:30pm	Off	9:30am-5:30pm	9:30am-5:30pm	9:30am-5:30pm	9:30am-5:30pm	=	40
Pot & Pan Cleaner 2	Off	Off	9:30am-5:30pm	9:30am-5:30pm	4:00pm-12:00am	4:00pm-12:00am	4:00pm-12:00am	=	40
Pot & Pan Cleaner 3	7:00pm-12:00am	7:00pm-12:00am	7:00pm-12:00am	7:00pm-12:00am	Off	Off	Off	=	20
Labor Hours per day	63.5	63.5	63.5	79.5	124.5	130	132	656.5	656.5

* Supervisors are salaried personnel and not included in the labor hours calculation .

Targeted Sales Per Manhour = $233
Sales Required to meet Target = $1,52,964.50

FIGURE 5.8 Chef Bert's Food Emporium.

expected to generate. This 1 hour of labor is generally hourly labor not salaried management. A company will often set a standard for sales-per-labor-hour such as when scheduling no more than 1 hour of labor can scheduled for every $55 in the projected sales. If this is the standard then if the projected sales for the day are $3,200 then no more than 58.18 hours of labor time can be scheduled. The scheduler, manager, must determine where to apply the hours available. An example schedule is shown in Figure 5.8.

Summary

While many of the details addressed in this chapter may be delegated to a human resource department in a larger operation, the full management team should be involved. Compensation benefits and scheduling are of critical importance to the continued operation of any business. In today's world, profit margins are often slim. This makes consideration, planning, and execution in this area of even greater importance. The goal is always to attract and retain the finest possible staff. Compensation, benefits, and scheduling play an important part in accomplishing that goal.

Study Questions

Summarize the principles of compensation structure.

1. Define the following terms associated with compensation:
   i. Hourly
   ii. Salaried
   iii. Exempt
   iv. Nonexempt personnel
2. Outline the regulations governing overtime pay.
3. State the process of determining job worth.
4. List and discuss four types of benefits common in hospitality operations.
5. Outline the requirements of each the following government mandated benefits:
   i. Health insurance
   ii. Workers' compensation

    iii.   Social security

    iv.   Medicare

6. List and discuss a minimum of two types of incentive programs associated with the hospitality industry.

7. State the purpose and components of an EAP.

8. State the steps in scheduling employees.

9. Create a schedule for your kitchen employees at Chef Bert's Food Emporium based on the following information (Figure 5.8).

    i.   kitchen supervisors

    ii.   line cooks

    iii.   cooks' assistants

    iv.   preparatory cooks

    v.   dishwashers

    vi.   pot and pan cleaners

The operation is open from 11 a.m. to 11 p.m., 6 days per week. The busiest times are from 11:45 a.m. to 2 p.m. and from 7:30 p.m. to 10 p.m. Prep begins 3 hours before opening each day. Clean-up finishes each night within 1 hour after close.

Your goal is to have a kitchen supervisor present whenever kitchen staff is working.

Case Studies

The case studies listed below relate to the information presented in this chapter and reading, answering the case study questions and participating in discussion of a case will reinforce and expand what you have learned in this chapter. All case studies are provided in this text after the last chapter.

    Shady Lane Inn

    Grand Adventure Park

    Shepherd Mountain Hotel

Notes

1. United States Department of Labor, Wage and Hour Division. Retrieved November 2, 2014, from http://www.dol.gov/whd/regs/compliance/fairpay/fs17a_overview.pdf, Revised July, 2008.

2. United States Department of Labor, Wage and Hour Division. Retrieved November 2, 2014, from http://www.dol.gov/whd/regs/compliance/whdfs14.htm, Revised July, 2009.

3. Social Security Administration. Retrieved November 2, 2014, from http://www.ssa.gov/oact/cola/cbb.html

4. Ibid.

5. Ibid.

6. Ibid.

7. Ibid.

8. United States Department of Labor. Retrieved November 2, 2014 from http://www.ows.doleta.gov/unemploy/uifactsheet.asp, Updated January 13, 2010.

9. California Department of Industrial Relations. Retrieved November 2, 2014 from http://www.dir.ca.gov/sip/sip.html.

10. Washington Council Ernest and Young. (February, 2013). *The Affordable Care Act: Summary of employer requirements*. Retrieved November 2, 2014 from http://www.nahu.org/meetings/capitol/2013/attendees/jumpdrive/Employer_ACA_Reference_Deck_02_14_2013.pdf.

11. Ibid.

12. *Almanac of policy issues*. Retrieved November 2, 2014 from http://www.policyalmanac.org/social_welfare/archive/unemployment_compensation.shtml

13. United States Department of Labor, Bureau of Labor Statistics. Retrieved November 2, 2014 from http://www.bls.gov/news.release/ecec.nr0.htm, March 9, 2011.

14. Scorza, J. (April 1, 2011). *Benefits can boost employee loyalty*. Society for Human Resource Management. Retrieved November 2, 2014 from http://www.shrm.org/hrdisciplines/benefits/Articles/Pages/Benefits_Loyalty.aspx.

15. The California Division of Labor Standards Enforcement. Retrieved February 3, 2015 from http://www.dir.ca.gov/dlse/ab1522.html.

16. Scorza, J. (April 1, 2011). *Benefits can boost employee loyalty*. Society for Human Resource Management. Retrieved November 2, 2014 from http://www.shrm.org/hrdisciplines/benefits/Articles/Pages/Benefits_Loyalty.aspx.

17. Taylor, L. (October 10, 2004). *Recipe for retention*. San Antonio Business Journal. Retrieved November 2, 2014 from http://www.enewsbuilder.net/peoplereport/e_article000326611.cfm?x=b11,0,w.

Staff Training 6

CHAPTER OUTLINE

- ▶ Introduction
- ▶ A Systems Approach to Training
- ▶ Types of Training
- ▶ How People Learn
- ▶ Adult Learning
- ▶ Barriers to Learning
- ▶ Conclusions
- ▶ Summary

LEARNING OBJECTIVES

When you complete reading this chapter, you should be able to:

- ▶ relate the concept of training as an investment
- ▶ describe a systems approach to training and explain how training interacts with the goals of the company
- ▶ define the types of training and their strengths and weaknesses and describe situations appropriate for each method
- ▶ list the learning domains
- ▶ understand the concept of andragogy and outline the challenges in this area for the trainer
- ▶ identify factors that inhibit learning.

Introduction

Quality is the key to success in any business. A critical factor in achieving success is training and development of staff. In any hospitality operation it is the quality of the execution of every task that ultimately determines the quality of the product or service delivered to and experienced by the guest. The goal must be for each guest experience to meet or exceed the guest's expectations. When the guest enters their hotel room the goal is for them to think "this is perfect from the décor, to the feel of the linens and mattress, to the cleanliness and operational order." When the guest is served their meal in the restaurant the goal is for them to think "this looks great" and when they taste food to think "this is really good." Training and staff development are a major part of the foundation that makes these pleasurable guest experiences possible. The management must clearly communicate its vision for the property and establish and maintain the standards of performance that will deliver on that committed vision. The standards must obviously be supported by well-developed processes and procedures that lead to achievement of the standards. Training must be developed and conducted to make staff experts and standard bearers in their assigned tasks.

To achieve the desired outcomes in this regard, there are numerous steps that must be strictly followed. At the hotel and the restaurant the designer understood the management's vision. The purchasing agent developed clear purchasing specifications and based product selection on that vision. The building engineer had the technical knowledge and demonstrated belief and support in the vision by insuring all operational aspects of the property. The hotel housekeeper's work demonstrated their sincere desire for the guest to have an outstanding experience as envisioned by the owners and managers of the property. The restaurant's culinary team prepared every dish with a sincere concern for the guest's enjoyment. Staff training in position-specific knowledge as well as skills and development of staff–beginning with orientation through specialized instructions in areas of importance to all staff such as harassment, safety, and company policies—are the foundations that allow the desired outcomes to be achieved.

It is an established fact that training is an investment. It is an infrastructure investment that leads to a tangible return on investment (ROI). Figure 6.1 shows the ROI for training. Commitment to staff training must begin from the top management of the company. It should be communicated clearly and consistently. A culture of continuous

FIGURE 6.1   ROI: Training is an Investment.

learning must be established. The commitment must be reflected in all of the company's actions including recruitment, pay, recognition, and promotion.

The aim of training is to provide services and products both internally and externally which meet and hopefully exceed expectations of the guest(s) and company standards every time. The company must deliver what is promised both to the guest and to the staff.

Training is an investment in the long-term health and well-being of the organization.

A Systems Approach to Training

Training is a learning process that involves the acquisition of skills, concepts, rules, and attitudes so as to optimize the performance of each team member. Training is the process of integrating personal and organizational goals. The focus is on establishment of a culture in which parts of the staff member's personal goals are in sync with the company's goals. Training is the way to bridge the gap between current and desired performance of individual team members and teams.

Training is not a singular action; in contrast, it is a system, that is, a cycle with interrelated elements. These elements closely parallel the steps a person uses in solving a problem. The five steps, shown in Figure 6.2, comprise this closed-loop continuous process. We now discuss each of these five steps.

Analysis of Training Needs

This step is sometimes called needs analysis and has two main purposes: (1) to determine what is needed in the first place and (2) to ensure that the training that does occur is based on sound requirements.[1] Therefore, the needs analysis process is the most important step in the development of a training program because all other activities involved in the design, delivery, and evaluation stem from this process. A needs analysis typically contains the following steps:

- identify performance problems
- identify knowledge, skills, and attitudes to perform job
- assess team member knowledge and skill
  - determine methods of gathering data

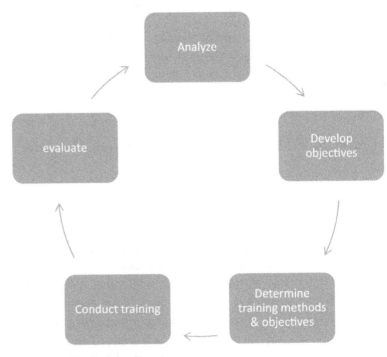

FIGURE 6.2 The Training Process.

- gather data
- analyze data
- prepare training plans based on data analysis.

The needs analysis assists in determining the difference between present performance and desired performance, that is, the gap between what is and what ought to be. "Performance problems might be reflected in high employee turnover, a decline in productivity, grievances, poor teamwork, and/or customer complaints. If this is the case, the following questions should arise as part of the needs analysis.[2]":

- What are the specific problems?
- What exactly is the desired outcome of training?
- What would the effect of no training be?
- Is training the best method of resolving the problems?

Once the problem or problems have been identified and it has been determined that it is training related, then the following steps are to be followed in the needs analysis process:

- Identify the knowledge, skills, and attitudes essential to performing the job.
- Assess individual team members. Analyze their strengths as well as their weaknesses.

These strengths and weaknesses are measured against the specific job requirements identified in the needs analysis step.

- Design an instrument or methods of gathering information. The basic rule in a systematic approach is to collect only that information that is necessary to design the training program.
- Principal methods of data collection are listed hereunder:
  - Observations: The process of observation involves observing team members, that is, their work routines and behaviors and how each person interacts within the team.
  - Interviews: The face-to-face interview is also a useful method of gathering information on training gaps. The interview technique, like the observation process, can take the form of informal interviews to discuss problems or issues related to training.
  - Work samples: Samples of work produced by the team member can be evaluated by having the individual perform a task.

Once the data have been collected, it is necessary to analyze the information so that specific training plans and strategies may be formulated.

The training plan should be prioritized on the basis of the needs analysis. In the needs analysis segment of a systematic approach to training, the basic purpose is to uncover the quality gaps: what it is that prevents a quality dining experience, hotel stay, or attraction experience. It is also about utilizing scarce resources of time, money, and people to maximize the training effort in a planned, systematic, and sequential way.

Training Objectives

Systematic and sequential planning of the training program is critical to its success. The development of precise and measurable training objectives is crucial in instructional delivery.[3] Good objectives ensure that learners are aware of what will occur during training. Objectives will also provide learners with information on what they will be able to do upon completion of the training session. In addition, objectives often serve as the basis for program and trainer evaluation. Training objectives are intended not to limit what a team member learns, but to provide a minimum level of expected achievement.

Training objectives are also called performance objectives or behavioral objectives. Whatever terminology is used, it is the concept that actually counts. The concept is that stating objectives for whatever type of training is undertaken will ensure that all efforts are directed to achieving only the desired results. The objective allows the manager or other trainer to determine whether the desired training objectives have been achieved. The performance of the team member is compared to the standard set by the objective to validate their mastery. The objectives guide both the trainer and trainee in the training process.

A statement of objectives may be viewed as an agreement between the team member or team and the manager/trainer. It is the primary and sole responsibility of the manager/trainer as an instructor to provide training and coaching in a positive environment. The team member's responsibility is to listen and work hard in the training sessions.

Problems of product and/or performance quality can be redefined as objectives that can be used to develop plans for training. Critical to a training objective is the statement of what the team member or team will be able to do after completion of a training session. Objectives should build the training needs of each team member in a logical and systematic way.[4] Example objectives are shown in Figure 6.3.

> **Example Objectives**
>
> * Upon completion of the training session on sauce making, the kitchen team member will be able to correctly prepare within 10 minutes 2 quarts of Hollandaise sauce from the recipe provided using the kitchen blender following all safety/sanitation procedures indicated within the lesson.
> * After completion of the training session on use of a type C fire extinguisher the staff member will be able to identify a type C fire extinguisher, state the type of fires for which it can be used and demonstrate proper use of the C type extinguisher.

FIGURE 6.3 Example Objectives.

Determine Training Materials and Instructional Method

Development of the training materials and instructional method are based on a training plan developed from the training objectives. Training materials must be matched to the training outcomes and the instructional technique selected for the training. Instructional methods include job talk, demonstration, role-play, or lecture. Instruction can be trainer driven, self-guided, or independent study. Instructional materials whether print or technology based should include complete student materials such as reading materials, activity sheets, job-specific information such as recipes, room cleaning procedure and other guide sheets, reference sheets, assignments, and practice quizzes and exercises. The materials should also include instructor lesson plans, tests and quizzes with answers, exercises and assignments with answers, equipment lists, work guide sheets, and timelines. Technology used for instruction and instructional materials is rapidly expanding and changing and currently includes digital video disc, online, and other computer based instructional programs. Only the time spent on the training itself is greater than the amount of time spent on the development of training materials. The quality of the training materials contributes substantially to the overall quality of the training.

There are totally eight steps in the planning and development of the training session. The following is an example of building a training session. The training session is on "the Frenching of a lamb rack."

Step 1: The objectives. This is the starting point for all planning of training activities. The instructor must realize from the start just what can be accomplished and the limits of time. The objective when well developed and written will serve also as a tool to evaluate the training.

- The time for the Frenching demo will be limited to 15 minutes with a 10–15 minutes follow-up supervised practice. The objectives for the demo are as given hereunder:
  - Upon completion of this demo the team member will be:
    - able to demonstrate the ability to French a 204A lamb rack
    - able to demonstrate the ability to cut the Frenched rack into chops
    - able to identify fat cap
    - able to identify lifter meat
    - aware of the use of trim from a lamb rack
    - aware of the characteristics of a lamb hotel rack.

Step 2: Analysis of the training topic. This involves determining the specific objectives, skills, knowledge, or techniques the team member must learn for successful performance of the task. For example, the objective of a training session may be using the proper making of a bed in a guest room. An analysis of this subject, or breaking it down into instructional steps, would result in these teaching points: Describe the component materials involved in the task, mattress cover, sheets and pillow cases, blanket, comforter, bedspread, or other topper, pillows. Show and explain each component. Demonstrate the steps in making the bed including how to make a hospital corner. Assign team members to make a bed. Evaluate the perfowrmance of each team member and allow for repetition of the task. Each step would have subpoints in the presentation, but in the analysis only the major instructional steps required to accomplish the training are considered.

- The steps in producing Frenched lamb chops are as given hereunder:
  - remove fat cap
  - split membrane on rib (from 1.5 to 4 inches trim)
  - push or cut rib free of membrane and surrounding muscle and fat
  - trim to eye
  - Frenched chop—cut chop.

Step 3: Equipment, facilities, and training aids. Requirements for and availability of training aids, equipment, training areas, and facilities need to be considered. Advance notice may be required to obtain training aids such as access and permission to use online programs, demo components such as equipment parts, tools, or recipe ingredients. Time should be allowed to carefully check all supplies and equipment before the training begins.

- The facility to be used for the Frenching demo is the prep table close to the protein cooler. The group of team members will be limited to 4 so each will be able to have a clear view of the procedure. The ingredients needed for the demo are limited to 5 prime, 204A hotel lamb racks. The lamb racks used for the demo and practice session will be part of the standard dinner preparation. The equipment list for the demo includes cutting board with anti-slip mat; boning knife; steel; sanitation bucket with sanitizing liquid; 4 side towels; 1 in the sanitation bucket, 3 dry; two ½ sheet pans with parchment paper liner, 1 for cut chops and 1 for trim; and a lamb chart if available. The equipment list for the practice session is 4 cutting boards with antislip mats; 4 boning knives; 1 steel; 2 sanitation buckets with sanitizing liquid; 6 side towels, 2 in the sanitation buckets, with 4 dry. The practice chops and trim will go on the ½ sheet pans used for the demo.

Step 4: Availability of time. If time is short, the training subject matter should be limited to the items essential for accomplishment of the training objectives. If time is available, more team participation can be used and more supporting material can be included.

- Time for the demo is limited and cannot be allowed to interfere with dinner preparation. Two members of the lunch protein preparation team at the end of their shift and two members of dinner protein preparation team at the beginning will participate in the demo and this will be repeated as needed to train all appropriate team members. The chops being prepared will assist in the dinner preparation. The demo and practice are to be held to a maximum of 30 minutes.

Step 5: Training conditions. Instructions must be flexible enough to remain effective even when obstacles to training arise. The basis of such flexibility is careful planning.

- The schedule for the Frenching demo and practice session will be:

2:30 p.m.	Introduction: today's lesson and objectives
2:32 p.m.	Introduction hotel rack (204A): description, placement in carcass, characteristics
2:35 p.m.	Fabrication of rack: Frenching technique
	Fabrication of rack: use of trim
2:40 p.m.	Fabrication of rack: cut rib chop
2:45–3:00 p.m.	Practice session/Q&A

- Each team leader that has team members attending is to schedule work to allow for the absence of the team members. In case of interruption due to operational challenges the lesson will be rescheduled to the earliest possible date.

Step 6: Select and organize material. Identify essential manipulative skills and related knowledge, then organize the materials for demonstration. Examples and stories can be used to make the lesson presentation or skill demonstration more interesting and meaningful. They should be related to the overall quality objectives of the operation and should be used whenever possible.

- The purpose for this lesson is to insure consistency of the quality of one of the restaurant's top selling menu items, Moroccan grilled lamb chops. The follow-up to this demo will be a demo on the proper seasoning and cooking of the chops and pan gravy. The use of a live demo will most effectively communicate the knowledge and skills to the team members. The team members will specifically learn and/or refine their ability to French a lamb rack and produce consistent Frenched chops. The team members will also be introduced to or review the use of the trim from the chops. A secondary benefit will be refinement of team member's use of the boning knife and steel. The information and skills presented in the demo will be immediately reinforced with supervised practice. The use of a lamb chart to indicate the location for the 204A hotel rack on the lamb carcass would be helpful, but is not mandatory. No other materials or teaching aides will be used due to the confined space and short time period for the demo. If at a later date it is decided to make this a demo for a large group of team members, the use of closed circuit video cameras and PowerPoint would be highly recommended additions to the demo.

Step 7: Conduct the training. Training may be conducted by human resource personnel, a professional trainer, or a manager. Whoever is conducting the training, their role is to instruct, motivate, lead, enable, and facilitate learning. In addition to serving as a training instructor, they facilitate the logistics involved in the training sessions.

Every time a trainer enters the training room, what follows should be a dynamic and effective training session. An effective presentation can be the most exciting and rewarding aspect of the trainer's job. The time invested in determining the needs analysis and preparing training objectives pays off. In this process the trainer becomes an instructor and learns to interact, discuss, question, and work with the staff to reach the training objectives. Trainers who are able to maintain participant interest with a dynamic delivery using a variety of instructional techniques are more likely to be successful in helping the participants succeed.

The purpose of instruction is to communicate knowledge and skills from the trainer to the team member. It is only successful when at the end of the training the individual team member can safely perform skilled activity to the required standard and/or demonstrate the ability to apply knowledge to the required standard. To achieve these objectives it is essential that the trainer choose the instructional method most suited to the training objectives and the needs of the team member. Additionally, in preparation for conducting the training the trainer determines:

- training priorities
- when and how often training can take place
- how much instruction can be given at one time
- over what period of time training will take place.

The first few minutes of any training session are critical. The introduction should capture the interest of all the participants. Good introductions will prepare the team members, boost their confidence, and also set the stage for a positive learning environment. The training session introduction may be used to review the objectives, restate the company's mission, and describe the activities that will be occurring during the training session.

Plans for the training should include arrangements for meals or coffee breaks during the session periods. Time allocation must be strictly adhered to when it is made part of the training plan. Where will the training take place? Even the most dynamic trainer can fail in poorly prepared facilities. Whether training is to be conducted on site or off site, the facilities should be satisfactory:

- If the room to be used is too warm or too small, a poor instructional climate will result.
- Is lighting adequate? Can the room be darkened to show visuals, yet still allow participants to take notes?
- Is the required technology and demonstration equipment in working order?
- Is there a writing board or flip chart available with marking pens or chalk?

Step 8: Evaluate the training. The purpose of a training session is the growth and development of the team member. Specifically, the training should allow the team member to achieve the objectives of the training. The question that must be answered when the training is completed is: "Did the team member/s acquire the intended additional knowledge, skills, and attitudes?" The trainer needs a system to determine how successful the training has been. There is a need to assess team member performance and to check learning to determine whether the designed instruction has met the training objectives. Evaluation is an essential component of training. Materials that are used continuously need to be assessed so that improvements may be made. Without evaluation it is impossible to quantify the results of the training plan. Methods of evaluation include the following:

- Instructor evaluation of the training outcome when each segment is completed.
- Learner evaluation of the course. (What skills do I possess now that I did not have prior to training?)
- Third-party evaluation by guests or other work centers.
- Field evaluation to determine if the learners are performing well in the roles for which the training was to have prepared them. (Can they perform the skills at the level desired?) Field evaluation is often a suitable method to determine training effectiveness in the hospitality industry. Team members may be assessed on the job by their lead or manager. Coaching on the job is also facilitated through this method of evaluation.

Evaluation is part of the continuous loop that feeds back into the cycle.[5]

Types of Training

There are many types of training. Each has its own relative strengths and weaknesses. The characteristics of each method and its strengths and weaknesses are shown so that each may be evaluated relative to the appropriateness of the training mission.

Job talk is a speech by the manager with limited opportunities for open discussion.

- Strengths
  - clear and direct method of presentation
  - good for large groups
  - materials can be provided to each member in advance to help with preparation

- manager has control over time
- inexpensive training method
- little or no equipment is necessary.

- Weaknesses
  - information not easily assimilated
  - appeals to one sense only (hearing); therefore, overloading may occur
  - group can become easily bored
  - difficult to assess if your "message" has been understood and accepted by the team
  - difficult to pace to the learning rate of each team member.

Team meetings (group discussions) generally include a speech by the manager or lead with a lot of participation and interaction with the team. The meetings always require leadership. Team meetings are particularly useful for teams with mixed experience levels.

- Strengths
  - good for a small number of people
  - all team members have the opportunity to present their ideas
  - more ideas can be generated
  - good for total quality principles
  - quality gaps can be identified
  - effective for continuous improvements within the foodservice organization.

- Weaknesses
  - team may get away from the subject matter
  - manager may be inexperienced at guiding or leading the discussions
  - possibility of one strong individual dominating the meeting.

Role playing is the creation of a realistic situation and having team members assume parts of specific personalities in the situation. Their actions are based on the roles assigned to them. A role-play draws upon the participants' experiences and knowledge and forces them to apply theory to practice.[6] It is effective for attitude awareness training.

- Strengths
  - good if the situation is similar to the actual work situation
  - team members receive feedback that gives them confidence
  - good for interpersonal skills
  - teaches team members how to act in real situations
  - can be used to highlight sensitive topics such as personal hygiene and/or poor interpersonal habits.

- Weaknesses
  - team members not actors
  - role playing sometimes not taken seriously
  - some situations cannot be implemented in role playing
  - uncontrolled role-plays may not lead to any results
  - requires that incorrect and correct methods being role played both be described.

Demonstration is the use of actual equipment and materials to demonstrate an action. This is the most effective method for instructing manipulative skills. Demonstrations make use of the learner's visual sense.

- Strengths
  - great visual impact
  - instruction can be built step by step
  - demonstration ensures that instruction is given in sequence
  - difficult tasks may be shown in easy stages
  - makes use of the natural inclination to imitate
  - best if preceded by study assignment.

- Weaknesses
  - suitable for relatively small groups
  - requires a lot of preparation
  - pace is often too fast
  - learners often watch the demonstrator rather than the demonstration
  - should be avoided unless adequate time has been allowed for preparation and practice beforehand.

A case study is a written narrative description of a real situation faced by team members. Team members are required to propose one or more suitable solutions and/or make appropriate decisions.

- Strengths
  - individual cases can be very interesting
  - involves the team members in a lot of discussions and inter-actions since there is no absolute solution
  - develops kitchen team members' ability to communicate and encourages active participation
  - develops the ability to analyze factors that influence deci-sion making
- Weaknesses
  - a slow method of training

- often difficult to select appropriate case studies for specific training problems
- requires a high level of skill by both trainer and team members
- can sometimes be boring for some team participants

Lecture/discussion is training conducted in a classroom setting.

- Strengths
    - allows highly structured presentation of material
    - allows presentation of large amounts of material in a short period of time
    - involves the team members through dialogue
    - develops team member's ability to communicate.
- Weaknesses
    - often leads to trainer a dominated learning environment
    - team members are reluctant to participate in dialogue
    - encourages passive learning
    - requires a dynamic trainer to maintain learner interest
    - can sometimes be boring for some participants.

On-the-job training (OJT) is training conducted on the job using actual work situations with which the team member is involved.

- Strengths
    - can be individualized to suit the learning pace of the individual
    - provides immediate job application for the new team member
    - integrates the new individual into the team.
- Weaknesses
    - requires a good deal of preparation and application by the trainee/manager/lead
    - sequencing of OJT must be planned and then recorded
    - not all skills are addressed within one establishment.

How People Learn

No two people learn at the same rate. Some team members will pick up new skills very quickly, while others will require repeated instruction and supervised practice. The primary way to classify the types of learning is termed learning domains. These domains fall into the following four categories: cognitive, psychomotor, affective, and interpersonal skills.[7]

- Cognitive: This refers to knowledge learning and includes the mental skills of classifying, identifying, detecting, and making decisions.
- Psychomotor: These are the manipulative, or physical, skills that require the learner to do something.
- Affective: These skills reflect attitudes, values, and interests of the team member.
- Interpersonal skills: Learning focuses on people interacting with others.

Most learned capabilities actually contain elements of all domains. They entail voluntary display (affective) of some observable action (motor skill) that indicates possession of some mental skill (cognitive) and working with other people and through people to carry out the task (interpersonal), which in the hospitality industry very often involves interaction with a guest (interpersonal).

We learn through our senses: seeing, hearing, touching, smelling, and tasting. The most important training sense is seeing, but when giving instruction, as many of the five senses as possible should be used to relay the message. Show things as often as possible. For example, if demonstrating sauce preparation, the method is explained (learning), skills are demonstrated (seeing), what the texture should be is determined (touching), and finally the sauce is sampled (tasting).

Instructional techniques may be divided into two areas: passive and active. Passive techniques require little or no activity from the learner. It is therefore difficult to assess what learning has taken place. Passive instructional techniques involve:

- Telling: The use of words to explain the subject matter.
- Showing: Trainers perform the activity.
- Illustrating: The use of visual materials to demonstrate the procedure.

Active techniques require the learner to participate by saying or doing something:

- Question and answer: Checking through communication to see if information is understood.
- Participation: Involvement by the learner through actions.
- Discussion: Learners are involved through verbal communication.
- Practical exercises: Learners practice the techniques.

Most of the training in the hospitality industry involves the hearing, seeing, saying, and doing, which indicates that this is the desired training method for all skills instruction. Figure 6.4 shows the retention level associated with these learning activities. These methods involve breaking down training into steps that are paced to the learner's ability so that he or she may be able to assimilate this new information. Using this method allows difficult tasks to be shown in easy stages. Thus, the unknown becomes known. Training is about helping people learn and develop. It should be centered on the team member, and there are no reasons why it should not be enjoyable: "Individuals learn best when they choose what to learn—that is, when they learn things that interest them, which they find personally satisfying, and when the learning environment is in harmony with their own particular learning preference or style."[8]

Adult Learning

Andragogy is the concept of adult education. At the heart of this concept is the assumption that adults want to learn. Adults prefer training sessions that will assist them in the successful completion of their daily work tasks. Therefore, instructions should be designed relative to the needs of each participant.[9] If the need or relevance of the training topic is not evident to adult team members from the start, they may soon become disenchanted with the training process. To meet this adult need, the objectives of the training session should be stated and linked to job performance in the introduction stage of the training program or module. For the most part adults enter training with a high degree of interest and motivation. Motivation can be improved and channeled by the trainer who can provide clear instructional goals. Adults learn by doing. They want to get involved. Adults relate their learning to

---

Retention and Learning Activities

Training experts generally agree that we retain:

* 20 percent of what we hear

* 50 percent of what we hear and see

* 70 percent of what we hear, see, and say

* 90 percent of what we hear, see, say, and do

FIGURE 6.4 Retention and Learning Activities.

what they already know. This presents a challenge for the trainer to incorporate participative activities into training such as hands-on work, discussions, or projects. Variety of training topics and methods tends to stimulate and open all five of the team members' senses.

The need for positive feedback is characteristic of all learners. Adults prefer to know how their efforts measure up when compared with the objective of the training program. Additionally, adult learners may have certain reservations when it comes to training; among these are doubts about their ability to learn and a fear of failure.

Each training session should be opened with a good introductory activity that will put everyone at ease. Adults prefer to be treated as individuals who have unique and particular talents, and they prefer an informal environment.

The establishment of a positive training environment hinges on understanding the characteristics of adult learners. The dynamics of the training process are dependent upon the instructor having a clear understanding of these characteristics. For adults, training should be a highly motivating experience, after which they should be inspired and committed to trying out new ideas and approaches. Effective adult training should be relevant, practical, inspirational, dynamic, informative, and solution centered.

Barriers to Learning

There are a number of barriers to learning. One of the most common is fatigue. When the team members are tired their physical and mental ability to accept and assimilate new information is reduced. It is therefore essential that training be planned and implemented at appropriate times. It should not be conducted at the end of work shifts when fatigue is probably a reality but additionally the team member's mind is on leaving for the day not the information being presented by the trainer.

Monotony is also a barrier to learning. If the trainer finds the training boring, it is highly probable that the team members will also find it boring. It is important for the trainer to keep the sessions lively and interesting.

Distractions also inhibit learning. Time for training should be planned to avoid work-related distractions. The location should not make the trainer compete for the attention of the team member.

The learning environment should put the participants at ease. People are usually tense when confronted with the unknown. It is up to the trainer to create a positive training environment that is motivational and encourages quality performance. Questions to consider with regard to creating the training environment include the smooth transition from a work-driven atmosphere to a training-driven atmosphere. Training sessions need not take up large chunks of the workday. They can range from 30-minute to 2-hour sessions but must be conducted regularly to reinforce their importance. What is vital is that the training period be totally uninterrupted by the requirements of work.

Summary

Investment in training is investment in the health and well-being of the operation and company. It is an investment in the future and therefore success cannot be achieved without it.

Training is the systematic application of:

- analyzing training needs
- developing training objectives
- determining appropriate training methods
- and conducting and evaluating training.

There are many types of training. Training methods that are suitable for hospitality training include job talks, demonstration, role-play, case study, and OJT. Each has strengths and weaknesses. Experienced trainers/managers can assess the training needs and determine the most appropriate training methods. The trainer/manager needs to develop skill in using a variety of these training methods. A role of the manager or lead is counseling team members through the learning process and being a subject matter expert, teacher, and motivator as they rotate through the training process.

Understanding how people learn is the key to effective training. No two people learn at the same rate or in the same way. There will be peaks and valleys in individual team member's progress. Training sessions should be stimulating and inspiring and be separate from the usual work schedule. The environment in which the training session is to be conducted should be one that is conducive to learning. The duration and timing of training are important. Training must be planned in a sequential and logical way and should not last too long. Dynamic presentations will always ward off monotony and fatigue.

Study Questions

1. Relate the concept of training as an investment.
2. Describe a systems approach to training and explain how training interacts with the goals of the company.
3. Define the types of training and their strengths and weaknesses and describe situations appropriate for each method.
4. List the learning domains.
5. Discuss the concept of andragogy and outline the challenges in this area for the trainer.
6. Identify factors that inhibit learning.

Case Studies

The case studies listed below relate to the information presented in this chapter and reading, answering the case study questions and participating in discussion of a case will reinforce and expand what you have learned in this chapter. All case studies are provided in this text after the last chapter.

Shady Lane Inn

Shandong House Restaurant

Notes

1. Sullivan, R., Wircenski, J., Susan S., Arnold, S., & Sarkeess M. (1990). *Practical manual for the design, delivery, and evaluation of training* (p. CD 1). Aspen, MD: Rockville.
2. Ibid., p. CD 2.
3. Mager, R. (1971). *Preparing instructional objectives* (2nd ed.). Belmont, CA: Fearson.
4. Ibid., p. CD 37.
5. Goad, T. (1991). *Delivering effective training* (p. 169). San Diego, CA: Pfeiffer & Co.
6. Hart, L. (1991). *Training methods that work* (p. 65). London: Crisp.
7. Vision, C. *Learning domains and delivery of instruction*. Retrieved October 14, 2014, from http://chettourhorizonsforteaching.blogspot.com/2009/05/learning-domains-and-delivery-of.html
8. Thomas, B. (1992). *Total quality training: The quality culture and quality trainer* (p. 73). Berkshire, England: McGraw-Hill.
9. Laird, D. (1985). *Approaches to training and development* (p. 25). Reading, MA: Addison-Welesey.

Orientation and Socialization 7

CHAPTER OUTLINE

- ▶ Introduction
- ▶ Orientation
- ▶ Socialization
- ▶ Duration of Orientation Training
- ▶ Conducting Orientation Training
- ▶ Follow-Up and Evaluation
- ▶ Summary

LEARNING OBJECTIVES

When you complete reading this chapter, you should be able to:

- ▶ differentiate between socialization and orientation
- ▶ identify the elements of orientation
- ▶ identify the elements of socialization
- ▶ describe topics for inclusion in orientation training programs
- ▶ discuss the duration of orientation training
- ▶ recall the principles of conducting orientation training
- ▶ illustrate the principles of follow-up and evaluation of socialization and orientation training.

Introduction

A new staff member's first impressions about his or her job can make all the difference. Orientation is the foundation for attitudes that may stay in place as long as that staff member remains with the company. Orientation describes the initial type of training given to a new staff member. It provides information about the job, working conditions, and covers the main activities and duties in which the new staff member will be involved. Orientation clarifies the area of training in which the new staff member will be instructed and the levels of performance expected. Orientation also involves socialization which includes the culture, mission, and philosophy of the organization. Socialization is part of orientation but a very distinct part. It also provides a systematic plan to accomplish these goals. By providing an orientation program, the company communicates to new employees what is expected of them and how their jobs fit into the overall operation. It also helps employees fit into their jobs faster, be more productive, satisfied, and realize that the company cares. Also, remember that how employees treat customers is often a reflection of how they are treated by management.[1]

Orientation

Orientation is a systematic method to acquaint the new staff member with all aspects of the new job. Orientation can be defined as a two-way informational and introductory session conducted by the employer to educate and excite all participants.[2] Its purpose is to make the new staff member an effective contributor to the team in the shortest time available.

New staff members receive orientation from their fellow staff members in an informal way and from the organization in a formal manner. The informal orientation received from fellow staff members is usually unplanned and unofficial. This type of orientation often provides the new staff member with misleading and inaccurate information. This is one of the reasons why the official formal orientation provided by the company is so important. An effective orientation program has an immediate and lasting impact on the new staff member. It can make the difference between a new staff member's success and failure. Studies have identified a strong correlation between customer satisfaction and the employee's view of service quality. Employees that have a positive perception of the organization's human resource policies carry that positive attitude into the service they deliver to the guest/customer.

It is ultimately the responsibility of the human resource personnel and/or the manager to carry out socialization and orientation training. Each new staff member brings to the workplace his or her own set of values. The new employee's values and attitudes may be quite different from those of the company, the manager, and other employees. The background of the new employee will have some effect on the way this person relates to the manager and to the new job.[3] In view of this, orientation training should be prepared with the same attention to detail as any other training program. It can be one of the best and most complete training investments made by the company.

The first three days at work for the new staff member is a critical time and will have a definite effect on his or her future performance. The first day is an opportunity to set a positive tone which can avoid future problems.[4] The highest proportion of employee turnover occurs within the first 30 days. This is due largely to poor or nonexistent orientation training program. The return on investment (ROI) from a planned approach to orientation takes many forms as shown in Figure 7.1. The type of operation impacts who does the training and the format of the training. Regardless of the type or size of operation orientation training is critical to employee success and reduction of turnover.

In the large restaurant or hotel the training may take place in a formal setting and is highly structured. There are a large number of staff members to be oriented by the company, the property, and their specific department. The consistency of the program is based on materials developed strictly for that purpose both at the company and

---

Planned Orientation ROI

* All new staff members receive information that allows them to fit into the organization/operation as quickly as possible.

* The new staff member quickly develops a sense of belonging creating a positive morale and motivation.

* The new staff member is aware of their assigned duties and the performance standards expectations from the beginning.

* The new staff member is working productively from the first day.

* The scene is set for further training.

* The potential increases for the staff member's and the organization's expectations being fulfilled.

* The new staff member is more inclined to be confident and loyal.

FIGURE 7.1   Planned Orientation ROI

property levels. The initial part of the program may be conducted by the human resource department and cover information about the company and property for all new staff members. The more specific orientation related to the staff members assigned department and position would be conducted in the department. The orientation of the new department staff members would be conducted by the department manager following the general orientation. In a chain property, there are generally standardized orientation materials for each department. If there are not materials available they would be developed by the department manager in conjunction with the human resource department. In larger properties, the total orientation will generally take a half to a full day.

In smaller properties where there is no human resource person in house the orientation is generally conducted by a designated manager with possible inputs from the general manager. Development of materials would be done by the designated manager with inputs from the general manager. Conduct of the orientation becomes more of a challenge in the smaller property because often the need for the new staff member in their assigned position is immediate. The need must be recognized as a reality of the operation. The manager that is quality focused will not allow the orientation to be sidelined because of the need. The ROI on the orientation training is too great and its impact on future quality and turnover too certain to dismiss it because of time challenges. In the small operation the mark of the excellent manager will be their scheduling of time for and conducting orientation training for all new staff members. Suggestions for conducting orientation training in smaller, time-challenged operations are shown in Figure 7.2.

The topics presented in the training plan should be based on the needs of the organization and the new staff member. The foundational information covered in an orientation session includes vision and mission; company and departmental goals; benefits information;

Orientation and the Smaller Property

* Schedule orientation time as part of the new staff members first day and first week.

* Prioritize orientation information into 3-4 levels and spread the information over shorter orientation sessions through-out the new team member's first week.

* Create orientation materials that can be used repeatedly.

* Develop a handbook for the basic information that a staff member needs to know and require the new staff member to read the handbook before reporting for duty the first day.

FIGURE 7.2   Orientation and the Smaller Property

attendance policy; meals and break policy; facility tour; general performance expectations; evaluation policy; payroll information; uniform requirements or dress code; harassment policy; emergency procedures; employee assistance programs, and other matters. Generally, the company is concerned with meeting the needs of its customers, making a profit, satisfying staff member needs, and being socially responsible. New staff members, on the other hand, are generally more interested in pay, benefits, and specific terms and conditions of employment.

A good balance between the company and the new staff member needs is essential if the orientation program is to be successful. Arrangements should be made to tour the facilities. In addition, comprehensive orientation kits should be prepared for all new staff members and should include the type of information shown in Figure 7.3. The trainer/manager might want to conclude the explanation of the orientation handbook policies and procedures by reviewing the most important points. Many companies require staff members to complete a questionnaire on the handbook. The questionnaire is not graded, but it is checked. Others require passing a test on safety and sanitation, emergencies, hazardous materials handling, and harassment policies. Additionally, the forms that the new staff member will need to complete should be highlighted within the orientation. The new employees should be assured that they are confident; they can do the job; and that they will get all the support they need to succeed.

Socialization

Socialization implies the absorbing of a new staff member into the culture of the company. It is separated deliberately from other orientation as a focus. Orientation is more process oriented. Socialization is more culture and attitude oriented. Training targeted to socialization will cover issues such as customer focus, philosophy, team focus, mission statement, corporate culture, commitment to goals, concepts of empowerment, and individual attitudes toward these goals. Socialization does not need to cover specific job details since the purpose is to evoke feelings and generate commitment. The trainer/manager conducting the socialization should sell the organization's philosophy along with security, caring, and peace of mind by talking in general terms about benefits, recognition programs, and salary policies. New staff members want to be part of a successful organization.

Socialization begins on the first day the staff member begins the new job. It takes place formally through training. It takes place

Orientation Kit Content
* Map of the facilities
* Organizational chart
* Organization's policies and procedures handbook, which typically features information and guidance on the following topics:
* Safety and sanitation procedures
* Uniforms, dress code & grooming policies
* Union policies (if applicable)
* Payroll procedures
* Vacation, public & religious holiday policies
* Group health insurance
* Meals & break policies
* Pension/savings plan
* Attendance, hours of work
* Incentive programs
* Performance evaluations
* Emergency procedures
* Promotion policy
* Harassment policy
* Employee assistance programs
* Security department's authority
* Disciplinary rules & actions
* Key telephone numbers
* Training programs

FIGURE 7.3   Orientation Kit Content

informally as the new staff member becomes immersed in the environment of the workplace.

While written policies concerning these issues are contained in an orientation kit, most socialization training is conducted by the team. It is not just a series of slogans but a calculated rationale that is lived by each member of the team daily. Socialization may begin with training but it matures with time and experience. When an employee leaves an organization, needless staffing expenses are incurred and service to customers is likely to decline. Potentially good employees may be "turned off" through improper orientation and poor training.[5]

Ensure employees are told about company goals and visions and their role in the dream.[6] When tactfully and correctly implemented, socialization will result in a committed staff member armed with the expectations of the mission of the organization.

Duration of Orientation Training

It is impossible for a new staff member to absorb in one long session all of the information in the company's orientation program. Sessions of no more than 2 hours should be used. These should be conducted over multiple days. This increases the likelihood that the new staff member will understand and retain the information presented. Orientation sessions can be reinforced by providing a handbook containing important company and departmental information. The new hire is instructed to read the handbook and is tested over the content in one of the orientation sessions. Position orientation should be carefully planned and conducted by the department manager using appropriate materials. The length of time allowed for position orientation will be based on the amount of time required to provide the introduction the new hire needs to effectively carry out their assigned duties. The length of time for the position orientation should still take in consideration the use of multiple shorter, 2 hours or less, sessions to improve employee retention of the information presented.

It is important to introduce the new staff member to the other staff members on the first day. These introductions should include each staff member's function, position within the team, and an explanation of how each fits into the department.

As with any training, time is involved, that is, the new staff member's time and the manager's time. Orientation training is a quality investment of time. It is one that can contribute to effective integration of the new staff member and set the foundation for a long association with the company.

Conducting Orientation Training

If management does not communicate and deliver an orientation program, other staff members will. This may not be the type of orientation you wish the new person to receive. Unplanned orientation can be harmful. Existing staff members can paint an unfavorable and untrue picture of the operation. Most people will have a tendency to relate and listen to those they feel are their peers, rather than the manager. Therefore, it is very important that the first impressions of the organization be created by the manager within the framework of real work situations.

New staff members come with a certain amount of anxiety. They will have feelings of insecurity regarding confidence in their abilities to do the job and fit into the team. The type of positive work environment the manager creates can reduce these anxieties and increase a feeling of worth and belonging in new staff members. It is much better to invest in training at this stage because the new staff member will become productive in a shorter period of time.

In communication, an open style should be adopted. Speak to the staff member in a manner that indicates "we picked each other." Speak clearly and directly as one human being to another. Provide any background information he or she will need. Explain any technical terms and avoid using jargon. Too much information at one time is as bad as too little. Provide information in manageable parts. Without making it obvious, repeat anything that is important for the staff member to remember. Use open questions as much as possible. Listening to the new staff member during the orientation is important, not just because of what might be learned, but because it means a lot to the new staff member. The intention is to communicate, not to intimidate, during this phase. Avoid "talking down" from a position of power. Show respect for the individual. A little awareness and genuine kindness go a long way. Develop an orientation program that not only goes over the rules but also stresses a "spirit of hospitality."[7]

Perception plays an important role in communication during an orientation session. It can help immensely and it can also devastate the most sincere effort to communicate effectively. The fact is that people often only hear what they want to hear. Knowing this, the manager should keep trying until the correct feedback is received. The negative aspect of this is that it can cause the new staff member to become defensive, which will obviously hinder the communication process. Problems in perception are often caused by differences in ethnic or cultural backgrounds, different educational levels, and difficulties with the particular language used. The cultural background of people has a strong influence on the communication process, which includes non-verbal and verbal communication. Investing time to start the new staff member on the correct path will make things easier for the manager.

Follow-up and Evaluation

Formal and systematic evaluation of the orientation training program is essential. New staff members should receive a set of contingency plans and contacts in the event they need further clarification or assistance to ensure their careful socialization and orientation into the company. The manager should regularly check on how well the staff members are doing and answer any questions that may have arisen after their initial socialization and orientation. A formal scheduled follow-up should take place within 1 month after the staff member becomes part of the team. The orientation training plan should be reviewed at least once a year. The purpose of this evaluation is to determine if the plan is meeting the company and new staff members' needs. The evaluation is critical to improving the current program.

Feedback from new staff members is one method of evaluating the socialization and orientation program. This can be achieved by asking new staff members to complete unsigned questionnaires or through in-depth interviews. Feedback of this type enables the manager and the company to adapt and modify the program. Socialization and orientation training programs for new staff members take priority in development and implementation; however, once completed, work on other training aspects can begin. The first day on the job is an opportunity for the manager and the company to set a positive tone and thereby avoid problems that might occur later. The way a new staff member is treated during the orientation period conveys an impression of the manager and the company as having a well-planned, well-executed orientation program.

Summary

Orientation training programs are vital to assimilating new staff members into the company's philosophy. They also provide for clear understanding by the staff member of their job and the performance expectations.

Socialization is a distinct part of orientation. It covers issues of corporate culture, philosophy, mission, customer focus, and expected staff member attitudes. Socialization is eventually conducted by the entire team. Orientation training is the umbrella under which socialization takes place. The purpose of the orientation training plan is to systematically and sequentially orient the new staff member to the company, job, and other staff members. This approach enables her or him to effectively contribute to the organization in the shortest possible time. The first 30 days of the new staff member's tenure in the job are vital. It is during this period that most employee turnover occurs, largely due to poor orientation training.

Orientation training should include an information kit that enables the new staff member to fit smoothly into the company. It is the manager manager's duty to ensure that the new member is armed with the necessary information to understand rules and procedures. Orientation training should take place over a period of time in a planned way, rather than as one long session. Formal and systematic follow-up should be planned. If the company does not conduct the orientation of the new staff member, others will. Unplanned orientation, including socialization, usually results in a negative view of the new job, the organization, and the manager by the new staff member.

The communication style of the trainer/manager during orientation should be open and concentrate on removing anxiety and building feelings of security in the new staff member. Topics for the orientation training sessions should include the department functions, staff members' duties and responsibilities, pay and benefits, rules and procedures of the organization, and a tour of the entire facility.

Formal evaluation of the orientation training program should take place annually to ensure it meets with the needs and requirements of the organization and its future employees. A systematic follow-up to the initial orientation should take place within at least 1 month to check on new staff members' comfort with their new position.

Study Questions

1. Discuss the differences between socialization and orientation.
2. Discuss the elements of orientation.
3. Discuss the elements of socialization.
4. Describe topics for inclusion in orientation training programs.
5. Discuss the duration of orientation training.
6. Recall the principles of conducting orientation training.
7. Discuss the principles of follow-up and evaluation of socialization and orientation training.

Case Studies

The case studies listed below relate to the information presented in this chapter and reading, answering the case study questions and participating in discussion of a case will reinforce and expand what you have learned in this chapter. All case studies are provided in this text after the last chapter.

Shady Lane Inn

Shandong House Restaurant

Shepherd Mountain Hotel

Notes

1. Drummond, K. (1992). *The restaurant training program* (p. 1). New York: John Wiley.
2. Eade, V. (1993). *Human resources management in the hospitality industry* (p. 173). Scottsdale, AZ: Garsuch Sciarisbrick.
3. Jernigan A. (1989). *The effective food service manager*. Rockville, MD: Aspen Publications.
4. Haynes, M. (1990). *Stepping up to manager* (p. 76). Los Altos, CA: Crisp Publications.
5. Zaccarelli, H. (1988). *Training managers to train* (p. 56). Los Altos, CA: Crisp Publications.
6. Weinstein, J. (December 1992). Personnel success. *Restaurants & Institutions*, 102(29), 92–113.
7. Hogan, J. (February 1992). Turnover and what to do about it. *Cornell HRA Quarterly*, 33(1), 40–45.

Performance Evaluation 8

LEARNING OBJECTIVES

When you complete reading this chapter, you should be able to:

- ▶ define performance evaluation
- ▶ state the elements upon which managers evaluate staff member's performance
- ▶ describe the benefits and the impact of performance evaluations on staff development
- ▶ identify methods of staff member evaluation
- ▶ recall the principles of evaluation interviews
- ▶ identify the factors in evaluating weak staff member performance
- ▶ relate the role of compensation in the performance evaluation process.

Introduction

Performance evaluation is the systematic process of developing criteria for job performance.

This involves outlining criteria for assessment of staff job performance relative to the criteria and clearly communicating the results to the staff.

However, many managers view performance evaluations as an unpleasant task. On the contrary, performance evaluations present the manager with opportunities to make valuable contributions not only to the team, but also to each individual staff member, thus improving the operation. It is usual for those managers who rise from the ranks to find it uncomfortable to evaluate another staff member's performance.

Performance evaluation is a continuous and sustained process and is under the responsibility of all managers. They are required to critically evaluate how well members of the team are doing their jobs. Through a critical and unbiased evaluation it may be decided who should be recommended for promotion, transfer, reassignment, further training, salary increases, or even termination. One of the most important aspects, however, is encouraging staff member performance improvement. In this regard, performance evaluations are used to communicate to staff members how they are doing and to suggest needed changes in behavior, attitude, skills, or knowledge. This type of feedback clarifies for each staff member the job task and overall quality expectations held by the manager. Additionally, evaluations often serve to validate the selection procedures used during the recruitment stage.

Performance evaluations should be conducted periodically to let staff members know how they are doing and to clarify whether their performance is satisfactory or unsatisfactory. This typically is done through an evaluation interview.

Evaluating Performance

It is true that performance evaluation is never an end in itself. It is the preliminary step prior to conducting meaningful feedback discussions, making appropriate administrative recommendations, and determining where performance improvement is required. Evaluation process of the staff members includes work productivity, work quality, dependability, team interactions, initiative, and leadership performance. Example areas of performance evaluation are shown in Figure 8.1.

```
                Areas of Performance Evaluation

        * Quality and amount of work performed

        * Adherence to company policies

        * Quality of job skill

        * Personal grooming or appearance

        * Attendance

        * Cooperation

        * Ability to work unsupervised

        * Initiative

        * Knowledge of rules and company procedures

        * Involvement as a team player

        * Leadership potential
```

FIGURE 8.1   Example Areas of Performance Evaluation

Generally, people are interested in how they are viewed by the manager. In the absence of specific feedback, staff members often form their own conclusions by comparing their experiences with others around them. This can sometimes lead to wrong conclusions. Clearing up doubt or uncertainty is a major purpose of the performance evaluation:[1]

A productive evaluation, along with providing a review of the employee's work, serves as a work session between manager and employee where new goals and objectives are set for the coming year. A productive evaluation recognizes that people are the most valuable resource of any organization.

The benefits of a good performance evaluation are shown in Figure 8.2.

```
                Benefits of Performance Evaluation


    * Staff members learn their strengths and weaknesses.

    * New goals and objectives are agreed upon

    * The relationship between the manager and the staff member is brought to a new level.

    * The staff member becomes an active participant in their professional development

    * New training needs are identified.

    * Time is set aside for discussing issues other than money.

    * Staff members feel they are taken seriously as individuals.
```

FIGURE 8.2   Benefits of Performance Evaluation

Performance evaluations also provide written records to substantiate personnel actions. Therefore, they can serve as an information and staff member feedback system. More and more administrative decisions taken by management are being subjected to review by outside parties. To verify the appropriateness of decisions made, it is necessary to document all meetings for review purposes. Performance evaluations serve as excellent records. Such documentation can also serve to confirm understandings between the manager and the staff member.

Methods of Evaluation

An evaluation decision is often made by comparison. Whatever is being evaluated is compared to something else, and it generally exceeds, equals, or falls short in comparison.[2] There are many methods of evaluation. Each has its own merits and some companies use more than one method. The following four methods are commonly used in the evaluation of staff members in both small and large operations.

The essay evaluation in its simplest form requires the manager to write a paragraph or more covering a staff member's individual strengths and weaknesses and potential for further development. A major weakness of this method is its inconsistency in length and content. However, essay evaluations are difficult to combine or compare.

The graphic rating scale typically evaluates a staff member on the quality and quantity of work. Both the quality and quantity of work are rated on a scale that allows some level of discrimination such as outstanding/above average/satisfactory/unsatisfactory. The scale is also used to rate a variety of other factors that vary but usually include traits like reliability and cooperation.

The critical-incident evaluation requires the manager to maintain a log of critical incidents of a positive or negative nature. The evaluation interview/discussion with the staff member is based on actual behavior recording in the log. One of the challenges to this method is that it requires the manager to write down incidents on a regular basis. The benefit of this method is the avoidance of appraising on only the most recent performance which is always top-of-mind.

The Behaviorally Anchored Rating Scales (commonly referred to as BARS) require that a job analysis has been conducted that identified performance behavior appropriate for different levels. The BARS method is objective in nature. Each staff member is rated against a predetermined specific set of behaviors identified on a job-by-job basis. The downside to this evaluation method is that it can be costly to initiate and time consuming for the manager.

Even though there are a variety of performance evaluation methods to choose from, it is still possible to end up with inaccurate information on the staff member or the team in general. To avoid this, managers should be trained in the techniques of performance evaluations. A common error in the performance evaluation process is the halo effect. This occurs when the evaluator allows a single prominent characteristic of a staff member to influence his or her judgment. Personal preferences, prejudices, and biases can also cause errors in performance evaluations. Managers with biases or prejudices tend to look for staff member behaviors that conform to their biases. Figure 8.3 is a simple generic example of a graphic rating scale.

Evaluation Interviews

The performance evaluation process is not complete until there is a conference between the staff member and manager. These interviews allow discussion about the period since the last evaluation. They typically review the previous year and set a course for the coming year. These discussions help answer such questions as "How am I doing?" "Where can I go from here?," and "How do I get there?" The first step in beginning an evaluation interview is to give the staff member a few days' notice of the interview date so that he or she may prepare for it. Managers should preview relevant data for the interview during this time period. A time and a place for the interview that will be private and free from interruptions should be selected.

The manager must work to create a positive feel during the interview. Traditionally, staff members view a performance evaluation with some level of fear. The process is generally viewed as an ordeal they must go through before they can find out whether or not they will receive a negative or positive evaluation. The goal should be to create a spirit of teamwork and collaborative problem solving.

Start the interview by creating the impression that the interview is considered very important. Next, help the staff member to feel that the interview is a valuable, constructive, cooperative process by placing emphasis on his or her development. Avoid any impression that the interview was arranged only for the purposes of warning or reprimanding. Assure the staff member that its purpose is to give constructive and objective feedback.

Graphic Rating Scale Performance Evaluation

Staff member: John Smith

Job Title: Purchasing Agent

Department: Purchasing

Check all items relevant to team member's position. Rate each item on a scale of 1–5. Circle number at right:

1=Needs much improvement; 2=Needs some improvement; 3=Satisfactory; 4=Very good; 5=Excellent

Part I: General work habits and attitude

Sanitation and safety	1	2	3	4	5
Attendance and punctuality	1	2	3	4	5
Meets deadlines	1	2	3	4	5
Cooperates with team members	1	2	3	4	5
Accepts suggestions	1	2	3	4	5
Uses equipment properly	1	2	3	4	5
Prioritizes work well	1	2	3	4	5

Part II: Job Performance

Quality of work	1	2	3	4	5
Ability to solve problems	1	2	3	4	5
Uses original ideas	1	2	3	4	5
Communications ability	1	2	3	4	5
Time management	1	2	3	4	5
Hands-on skills	1	2	3	4	5
Interpersonal skills	1	2	3	4	5
Ability to work on a team	1	2	3	4	5

FIGURE 8.3   Graphic Rating Scale Performance Evaluation

The interview portion of the performance evaluation should consist of a thorough review of the staff member's goals for the evaluation period, the degree to which these goals were accomplished, and setting new goals for the subsequent period. The discussion should be based on observed behavior and performance both positive and negative, not on the staff member's personal characteristics. Staff members accept criticism when it is based on fact rather than vague remarks.

The conduct of an effective evaluation process requires attention to six areas: (1) preparation, (2) environment, (3) focus, (4) engagement, (5) closure, and (6) documentation. Prior to the interview, the manager must do his or her preparation. The manager must:

- set a date and time and notify the staff member;
- ensure that all relevant data concerning the staff member has been reviewed and is available; and
- select for the interview only those accomplishments and problems relevant to the discussion.

The manager must establish an appropriate environment as elaborated hereunder:

- arrange the meeting area so the evaluator and the staff member can sit face to face, without a desk between them, or with both sitting at the same side of the desk;
- make the area comfortable, with the right temperature and comfortable chairs; and
- during the interview create a positive, nonthreatening environment and display a supportive attitude.

The focus established by the manager must be on the behavior rather than the individual. Performance is the subject and basis for the interview.

- Focus on feedback on the behavior rather than on the individual.
- Get the staff member to commit to future goals and set benchmarks for accomplishment.

The greater the engagement of the staff member in the interview the more likely it is that the outcome of the interview will lead to improved performance. The following will help encourage engagement of the staff member.

- Ask staff members for their opinions on work-related issues. Interviews are two-way streets. Therefore, encourage continued conversation.
- Allow for individual differences in the ratings. Do not compare an average but competent staff member with a superstar.
- Evaluate honestly and carefully. Do not say, "I don't like your attitude." It is more appropriate to say, "Your behavior shows that you seem to resent doing the work that is asked of you. If that is true, you need to change your behavior." Give specific examples.
- Some questions encourage while others limit. State questions so that the staff member will think and give detailed responses.

Generally avoid closed-ended questions that require yes or no answers. Actively listen and avoid forming conclusions on too little data.

- An interview cannot be conducted only as a series of questions. It is appropriate for the manager to add thoughts on various topics discussed. This will be either confirmation or clarification of the staff member's understanding of the points discussed. Always allow the staff member ample time to respond to any questions.

Closure is a critical step in the interview. It should be viewed as solidifying what the expectations are for future performance. When all the points have been covered that were planned, close the discussion. However, three important issues need to be addressed at this stage as listed hereunder:

- Summarize the key points and check for staff members' understanding. Invite them also to summarize.
- Compare the points agreed upon.
- Staff members should have a chance to review their problems and outline any concerns or work-related problems that they may have.

Following the interview closing, the manager must document the interview by writing a brief summary of the discussion. This should include action plans that make it clear what actions are expected of the employee. These plans are based on specific action points. Action points are the specific performance factors targeted for improvement. The manager and staff member should both sign the plan indicating it was not only discussed but also understood. If it was agreed to do anything during the course of the interview, then follow through. If something that was agreed to is not acted upon, it can have a serious impact on the staff member's morale. It sends a message that the manager does not care. Follow-up is important with all staff members, but it is crucial when dealing with weak staff members. They need continued guidance and support from the manager. The goal is always to grow the employee. This is only possible when both direction and guidance are given.

Documenting evaluation interviews serves a secondary purpose also. It can also be used to protect the manager and the company if they are accused of bias or improper behavior by an individual or by another manager and a lawsuit is initiated: "Any incidents that are out of the ordinary or that involve a significant clash of tempers or personalities should be included in the documentation."[3] The documentation of the interview should be finalized by allowing the staff member to review and sign the report on the interview. The staff member's signature line should have the statement next to it that their signature is solely acknowledgment of having seen the document but not their agreement with the document. The staff member should be given the opportunity to respond to the report in writing. If the staff member provides a written response it should be placed in the staff member's personnel file with the manager's report on the interview.

Conducting the performance evaluation of a poorly performing staff member can be particularly challenging. Performance evaluations do not always bring good news to a staff member. Good and bad employees must be briefed regarding how they are doing. Handling the bad news requires some special techniques[4] such as those listed hereunder.

- Have the relevant documentation available to demonstrate previous discussion on poor performance.
- Give specific examples of where work failed to match the set quality standards.
- Prepare a list of changes the staff member is to make in his or her performance.
- Be positive about each staff member's ability to improve. Arrange for further training sessions.
- Set short-term goals that are within the ability of the individual. Progressively build upon successes.
- Be honest with staff members. Spell out clearly what they have to do and outline the consequences if they do not improve.
- Make a short-term agreement with the staff member on measurable performance improvements set against a specific time period. Agree to meet again after the short time period to assess progress.

End the meeting on a positive note. Point out the staff member's accomplishments. Reaffirm a willingness to continue to work with the staff member until he or she reaches a satisfactory performance level. It is vital to get the staff member's attention if the performance is unsatisfactory. Managers should not gloss over prior performances and go easy on the staff member. The staff member may see what the manager may view as a tough review as an acceptable evaluation unless the unsatisfactory behavior is clearly stated.

Compensation

It is natural for the employee to directly associate both compensation and performance evaluation. The reality is that discussion of pay should be separated from the performance evaluation interview. Productive performance evaluations focus entirely on issues of strength and weakness and the development of new goals and objectives. Once money becomes part of the discussion, interest in improvement tends to dissipate. If the staff member does bring up the question of money during the evaluation interview, state that this will be discussed later and that now the interview will concentrate on performance only.

While pay should be discussed in a separate conference with the employee, the connection between performance evaluation and pay must exist. Policy for pay increases that is tied to performance evaluation should be established. Compensation after initial employment is generally classified as either cost-of-living or merit pay increases. Cost-of-living pay increases are not based on performance. They are adjustments based on the purchasing power of money in the market place. This purchasing power can decrease or increase because of changes in the economy. Merit pay increases are based on an employee's performance. When a merit format is used the employee/s who performs at the highest level receives the greatest pay increase.

Summary

A sound performance evaluation system draws on both the manager and the staff member. Together, they negotiate performance expectations for the future. Through evaluation it may be decided who should be recommended for promotion, transfer, reassignment, further training, salary increases, or termination. Performance evaluations are generally used to communicate to staff members regarding their strengths and weaknesses as evidenced from their job performance. When used correctly and appropriately, performance evaluations may be an asset in identifying gaps in the training stage and act as information-gathering systems and morale boosters for the team. The performance evaluation interview is an opportunity for the manager with the staff member to craft plans for future development. Performance evaluations should be conducted at established intervals. They usually include aspects of work quality, attitude, and cooperation.

There are various performance evaluation methods such as the supervisor-produced essays, graphic rating scales, critical incident evaluation, and BARSs. Every effort should be made to eliminate areas of bias and prejudice when evaluating staff members. Evaluation interviews are used to apprise the staff member of acceptable or unacceptable behavior. They should contain a thorough review of the staff member's performance outlined during a matter-of-fact, friendly interview. When the interview is concluded, both parties "sign off" on agreed goals. Issues discussed and agreed upon should be documented.

Performance evaluation is, therefore, critical to the success of the company.

Study Questions

1. Define performance evaluation.
2. State the elements upon which managers evaluate performance of the staff member.
3. Describe the benefits and the impact of performance evaluations on staff development.
4. List and discuss methods of staff member evaluation.
5. Recall the principles of evaluation interviews.
6. Identify the factors in evaluating weak staff member performance.
7. Relate the role of compensation in the performance evaluation process.

Case Studies

The case studies listed below relate to the information presented in this chapter and reading, answering the case study questions and participating in discussion of a case will reinforce and expand what you have learned in this chapter. All case studies are provided in this text after the last chapter.

C&L Restaurant

Naples by the Sea

Shandong House Restaurant

Summit Resort

Notes

1. Haynes, M. (1990). *Stepping up to supervisor* (p. 84). Los Altos, CA: Crisp Learning.

2. Sachs, R. (1992). *Productive performance evaluations* (p. 5). New York: AMACOM.
3. Ibid., p. 43.
4. Travers, A. (1993). *Supervision, techniques and new dimensions* (p. 181). Englewood Cliffs, NJ: Prentice-Hall.

Environment in the Workplace 9

CHAPTER OUTLINE

- ► Introduction
- ► Job Satisfaction
- ► Frustration
- ► Complaints
- ► Safe Work Environment
- ► Health and Wellness
- ► Conclusions
- ► Summary

LEARNING OBJECTIVES

When you complete reading this chapter, you should be able to:

- ► identify the issues that contribute to staff member frustration
- ► describe steps to deal effectively with staff member complaints
- ► define the connections between motivation and job satisfaction
- ► identify the basic steps in health, safety, and accident prevention
- ► relate the companies roll in employee health and wellness

Introduction

The performance of staff members is impacted by many factors and some of the most important and most often abused of those factors relate to the environment in the workplace. The nature of the work environment, positive versus negative, has a major impact on staff member performance and development. A positive work environment generates a more positive attitude among staff members and leads to higher levels of productivity and service of greater quality.

A positive environment can only be achieved when the foundation has been established to support that type of environment. The manager's ability to address conflicts is critical to a positive work environment and a positive attitude among staff members. The goal in a positive work environment is not to have conflict staff member to staff member or staff members to management. The reality is that there will always be some conflict. The maintenance of the positive environment requires quick and effective conflict resolution.

Also key to the positive environment is the physical work environment. Employers are required by the Occupational Safety and Health Act (OSHA) to provide a safe work environment. The company and the manager as the representative of the company are responsible for meeting the requirements of the law. Complying with the law does contribute to a positive work environment. The greatest contribution to the positive work environment is achieved, however, when the company, including the manager, sincerely cares about the safety of staff members.

The other foundational piece for a positive work environment is that of employee wellness. Safety addresses the physical safety of the staff member. The concept of "employee wellness" addresses both the psychological and physical well-being of the staff member.

A well-laid foundation combined with a clearly delivered message of concern for the well-being of the employee will help to minimize staff member frustration. The result will be staff member job satisfaction. The goal of the manager should be to create and maintain a positive work environment. The result of pursuing this goal will be quality staff member performance and high levels of guest satisfaction.

Job Satisfaction

Like motivation, job satisfaction means different things to different people. At its highest level, it is the staff member who derives happiness in the knowledge that no matter what the job, the job is well done. In hospitality we most often equate a job done well with an outstanding guest experience. Generally, the satisfaction individuals receive is dependent upon the extent to which the job and everything associated with it meets their needs and wants. We elaborate in this regard in the following:

- The "wants" are items the individual feels will deliver satisfaction. The wants are perceived differently within the team and are based on differences in age, educational level, gender, health, family relationships, personality, and other factors. Wants are very often of an intrinsic nature.
- Typically, "needs" represent tangible rewards such as pay and benefits.

Job satisfaction has been shown to be closely linked to turnover and absenteeism. The higher an individual's satisfaction, the less likely it is that he or she will leave the organization. According to The National Restaurant Association's Chief Economist Bruce Grindy, "The turn-over rate for employees in the restaurants-and-accommodations sector was 62.6 percent in 2013, compared to a 42.2 percent turnover rate in the overall private sector."[1] The link between turnover and satisfaction in the foodservice and lodging industry indicates that many employees are unhappy. The turnover rate in the rest of the hospitality industry is somewhat better but still above that of other industries. Is it pay or working conditions? To maintain quality in all aspects any operation requires a team that is stable and satisfied.

Replacing a staff member is time consuming and expensive. Replacement has a direct impact on the quality of the product and service delivered to the guest due to the ramp-up time required for a new staff member to achieve 100% mastery of processes and procedures. It is far better and more cost effective to invest in current staff members rather than constantly hiring and training new people. The intangibles of a dissatisfied staff member are costly. This includes the effect on morale within the team and its impact on customer satisfaction and the missed opportunities to utilize the staff member's talent and potential to grow.

Job satisfaction is affected by all of the elements discussed in this chapter. Managers should invest in the team through excellent management skills and by providing conditions within the operation that provide the basis for job satisfaction. Mentally challenging work with which each individual can cope successfully is of primary importance. Ideally each member should like what they do and have a strong sense of professionalism. The atmosphere in the operation should be open and nonthreatening, led by a firm but friendly manager who seeks input and support from the team and in which each staff member is valued. Satisfaction is not about winning popularity contests; rather, it is about the creation of a team and an environment where the individual is respected. Most studies in the area of job satisfaction conclude that a link exists between satisfaction and performance. The role the manager plays in this link is crucial.

Frustration

When examined, the working day of a staff member will reveal that all needs are seldom satisfied fully. They may be prevented from reaching a particular goal or objective or there may be conflicting goals. Either condition will produce a state of dissatisfaction and tension that may prevent a harmonious team spirit in the operation. Managers should understand the forces and factors that contribute to tension and dissatisfaction. Barriers to achieving individual goals produce a frustrating condition. A list of typical sources of frustration is shown in Figure 9.1.

A frustrated individual may respond by engaging in disruptive behavior. The distance between frustration and aggression is a short one. Aggression typically involves verbal or physical attacks against the person or persons perceived to be the cause of the frustration. Managers have a responsibility to be sensitive to the warning signs in this area. Not all sources of frustration are under the direct control of the manager. However, an awareness of potential areas of frustration and a sincere effort to handle them effectively through better organization,

---

Typical Sources of Frustration

* Antagonistic manager / supervisor

* Repetitious tasks

* Unpleasant working conditions

* Economic uncertainty

* Biased work assignments

* Manipulation of established working procedures

* Absence of orientation training

* Being unnoticed

FIGURE 9.1 Typical Sources of Frustration.

planning, and communication can help to remove many of the conditions that cause frustration.

When individuals sense that they are in danger, they may experience a feeling of anxiety. In contrast to fear, anxiety results when the source of danger cannot be identified. The physical symptoms of anxiety are similar to those associated with fear such as nausea, trembling, a pounding heart, and dryness in the throat. Anxiety is a form of stress that is emotionally and physically harmful. Anxiety may account for various staff members' behaviors that are often misunderstood or misinterpreted, particularly in individuals of different backgrounds and cultures. Anxiety is also frequently caused by the prospect of change. This activity can often be misinterpreted by managers as staff members being difficult rather than simply anxious or frightened.

Complaints

Complaints are an indication of discontent among the team. The manager is the key to addressing complaints before they develop into something they are not and become even more difficult to resolve. Speedy resolution of grievances and complaints is part of a positive work environment and a well-led operation. Wise handling of complaints affords the greatest opportunity to win staff members' respect and to gain their confidence.

Departments that have conflict or fail to focus on the objective of guest satisfaction will doom the entire hospitality organization to failure. Every member of the organization must be a committed team player totally focused on continuous improvements that facilitate the provision of high-quality products and service; however, both are inextricably intertwined.

Complaints from staff members concerning other staff members come to the forefront very quickly. Most people do not hesitate to complain about each other. It is a normal human phenomenon. Complaints about other people can be presented in a highly emotional way or in a cool, calculating manner. But usually this is done with a great deal of emotion, which colors the facts involved. This can make it difficult to determine the real problem as opposed to the symptoms.

In all cases, the issue should be dealt with as soon as possible. The longer the complaint remains unresolved, the more other people get involved and the more the quality of the work is affected. The quality of work immediately has an impact on guest satisfaction. If the manager has difficulty in resolving the complaint, then it is appropriate to seek further help from the human resource office/officer or senior management. There should be a process by which the complaining staff member can obtain a full and fair hearing, particularly if he or she is dissatisfied with the decision of the manager.

The "ideal" resolution of complaints avoids a "one loses and one wins" scenario and leads to a "win-win" scenario. A "win-win" scenario is achieved through participation by the staff member with the manager in resolving the issue. One of the most useful approaches is the application of a systematic approach to resolving complaints as shown in Figure 9.2.

Complaints are sometimes used by staff members to gain attention and to send messages regarding unfair wage scales, poor working conditions, and discriminatory actions against staff members on the basis of ethnic origin, gender, or sexual preference. The individual making the complaint is entitled to a fair hearing. Complaints that are not handled promptly and decisively can lead to problems of arbitration with labor unions. By bringing the complaint or problem to a win-win situation,

---

Systematic Approach to Resolving Complaints

The following steps can lead to a satisfactory resolution and investigation of the complaint:

* Check the team member's record in detail. Look for evidence of tardiness or absenteeism. Get the facts. Perhaps there are hidden reasons for seeking attention by complaining.

* Attempt to understand why the team member has made the complaint and what his or her feelings are. Allow the individual to "vent." Let him or her communicate freely and without interruption.

* Watch for body language and observe facial expressions.

* When other persons are involved, check for accuracy of information.

* Avoid an argumentative disposition when hearing the complaint.

* Keep senior management informed.

* Admit a management mistake. Do not try to conceal it if you have caused the complaint.

* Record the formal complaint; do not depend on memory. Be specific; include day, date, time, place, those involved, the type of complaint, and any other relevant facts.

* Prepare a written statement that includes the resulting decision and the rationale for this decision

* Establish facts and a definition of the complaint with the team member. Seek solutions, exhausting all avenues.

* Finally, bring the resolution to a mutually agreeable set of terms that includes steps for avoiding future problems in the area of the complaint.

FIGURE 9.2   Systematic Approach to Resolving Complaints.

the manager is dealing with the immediate problem. However, win-win solutions can involve a promise to submit the complaint to higher authority for resolution.

What is important in dealing with complaints is that the manager recognizes that the old-style Theory X type manager needs to be replaced with a Theory Y type, which in some instances represents a major shift in attitude for the manager. It replaces the notion that complaining staff members are adversaries and it focuses on solutions, assuming that both parties are aiming for the same goals. The win-win approach is consistent with an environment that encourages continuous improvement of product and service. In the hospitality industry, positive, motivated, happy staff members are critical to success.

Safe Work Environment

Hospitality employers are required by law to provide working conditions that do not impair the safety or health of operation employees. Therefore, they must provide an environment that protects employees from physical hazards, unhealthy conditions, and unsafe or dangerous practices by other staff members. Effective health and safety practices promote a positive work climate in the operation by providing for the physical and emotional well-being of all staff members as well as enhancing their economic security.

Safety hazards in the hospitality industry range from the use of knives in the restaurant and power-driven equipment in the hotel to slippery floors and chemical cleaning materials in theme parks. These hazards can produce accidents resulting in individuals falling, cutting themselves, burning themselves, receiving an electric shock, scalding themselves, or worse. These accidents occur because of ignorance of safety procedures, the carelessness of individuals, and the failure of the company to properly maintain the equipment and the facility.

In the late 1960s, the Congress became increasingly concerned that each year job-related accidents accounted for more than 14,000 deaths and nearly 2.5 million disabilities.[2] Eventually, these concerns led to the passage of the OSHA in 1970. This act was designed to "assure so far as possible every working man and woman in the nation safe and healthful working conditions and to preserve our human resources." The OSHA is administered by the Occupational Safety and Health Administration (OSHA). One of the responsibilities of OSHA is to develop and enforce mandatory job safety and health standards.

These standards cover workplace issues of machinery and equipment, materials, power sources, processing, protective clothing, first aid, and administrative requirements. Moreover, OSHA also requires that managers train and inform employees of any known safety hazard in the operation. The Hazard Communication Standard (HCS) requires employers to inform employees what chemicals they are working with and to detail their risks and what can be done to limit these risks. Further, HCS is achieved through training programs and detailed labeling on or near chemical containers. Material Safety Data Sheets are part of this standard. A system of priorities for workplace inspections (which includes operations) has been established by the OSHA[3] as listed hereunder:

1. inspection of imminent danger situations
2. investigation of catastrophes, fatalities, and accidents resulting in hospitalization of five or more employees
3. investigation of valid employee complaints of alleged violation of standards or of unsafe or unhealthful working conditions
4. follow-up inspections to determine if previously cited violations have been corrected.

The current OSHA regulations are available online at http://www.osha.gov/pls/oshaweb/owasrch.search_form?p_doc_type=STANDARDS&p_toc_level=1&p_keyvalue=1910.[4] However, OSHA provides a free on-site consultation service that helps employers identify hazardous conditions and corrective measures. According to the new law, a minimum fine of $5,000 is mandatory for intentional violations with a maximum fine of $70,000 for intentional or repeat violations. A maximum fine of $7,000 applies for all other violations, including failure by an employer to post the required OSHA notice.[5]

One of the best methods for identifying potential hazards in the operation is to simply consult the team. Ask the staff members to develop a list of items that need attention and accident prevention measures. They see hazards in and around the operation every day.

Managers may unintentionally reinforce unsafe acts by not correcting them when they are first observed. Through mandatory and proper supervision, unsafe work practices can be corrected. The nature of the hospitality industry requires that many staff members work with equipment that could do them harm if not used correctly or kept in good operating order or they use chemicals and have potential exposure to hazardous (bio) waste materials. The most common types of operation accident injuries are directly related to these types of physical elements and the element of human error. The most common type of injuries and their causes in the operation include the following.

- Lacerations: These are caused by improper use of chef's knives, slicers, choppers, broken ware, or glass, and other hand tools.
- Power-driven equipment: When used improperly, blenders, mixers, slicers, grinders, lawn mowers, laundry equipment, steam cleaning equipment to just mention a few can cause accidents. The manager is responsible for ensuring that each staff member is fully trained in the safe use of all power-driven equipment and that the equipment is properly maintained.
- Burn: Common injuries in the operation, burns and scalds of varying degree, can result from contact with the boilers, steam, chemicals, hot surfaces such as a grill and any other equipment that might get hot when used.[6]
- Slips and falls: Slips and falls in the operation are typically caused by wet or greasy floors left unattended. The danger from greasy or wet floors is compounded by staff members rushing about during busy periods. Staff members should be made aware by the manager of the necessity to keep floor surfaces safe. Staff members should wear shoes with rubber soles or ones made from neoprene to prevent slipping. Leather-soled shoes should never be worn in areas where floors are likely to be slippery. Safety shoes that have strong uppers without openings should be worn in areas such as the kitchen and laundry because they help prevent cuts or crushing injuries.
- Fires: Because most operations have open flames of some type the potential for fire is high. More fires occur in foodservice establishments than in any other type of business operation but a fire in a hotel can be extremely devastating. Managers should check these potential fire hazards regularly. Special fire protection equipment should be provided in all areas where fires are likely to occur. This equipment includes sprinkler systems, chemical fire suppression systems, and handheld fire extinguishers. Training in the use of fire extinguishers and evacuation procedures for guests and employees should be part of every new staff member's induction and orientation training.

Since training alone will not assure continual adherence to safety, managers should observe staff members at work and show approval for safe work practices. When unsafe actions are observed, immediate corrective action should be taken. Fatigue and stress can contribute to the cause of accidents. Simple changes can often be made in the operation to reduce the occurrence of fatigue and stress.

Establish a safety committee composed of staff members and other interdependent department managers. The safety committee provides

Methods for Promoting Safety
* Publishing safety statistics. Monthly accident reports should be posted. Ideas and suggestions should be solicited as to how these accidents can be avoided.
* Using bulletin boards and menu wall display areas throughout the property to display posters, pictures, sketches, and cartoons depicting safety situations.
* Setting high expectations for safety. Encourage the managers and staff members to recognize positive safety actions and acknowledge those who contribute to safety improvements.

FIGURE 9.3   Methods for Promoting Safety.

a means of getting staff members directly involved in the operation of the safety program. The duties of the committee include inspecting, observing work practices, investigating accidents, and making recommendations. The committee should meet regularly, at least once a month, and attendance should be mandatory. Additional ways to promote safety in this regard are shown in Figure 9.3.

Health and Wellness

Physical Health

Until the last two decades safety and accident prevention received far more attention than did employee health. However, this has changed. Statistics show that occupational diseases may cost industry as much or more than occupational accidents.[7] Many hospitality organizations now not only work to remove health hazards from the work place, but also initiate programs to improve employee health. Some employers offer preventive health programs such as healthy eating and smoking cessation programs at no charge.

Stress

Stress comes from two basic sources: (1) physical activity and (2) mental/emotional activity. The physical reaction of the body to both is the same. The operation can be a stressful environment, particularly at busy periods but not all stress is harmful. Positive stress is a feeling of exhilaration and achievement. This can be associated with a successful busy service period, such as the check-in of a large convention group, during which

Causes of Negative Stress
* Conflicting expectations between manager and staff member
* An unpleasant work environment which could include high temperature, high noise levels, long hours, irregular hours, insensitive or hostile supervision
* Poor preparation for the job
* Performance appraisal
* Lack of social interaction
* Work that is challenging
* Personality conflicts
* Working holidays
* Group pressures

FIGURE 9.4   Causes of Negative Stress.

everything went well in the operation. Staff members performed well as a group, record numbers were served, and 100% guest satisfaction was achieved. On the other hand, negative stress may cause people to become ill. Some of the causes of negative stress are shown in Figure 9.4.

Arguments with managers or fellow staff members are a common cause of stress. Feeling trapped in a job to which a person is ill-suited can be equally painful. Other strains include lack of communication on the job and lack of recognition for a job well done. Stress has been linked to many things. It manifests itself in several ways such as increased absenteeism, job turnover, lower productivity, and mistakes on the job. Stress-related disorders include tension, high blood pressure, muscle tightness in the chest, ulcers, and others requiring medical attention.

Burnout is considered to be the most severe form of stress. It is fatigue, frustration, or apathy resulting from prolonged stress, overwork, or intense activity.[8] Career burnout usually occurs when work is no longer meaningful to the individual staff member. The factors that cause burnout are those that cause stress; in fact, burnout and stress are interconnected issues.

Counseling

The manager is in a position to counsel staff members regarding behavior that is affecting their job performance. Changes in an individual's behavior, such as excessive absenteeism, tardiness, hostility, moodiness, withdrawal, and a decline in job performance should be monitored. Good managers interact with their team on a constant basis and are usually in the best position to identify and observe these changes.

The role of the manager in this situation is to address the behavior from the standpoint of the impact on job performance, not to solve the staff member's personal problems. Within emotional and personal crises, alcoholism and drug abuse are considered to be personal matters. They do become the manager's problem when they affect the staff member's ability to perform satisfactorily in the workplace. The manager should make the staff member aware of the impact their behavior is having on their performance and that they are jeopardizing their position with the company. It is appropriate for the manager to recommend the staff member seek professional help but this must be done very carefully and with tact. Typically in large organizations, employee assistance programs (EAPs) exist. These programs are in place to help employees overcome problems, and they provide guidance and referrals to outside professional help.

The most prevalent problems among individuals are personal crisis situations involving mental, family, financial, or legal matters. These are problems that can be brought to a manager's attention. These types of issues should be referred to the EAP or an outside agency.

Managers should be aware that the behavior of some staff members might be adversely affected by some elements of the "physical" operation environment, which may necessitate reassigning, or rotating individuals to different sections of the operation.

Alcohol is the single most used and abused drug in America. According to the National Institute on Alcohol Abuse and Alcoholism, as of 2014 16.3 million people 18 years of age or older have a Alcohol Use Disorder (AUD)[9] Alcohol abuse has been a problem for the hospitality industry in general and the restaurant operation employee in particular. Many theories for its prevalence have been put forward, from the notion that its accessibility contributes to the problem to the idea that the hot operational environment encourages the use of alcohol.

The approach to handling alcoholism is to monitor all staff members regularly and systematically. Evidence of declining performance on the job should be carefully documented, so that the individual can be confronted with unequivocal proof that his or her work is suffering. Offers of help should be made available without any penalty to the individual. Mention of alcoholism should be avoided. The staff member should be allowed to seek aid as for any other health problem.

Drug abuse among employees is one of the wider societal issues confronting this industry. While alcohol is the most abused substance, marijuana, cocaine, heroin, crack, and varieties of abused prescription drugs are found to be in use in the hospitality industry. Various approaches are used to assist individuals with a dependency. They range from outpatient treatment for an extended period to inpatient treatment. "Nearly 75 percent of all adult illicit drug users are employed, as are most binge and heavy alcohol users. Studies show that when compared with non-substance abusers, substance-abusing employees are more likely to

- change jobs frequently
- be late to or absent from work
- be less productive employees
- be involved in a workplace accident
- file a workers' compensation claim."[10]

Wellness Programs

Wellness programs are becoming a common feature in hospitality organizations. The programs are designed to prevent illness and enhance the well-being of each individual. They include periodic medical exams, stop smoking clinics, improved dietary practices, weight control, exercise and fitness, stress management, immunizations, and cardiopulmonary resuscitation training. Documented results from these types of programs have shown a reduction in employee sick days and lower major medical costs. It is expected that as health care costs continue to increase, wellness programs will grow.

Summary

Job satisfaction has been shown to be linked to turnover and absenteeism. The greater the individual's job satisfaction level, the more productive he or she becomes. Job satisfaction revolves around the creation of an environment where each person is valued and respected. An environment where frustration is minimized and complaints are addressed quickly. The ideal resolution of complaints is a situation in which all feel they have won.

Managers have a responsibility to ensure that a safe work environment exists, a place free from physical hazards, unhealthy conditions, and unsafe or dangerous practices. Effective health and safety practices promote a positive work environment.

Managers need to be prepared to counsel staff when their behavior impacts their work. They should know their limitations in this area and know how and when to seek recommend the staff member to seek assistance through the EAP or outside professional help. As with all other considerations for a safe operation environment, stress and stressful situations must be recognized and avoided.

There are no good reasons why operations should be unpleasant places, even during busy service. Poor physical working conditions can be overcome. Considering the staff member in a holistic way, with all that entails, is now considered to be a worthwhile investment. Needless to say, when frustration on the job is dealt with effectively and a safe and healthy work environment exists in the operation, job satisfaction is possible.

Study Questions

1. Identify the issues that contribute to staff member frustration.
2. Describe steps to deal effectively with staff member complaints.
3. Discuss the connections between motivation and job satisfaction.
4. Identify the basic steps in health, safety, and accident prevention.
5. Relate the companies' roll in employee health and wellness.

Case Studies

The case studies listed below relate to the information presented in this chapter and reading, answering the case study questions and participating in discussion of a case will reinforce and expand what you have learned in this chapter. All case studies are provided in this text after the last chapter.

Bill & Jean's Restaurant

C&L Restaurant

Grand Adventure Park

L&J Cafeteria

Shady Lane Inn

Shepherd Mountain Hotel

Stone Lion Hotel and Conference Center

Notes

1. National Restaurant Association. (March 20, 2014). *Economist's notebook: Hospitality employee turnover rose slightly in 2013*. Retrieved October 16, 2014, from http://www.restaurant.org/News-Research/News/Economist-s-Notebook-Hospitality-employee-turnover

2. Sherman, A., Bohlander, G., & Crudden, H. (1988). *Managing human resources* (8th ed., p. 576). Cincinnati: South-Western.

3. Miller, J., Porter, M., & Drummond, K. (1992). *Supervision in the hospitality industry* (2nd ed., p. 98). New York: John Wiley.

4. United States Department of Labor, Occupational Safety and Health Administration. Retrieved October 6, 2014, from http://www.osha.gov/pls/oshaweb/owadisp.show_document?p_table=OSHACT&p_id=3371

5. Ibid., p. 259.

6. Bryars, L., & Rue, L. (1994). *Human resources management* (4th ed., p. 499). Boston: Irwin.

7. Sherman, A., Bohlander, G., & Crudden, H. (1988). *Managing human resources* (8th ed., p. 592). Cincinnati: South-Western.

8. Dictionary.com. Retrieved August 29, 2014, from http://dictionary.reference.com/browse/burnout?s=t

9. Institute on Alcohol Abuse and Alcoholism. Retrieved January 17, 2015, from http://pubs.niaaa.nih.gov/publications/AlcoholFacts&Stats/AlcoholFacts&Stats.htm

10. U.S. Office of Personnel Management. *Work-life reference materials: Alcoholism in the workplace: A handbook for supervisors*. Retrieved October 16, 2014, from http://www.opm.gov/policy-data-oversight/worklife/reference-materials/alcoholism-in-the-workplace-a-handbook-for-supervisors/

Motivation 10

CHAPTER OUTLINE

- ► Introduction
- ► Defining Motivation
- ► Theories and Motivational Philosophies
- ► Morale
- ► Stimulus and Motivation
- ► Feedback
- ► Conclusions

LEARNING OBJECTIVES

When you complete reading this chapter, you should be able to:

- ► define motivation
- ► list the major theories and philosophies of motivation
- ► explain the elements that contribute to a motivated team
- ► describe factors of morale within the operation
- ► recall the elements of positive stimulus
- ► describe the elements and effects of negative stimulus
- ► explain why feedback is an important element of morale.

Introduction

A foundational aspect of the manager's role in the operation is that of motivator. It is through motivating the team that the manager achieves the goals of the operation. However, motivating people is both a simple and complex task. It is achieved by directing, praising, rewarding, and even correcting and disciplining. The critical factor in motivating anyone is using the right method of motivation at the right time. The goal must always be to create an environment that encourages and supports while continuing to move always in the direction of the goals to be accomplished.

Defining Motivation

Defining motivation requires looking at the root of the word. Motivation, the term, was originally derived from the Latin word *movere*, which literally means to move.[1] The goal of the manager is to move the staff member and the team as a whole forward to their assigned goals. To accomplish this, the understanding of what motivation is must go beyond the root of the word to include understanding of the terms motive, motivate. and motivator. A motive is something that causes a person to act. A motivator is someone or something that provides the motive for others to act. It is important to note that often the best motivator (something) is part of the staff member's nature, their inner drive. The action resulting from a motivator is called motivation. Motivation is the process of motivating and also the condition of being motivated.[2] One of the motivators in the operation will be the manager. The manager provides the motivation or taps into the inner motivation of the individual to move the staff member and the entire team forward to accomplish goals.

Motivation is concerned with three factors: (1) what energizes behavior, (2) what channels such behavior, and (3) the conditions under which this behavior is maintained. The triggers and drivers of motivation are the same for all individuals. It is clear that the characteristics of the work environment and the characteristics of the manager (the particular disposition and leadership style) affect the elements of motivation. The more the manager understands the staff member's behavior, the better he or she should be able to influence that behavior and make it more consistent so as to align with the goals of the company. Since quality service and productivity are central to the success of the hospitality manager, the creation of the appropriate motivational environment is critical to this success.

Each person sees the world from an individual viewpoint. An individual's perception of the world is determined by his or her background and personal experiences, among other variables. The operation, company, and the world generally are viewed through this personal and individual lens. The manager needs to work to learn how each staff member is likely to respond to different events. Each staff member perceives and interprets instructions, actions, and communications in a unique way. He or she must strive to understand the diverse cultural issues that occur in their department and company.

A staff member's values and cultural background are a strong determinant of behavior. A value is any object, activity, or orientation that individuals consider very important to their way of life. Culture, on the other hand, refers to the beliefs, practices, traditions, ideologies, and lifestyles of a particular group. Each culture has its own cultural values which are commonly held standards of what is acceptable or unacceptable, important or unimportant, and right or wrong. Values and culture have been shown to be related to decision making, motivation, communication, and supervisory success. One of the challenges for management is the creation and then maintenance of a culture in the workplace that is based on cultural values that drive quality performance, team work, and loyalty.

The makeup of today's workforce in the United States is very diverse. According to the United States Bureau of Labor Statistics, population survey for 2013, 57.5% of the individuals employed in the accommodation category were women, 14.9% were African-American, and 25% were Hispanic.[3] The foodservices and drinking places category was similar with 51.8% women, 11.7% African-American, and 24.4% Hispanics.[4] According to Forbes in 2012 globally the hotel and catering (in the US restaurants) industry is in the top three for diversity.[5] The diverse nature of the industry workforce is changing the culture of the workplace in the hospitality industry. This diversity will continue to grow in the future.

Humans function in an integrated manner, not in individual parts. It is the total of the staff member we are interacting with. While sometimes it is useful to focus our attention on certain segments of the individual's personality in order to have a better understanding of the person, in the final analysis the staff member should be viewed as a complete package.

Managers must recognize that they cannot know the nature of many of the factors influencing the behavior of individual staff members. Staff members often do not reveal what they are currently experiencing in their lives away from the job. What happens to staff members at home or through other activities will affect how they feel about their work and other aspects of their lives. What happens away from work also influences how well they perform at work. Remember, it is impossible to have the highest-quality team without a respect for people, their differences, and the strengths this diversity brings to the company's motivational environment.

Theories and Motivational Philosophies

Maslow: Hierarchy of Needs

Probably the most widely accepted description of human needs is the hierarchy of needs concept put forward by Abraham Maslow. Maslow states that we as humans possess five basic needs and that these needs can be arranged in a hierarchy of importance that relates to the order in which individuals generally strive to satisfy them. The needs (see Figure 10.1) listed in Maslow's hierarchical order are (1) physiological, (2) security, (3) social, (4) esteem, and (5) self-actualization needs.[6]

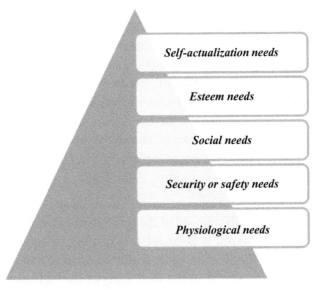

FIGURE 10.1 Maslow's Hierarchy of Needs

Physiological needs relate to the normal functioning of the body and include the need for food, water, air, rest, and sex. However, until these needs are met, a significant portion of an individual's behavior is aimed at satisfying them. If these needs are satisfied, then behavior is aimed at the next level, the security needs.

Security or safety needs are the needs individuals require to keep themselves free from bodily and economic disaster. The organization can best help employees to satisfy their security needs through good and fair salaries, since it is with these salaries that employees can buy items such as food and housing. When security needs are satisfied, then behavior tends to be aimed at satisfying social needs.

Social needs include an individual's desire for love, companionship, and friendship. Overall, these needs reflect a person's desire to be accepted by others. As these needs are satisfied, behavior shifts to satisfying esteem needs.

Esteem needs consist of an individual's desire for respect and are generally divided into two categories: (1) self-respect and (2) respect for others. Once esteem needs are satisfied, an individual emphasizes satisfying self-actualization needs.

Self-actualization needs are the desire to maximize whatever potential an individual possesses. For example, a motivated staff member who seeks to satisfy self-actualization or self-realization needs might strive to become a manager. Self-actualization needs are at the highest level of Maslow's hierarchy.

These needs are the same for everyone. They apply when staff members are at work, at which time there may be problems with how well they work. Maslow's need hierarchy theory is consistent with the reasons people work. In the right environment individuals move from one level to another and do not remain at any one level for their entire life.

Herzberg: Two-Factor Theory

Frederick Herzberg put forward the motivator-hygiene theory. Proposed in 1959, this theory emphasizes the roles of motivator factors and hygiene factors (also known as maintenance factors). It is also known as the *two-factor theory* of work motivation which is shown in Figure 10.2. The factors ensure produce job satisfaction are called motivator factors because they satisfy a staff member's need for

FIGURE 10.2   Herzberg's Two-Factor Theory

self-realization. According to this theory, hygiene factors are important, but they are not motivators.

Dissatisfaction: contributing hygiene factors are as listed hereunder:

- company policy and administration
- supervision
- relationship with supervisor
- relationship with peers
- working conditions
- salary
- relationship with subordinates.

Satisfaction: contributing motivation factors are as listed hereunder:

- opportunity for achievement
- opportunity for recognition
- work itself
- responsibility
- advancement
- personal growth.

When hygiene factors deteriorate to a level below what a staff member considers acceptable, then dissatisfaction is imminent. If staff members are required to work in an environment that is unpleasant, unsafe, and/or hostile, then a motivational climate cannot be created until such time as the hygiene factors are at an acceptable level. Bringing the hygiene factors to an acceptable level for the staff member can remove dissatisfaction but it will not create full job satisfaction, and certainly it will not motivate performance in the long term. When the hygiene factors of policy, supervision, working conditions, relationships, and pay are good and adequate, the stage is then set for the motivating factors.[7] The motivating factors help create job satisfaction, which in and of itself is the primary motivating factor. In Herzberg's theory, the opportunity for staff members to advance will require them to seek recognition, assume responsibility, and achieve success through the job. Recognition is the most important factor, more important than pay or any other element of the hygiene factors. If the job or position of a staff member can be enriched to include more motivators, then the opportunity exists to have a motivated, participative member fully committed to the principles of success.

Herzberg is the person associated with the concepts of job enrichment. In 1968 he stressed that "the only way to motivate employees is through challenging work in which they can assume responsibility."[8] This he proposed as a reaction to what he called the KITA (kick in the ass) methods used widely by most managers and supervisors. Central to these proposals is the idea that strategies that modify jobs can offer a more meaningful role for employees and can give them the opportunity for recognition and ultimately greater responsibility.

Theory X–Theory Y

Another motivational theory involves the manager's assumptions about employees and the nature of people. Douglas McGregor, a Massachusetts Institute of Technology professor, identified two contradicting sets of these assumptions. Theory X involves assumptions that McGregor feels managers often use as the basis for dealing with people, while theory Y represents the assumptions that McGregor feels managers should strive to use.[9]

Theory X, according to McGregor, assumes that the average person has an inherent dislike of work and will avoid it if possible. Because of this natural human dislike for work, most people must be coerced, controlled, directed, and threatened with punishment to get them to put forth adequate effort toward the achievement of organizational objectives.

The Theory X manager assumes that the average person prefers to be directed, wishes to avoid responsibility, has relatively little ambition, and wants security above all. The Theory X manager motivates staff primarily through fear. This type of manager closely controls the staff. The Theory X manager believes that he or she must protect the employees from their own shortcomings. This type of manager does this with heavy-handed control and coercion.

Theory Y assumes that the expenditure of physical and mental effort in work is as natural as play or rest. People will exercise self-direction and self-control in the service of objectives to which they are committed. Commitment to objectives is a function of the rewards associated with achievement.

The Theory Y manager assumes that under proper conditions the average person learns not only to accept but also to seek responsibility. The capacity to exercise a relatively high degree of imagination, ingenuity, and creativity in the solution of organizational problems is widely and normally distributed in the population. The Theory Y manager believes that he or she should lead by including the staff in planning. This type of manager encourages staff to experience personal satisfaction as they contribute to the achievement of objectives.

Theory X has a part to play in situations that require a firm but necessary position of authority. But it has no part to play in team building, or the creation of a team where each member is expected to contribute to the overall success of the team. The empowering of staff members to take an active part in all aspects of the team is certainly not a part of theory X. Rather, the successful team will fall into McGregor's category of theory Y that relies on the assumption that people are naturally primed and ready to contribute; however, the only missing pieces are great leadership and a motivated environment.

Theory Z

Theory Z is a motivational philosophy that emerged in the 1970s. It was first fully presented in a book by William Ouchi in 1981.[10] Theory Z is a humanistic approach more similar to Theory Y than to Theory X. The difference between Theory Z and Theory Y is the perspective. Theory Y looks at management from a view of employer to employee. Theory Z looks at management from an organizational view. Theory Z is based on long-term employment and slow, but continuous growth and progression. Employees are included in decision making for the organization but are still responsible for their own performance and development.

The Theory Z manager believes in encouragement and development of the individual. This manager also constantly considers the future of the total organization when working with staff. The manager views the welfare of the individual as directly connected with that of the organization.

Expectancy Model

Victor Vroom's expectancy model is based on the premise that needs cause human behavior. The model addresses the issue of motivation strength. Motivation strength is an individual's degree of desire to perform a behavior. As this desire increases or decreases, motivation strength is said to fluctuate correspondingly.[11]

Motivation strength = perceived value of result × perceived probability of successful completion

According to this model, motivation strength is determined by two factors as listed hereunder.

1. The perceived value of the result of performing a behavior.
2. The perceived probability that the behavior performed will cause the result to materialize.

As both of these factors increase, an individual's motivation strength and desire to perform also increase. In general, individuals tend to perform those behaviors that maximize personal rewards over the long run.

An illustration of expectancy theory applied to hotel operations might be as follows: A staff member believes that if he or she provides guest service at the front desk that satisfies the hotel's standards and meets the needs of the customer consistently, then the perceived value of maintaining quality service will produce for the individual a perceived probability of further reward.

Pygmalion Effect

The Pygmalion effect states that the expectations the staff members have of themselves will determine how well they perform. If you expect great things, great things will happen. If you expect mediocre performance, mediocre performance is what you will get. This is also known as the self-fulfilling prophecy. If you emphasize the positive and exhibit belief in the individual's and team's ability to succeed then staff members will begin to believe in themselves. The more the manager tells the team how successful they can become, the more competent the team will be. When high performance and quality standards are set and staff members are told they can rise to the occasion, the self-fulfilling prophecy determines that they will. Positive expectations equal positive results.[12]

MORALE

Morale is defined as the mental and emotional condition of an individual with regard to the function or task at hand.[13] So far in this module we have examined some of the theories pertaining to motivating people in the workplace. These are important because they provide insight into why some individuals perform well while others do not. Motivation contributes to morale. There can be no great "company morale" without the application of motivation by the manager. The hospitality operation is often a pressure-filled place of work during busy periods. Good team morale can reduce this pressure, increasing the confidence, ability, and harmony of the team and helping to deal with busy periods.

The first and most important element of morale is the leadership style of the manager. The focus should be a leadership style that continuously demonstrates respect and a caring attitude toward the staff members. The manager who will make the greatest impact on morale is the one who believes in people. This belief is demonstrated by being approachable and sensitive to individual difficulties in achieving goals.

There are elements that contribute to the morale of the staff member and the team. These elements include leadership attributes and a manager who can:

Create

- a comfortable atmosphere in which everyone is clear on what to do, when to do it, and how to do it.
  - a climate that challenges each staff member to contribute the best.
  - healthy competition.
  - individual passion and a pride in being the best.
  - a team morale that provides a sense of belonging.
  - an atmosphere in which individuals are encouraged to share opinions and ideas.

Show

- a caring awareness of individuals' problems.
  - sensitivity and understanding of ethnic diversity and the special problems of integration that may exist.
  - respect for individual staff members' dignity.
  - a sense of humor.
  - consistency of behavior in dealing with each staff member.
  - fairness at all times.
  - displeasure for poor performance when appropriate.

Give

- praise when it is merited.
  - reasons for uncompromising high quality standards.

Be

- an active listener.
  - a coach.
  - a team builder.

Morale is also about building trust and empowering staff members to make the right decisions. A key element to positive morale is giving a sense of real involvement to individuals. Figure 10.3 shows what the manager should do to activate trust and empowerment.

The manager must scrupulously avoid the appearance of favoring one person over another. This may be the most difficult challenge, as no human being is totally objective in dealing with another. We all have biases. Since we cannot be totally objective, we must recognize our subjectivities and compensate for them. To build morale, each individual staff member must be treated fairly.

Trust and Empowerment

Activators

* Give staff members important work to do.

* Allow staff members some freedom in how to get the work done.

* Give staff members the resources to do the work.

* Make staff members feel their input is given real consideration.

* Actively encourage teamwork.

* Be tolerant with failure.

* Celebrate successes.

FIGURE 10.3   Trust and Empowerment

Trust is critical to the morale of both the individual and the team. Trust is the foundation for respect and respect is the foundation for positive morale. When trust does not exist, morale will turn to the negative side. The goal is to achieve the highest possible level of Esprit de Corps. Esprit de Corps is the spirit of the group. It is the common enthusiasm and honor that drives the individual and team to success. This is a critical concept when building a team. When the team loses its spirit, performance quickly diminishes in quality.

Achieving Esprit de Corps also requires regular and effective communication. The staff members need to be kept informed of their individual and team progress to goals, the progress of other teams, and changes in the operation that will impact them. The standards and goals should be made clear initially and revisited on a regular basis. The opportunity to directly communicate with managers encourages trust and makes the staff members feel they are respected and have an active role in building the future of the operation. One of the greatest berries to a positive morale is a workforce that does not feel their jobs are secure, remember Maslow and Herzberg. A sense of ownership and the feeling their work is valuable and contributes to the operation's success is foundational to positive morale and positive morale is foundational to quality in all aspects of the operation.

As we have observed from different approaches to motivation, staff members generally perform at their best when they feel useful and needed, in an environment where they are contributing and valuable team players, and enjoy a sense of security and belonging. These elements make up individual and team morale. The creation and maintenance of this morale is part of the manager's job. It is easy to determine when poor morale or no morale at all is present in the department or company; however, although it is difficult to tell if morale is just average, it is obvious when good morale is present. Good morale is reflected in low employee turnover and a department/company that is well led and productive, where staff members show pride in producing high-quality customer experiences.

Stimulus and Motivation

Stimulus is something that causes action. Motivation and demotivation are the result of stimulus. Demotivation can be defined as something that reduces or removes the desire to complete a task or continue to carry out a function. Motivation is the result of positive stimulus such as praise or rewards. Demotivation is the result of negative stimulus such as put-downs, failure to make good on promises, or favoritism. Stimulus can be physical, verbal, nonverbal, or combinations of all the three. Most of the stimuli we get as adults are verbal and nonverbal as opposed to the physical ones we may have received as children. Normal stimuli is used to describe different aspects and factors that when applied to individual staff members are motivators and builders of morale. Negative stimuli in the form of put-downs, insensitivity, insults, sarcasm, poor working conditions, and poor leadership can damage relationships and destroy morale.

Positive Stimuli

Positive stimuli are necessary to satisfy the esteem and ego needs of individuals. At its simplest, a positive stimulus may be a smile from the manager or a nod of recognition. Figure 10.4 provides examples of nonverbal and verbal stimuli. Positive stimulus is also about catching staff members doing a good job. An example of high level positive stimuli is the staff member receiving praise from the manager in front of the team and other department staff.

Stimulus

<u>Nonverbal</u>

* Making eye contact

* Giving listening signals

* Shaking hands

* Waving

<u>Verbal</u>

* Using a person's name

* Checking for understanding

* Making reference to past experiences

* Praising

* Greeting

* Thanking

* Saying farewell

FIGURE 10.4   Stimulus: Verbal and Nonverbal

The highest performance or overall quality is achieved when there is buy-in by the staff members. This is achieved by involving staff members in determining team direction and goals. When the staff members feel that the company's vision is "their" vision, they will achieve. Creating buy-in is an integral part of motivating staff.

When a climate of cooperation and communication is established through organized, sensible motivational techniques, individuals become a team rather than just a work group. This is a challenge for the manager and the team, but the potential rewards for the establishment are great.

The prospect of earning more money does not motivate as much as recognition, responsibility, and the prospect of advancement. However, incentives can be used as methods of positive stimuli. Incentives and awards are positive stimuli and performance reinforcements. Small rewards may be more effective than large ones. The small rewards may become a cause for positive celebration. Awards, prizes, and ceremonies are important to staff members. What Tom Peters refers to as "little things with high impact"[14] are shown in Figure 10.5. Whatever programs, awards, or rewards are instituted, it must be ensured that all staff members are included and are eligible to participate.

Internal advancement programs, often called promotion from within programs, are important motivators. These types of programs allow management to develop a pool of trained candidates for future positions. In the process, the company clearly demonstrates that it wants a long-term relationship with its staff members.

Little Things with Big Impact:

Stimulus

* Keep a calendar of staff members' birthdays and recognize them with a cake, flowers, or a card or by simply wishing them a happy birthday.

* Celebrate happy family events with staff members.

* Celebrate achieving a goal.

* Create a player of the week or month program.

* Send out thank-you notes regularly.

* Create incentives to address gaps or needs in quality and production.

* Provide professional development opportunities for staff members.

* Promote from within when possible.

FIGURE 10.5 Little Things with Big Impact: Positive Stimulus

Negative Stimuli

Examples of negative stimuli are publicly reprimanding or belittling a staff member. These are also known as demotivators. If these are in widespread use in the department or company, then morale is nonexistent and the leader is probably operating in a Theory X mode, the manager who leads through fear. If no positive stimuli are available to staff members, then they will work for negative stimuli rather than suffer the least acceptable situation, no stimuli at all. Examples of common negative stimuli or demotivators that should be avoided are shown in Figure 10.6.

When people are unhappy at work, absenteeism increases, productivity goes down, the quality of work is lower, and employee turnover increases, all of which adds up to a failing business. Negative stimuli contribute to low morale. Stimuli are part of morale building, which together make up the motivational climate. As has been pointed out, motivation comes from within each individual. Simply removing negative stimuli and demotivators does not really motivate staff members; it simply brings them to average satisfaction. A manager's leadership qualities and supervisory style will exert a great influence over the team and will determine whether individual staff members motivate themselves.

Things to Avoid:

Negative Stimulus

* Inconsistent behavior by the manager/management

* Abusive or abrasive behavior

* Poor working conditions

* Fear of supervisor, loss of job, or change

* No team atmosphere

* Lack of recognition

* Poor leadership

* Lack of incentives, ambitions, or goals

* Use of ridicule or sarcasm

* Micro-management, clearly communicated lack of trust

* Unfair job allocations

* Lack of communication

* Lack of respect for persons of different age, ethnicity, gender, physical abilities and qualities, and sexual preference

---

FIGURE 10.6 Things to Avoid: Negative Stimulus

Feedback

Feedback is not only a useful method of providing information to the staff member on performance but also an excellent method of giving reinforcement and positive motivation. Quality feedback is driven by a number of factors. The first and most important of these is that feedback must be intended to help both the person and the operation. Additional characteristics of a quality feedback are shown in Figure 10.7.

The purpose of giving feedback is to reinforce the staff member's commitment and abilities. It should be given when requested by a staff member. Feedback should be given on two positive levels: needs improvement or is doing well.

Excellent morale within the department or company is instilled by a manager who believes that most staff members want to do a good job and in most instances will do a good job. The achievement and success of the team are the results of each staff member at all levels of the team. As Daryl Hartley Leonard, the chief executive officer of Hyatt Hotel Corporation, states: "If there is anything I have learned in my 27 years in the service industry, it is this; 99 percent of all employees want to do a good job. How they perform is simply a reflection of the one for whom they work."[15]

Quality Feedback

Characteristics

* It is intended to help both the person and the operation.

* It is given directly to the person (face to face).

* It actually describes what the staff member is doing and the effects the actions are having.

* It is a description of a person's actions, not a type of person.

* It is specific, rather than general, with good, clear, recent examples.

* It is given at a time when the staff member appears ready to accept it and as soon after the event as possible.

* It is given in private where other staff members cannot overhear.

* It includes only those things that the staff member can reasonably be expected to do something about.

* It does not cover more than the staff member can handle at any one time.

* It is always given when asked for.

FIGURE 10.7   Quality Feedback Characteristics

Conclusions

What motivates? As we have learned, each person requires different things. The expression "different stimulus for different folks" is perhaps the best way of summing up motivation, morale, and stimuli. In general people want to join a team or pursue quality objectives that will enable them to realize their value and potential. They need to see that what they are doing is not a wasted effort but is making a contribution to the team's and operation's goals. They must see value in what they are doing. Motivation comes not only from activity but also from the desire to actively contribute and be part of something. As the positive work environment develops and gains momentum, staff members will support what they create. When employees are given the opportunity to provide input, they have a stake in the issue. Seeing objectives reached and becoming a reality along with helping to shape the future is fulfilling.

Recognizing staff members for the accomplishment of particular tasks also contributes to team morale. Staff members want credit for personal achievements and appreciation for their participation in the overall team objectives. Recognizing the achievements of staff members is another way of saying thanks. Staff members are motivated when they know exactly what is expected of them and the manager expresses confidence that they will be successful.

Motivation rises when the goals and individual responsibilities are made clear by the manager. Encourage the staff member to stretch; give them opportunities to try new things and acquire new skills. Managers should not feel threatened by the achievements and successes of individuals but should be supportive of their success.

Motivational theories have demonstrated that most individuals are highly motivated when they can see their value to the goals of the company. Among these theories are Maslow's needs hierarchy theory, Herzberg's two-factor theory, Douglas McGregor's Theory X and Theory Y, Ouchi's Theory Z, Victor Vroom's expectancy theory, and the Pygmalion effect.

Morale within the department and company is closely related to the leadership ability of the manager, who can create a positive atmosphere, show respect for individuals, seek their opinions, and build a team environment. Stimuli contribute to motivation and morale. Negative stimuli such as put-downs, insensitivity, insults, sarcasm, and poor working conditions are considered demotivators, which damage relationships and destroy morale within the department and company. Positive stimuli are necessary to satisfy the esteem needs of individual staff members.

Feedback is an important element in creating an environment where positive stimuli encourage staff members to motivate themselves and the team. Allow the staff members to fail as well as succeed. Build the team's *esprit de corps*, which says to each member of the team, "If you grow, we all benefit." Managers can establish morale through trust, direction, high standards of conduct, encouraging innovation, providing adequate training, treating each member with dignity, and being a champion of the team.

Managers cannot motivate individuals, but they can create an environment in which individuals can motivate themselves. Each person sees the world from a different and individual viewpoint. Managers therefore should learn how each staff member is likely to respond to different events.

Study Questions

1. Define motivation.
2. List and state the elements of the major theories and philosophies of motivation.
3. Explain the elements that contribute to a motivated team.
4. Describe factors of morale within the operation.
5. Recall the elements of positive stimulus.
6. Describe the elements and effects of negative stimulus.
7. Explain why feedback is an important element of morale.

Case Studies

The case studies listed below relate to the information presented in this chapter and reading, answering the case study questions and participating in discussion of a case will reinforce and expand what you have learned in this chapter. All case studies are provided in this text after the last chapter.

Bill & Jean's Restaurant

C&L Restaurant

Grand Adventure Park

L&J Cafeteria

Naples by the Sea

Prairie View Country Club

Shady Lane Inn

Shandong House Restaurant

Shepherd Mountain Hotel

Notes

1. Merriam-Webster. (2011). Retrieved October 21, 2014, from http://www.merriam-webster.com/dictionary/motivation
2. Sherman, A., Bohlander, G., & Crudden, H. (1988). *Managing human resource* (8th ed., p. 290). Cincinnati, OH: Southwestern.
3. United States Bureau of Labor Statistics. *Labor force statistics from the current population survey: Household data annual averages—18. Employed persons by detailed industry, sex, race, and Hispanic or Latino ethnicity.* Retrieved October 18, 2014, from http://www.bls.gov/cps/cpsaat18.htm
4. Ibid.
5. Forbes. (2012). Insights: *Diversity & inclusion: Unlocking global potential—Global diversity rankings by country, sector and occupation.* New York: Forbes.
6. Maslow, A. (1970). *Motivation and personality* (2nd ed.) New York: Harper & Row.

7. Herzberg, F. (1966). *Work and the nature of man*. Cleveland: World Pub co.
8. Herzberg, F. (2003). One more time: How do you motivate employees? 1968. *Harvard Business Review*, 81(1), 87–96.
9. McGregor, D. (1960). The *human side of enterprise*. New York: McGraw-Hill.
10. Ouchi, W. (1981). *Theory Z: How American business can meet the Japanese challenge*. Reading, MA: Addison-Wesley.
11. Encyclopedia O Management. *e Notes*. Retrieved October 21, 2014, from http://www.enotes.com/management-encyclopedia/theory-z
12. Vroom, V. (1964). *Work and motivation*. New York: John Wiley.
13. Tanke, M. (1990). *Human resources management for the hospitality industry* (p. 204). Albany, NY: Delmar Publishing.
14. Peters, T. (1988). *Thriving on chaos* (p. 371). New York: Harper & Row.
15. Leonard, D. (August 24, 1987). Perspectives. *Newsweek*, p. 19.

Building Teams **11**

CHAPTER OUTLINE

- ▶ Introduction
- ▶ Team Development
- ▶ Attributes of Effective Teams
- ▶ Eliminating Barriers
- ▶ Empowerment
- ▶ Conclusions

LEARNING OBJECTIVES

When you complete reading this chapter, you should be able to:

- ▶ identify and describe the rationale for a team approach
- ▶ know and understand the principles of building a team
- ▶ identify the crucial elements of developing a team commitment
- ▶ define the elements of establishing goals and objectives for team building
- ▶ describe the key aspects of facilitating teamwork
- ▶ list the major criteria associated with effective teams
- ▶ explain the requirements of understanding and trust in relation to team building
- ▶ list the steps essential to improving teamwork
- ▶ explain the requirements of team to team/department to department dependence in the hospitality industry

► identify and describe the elements that contribute to the creation of an organizational "vision."

Introduction

Through teamwork, common people produce uncommon. The environment created is one in which no individual is more important than any other individual. People in the team share varying degrees of responsibility, but the success of the team is really determined by the performance of each individual, and the contribution of the individual makes the team effort.

> Never tell people how to do things. Tell them what you want to achieve and they will surprise you with their ingenuity.

> —General George S. Patton, 1944.

Teamwork has become the leading form of operational design. The underpinnings of teamwork are the individual's drive to be a team player and eventually a team leader. Managers achieve better, more-inclusive interaction with staff in a team environment. The team approach to management is about managers becoming coaches, facilitators, and teachers, rather than administrators, inspectors, and control agents. In the team environment the manager is a team builder, a creator of strategies to generate staff member commitment to the team. Establishment of an active and effective team environment requires that staff members have a clear understanding of what is required of them and how their work relates to the operation/business as a whole. The more staff members understand the total operation/business the greater the role each can play in achieving success. Effective managers maximize the value of staff members by improving the organizational resources, by fostering teamwork, and by rewarding contributions by individual staff members to the team.

According to Marshall J. Cook:

> "You don't want compliant subordinates. You want committed co-workers who identify their self-interest with yours and want excellent job performance. They'll work just as hard and just as well when you're not watching—because they're not working for you, they're working with you."[1]

An important reason why hospitality organizations seek to develop teams is because teams are more effective at improving work methods and providing high-quality products and service. A mature, well-trained hospitality operation's team is capable of making better decisions than are individuals. The use of a team approach improves the overall quality of decision making, and the level of commitment becomes much higher. When staff members are involved in problem solving as a team, they are more likely to "buy-in" to the resulting plans and to do everything possible to transform the plans into reality.

There is a difference between a group and a team. A group is a random group of people. The people you are standing with at a stoplight when crossing the street is a group. People in a group do not necessarily share common values or goals. A team, on the contrary, is a group of people who have common values and goals. A team has a definite common purpose.

Team Development

Groups and Teams

Developing a team begins with understanding that there is a difference between a group and team. The goal is to bring the staff members that make up the team to a point of buy-in to a common purpose. This is true whether the team is part of a specific department, such as the laundry team in the housekeeping department or the team is all of the staff of the hotel. In the case of the micro, the laundry team, the common purpose is to produce the highest possible quality in the laundry in the most efficient manner. In the case of the macro, the laundry team wants to achieve their common purpose because they want to actively contribute to the best possible guest experience and the success of the hotel. In both the cases the staff members must move from a group of individuals working as individuals to a team of individuals working together as a team. Ken Blanchard said of people, "We would like to find the most effective, most rewarding, and most productive way of working together."[2] Team building involves getting each staff member to feel a sense of belonging and ownership in what they are doing as a team. The desired outcome is a team effort that leads to synergy. Synergy is achieved when the interaction of team members combine to produce a total effect that is greater than the sum of the actions of the individual team members.

Woods said, "Teamwork can be seen and felt—it is a tangible thing. The real problem is very often people are organized into groups; they are called teams but do not act like a team."[3] It is quite easy to spot sets of individuals who are not yet a team. They meet, and someone says "What do we do now?" or "Who is going to start first?" or "Who is going to do what?" Barrie, Cooper, and Wilkinson said ". . . Teamwork is one of the key features of involvement and without it, difficulty will be found in gaining the commitment and participation of people throughout the organization."[4] When the concept of team building is adopted, it becomes easier to generate a continuous drive for quality. It also provides encouragement for each team member to work together to develop a team spirit. It helps people get to know each other so that they in turn can learn to trust, respect, and appreciate individual talent and abilities. According to Smith, "Teams bring together skills and experience that collectively exceed those of any individual. . . . Consequently teams can respond to a variety of challenges, for example, process improvement, product development, or customer service, more readily and more effectively."[5] When one person is unable to perform at 100%, the difference must be made up by the other team members. This places additional pressure on teammates because they will have to work harder to meet the team's goal. When this happens, it is clearly noticeable. It is extremely gratifying at the end of a successful day to know that all team members have pulled together and reached the goals.

Creating the Team

The development of a team requires the manager to think about a number of factors. One of these factors is why people become committed to a team. Figure 11.1 lists the primary reasons an individual commits to a team. The level at which each team member is affected by these primary reasons will ultimately determine the level of that member's commitment to the team. The more that team members feel it is in their best interest to be a member of the team, the greater commitment they will have to the team.

In the late 1970s, a "new" philosophy of service was introduced to the dinner house segment of the restaurant industry. This philosophy of service, which is very common today, was a team service system. The server was no longer assigned a specific set of tables and held responsible for that set. The server was expected to work as part of a total property service team with the common focus of providing the highest possible level of service to all guests. This service system required a commitment by all team members to the success of the whole rather than just their portion. This service system was readily adopted. It was a good fit to the dinner house, where efficiency of service was considered by the guest to be as important as the personalization of the service.

While the service of the table by multiple servers diminished the personal aspect of the service to some degree, it made up for that in the efficiency of the service. Food came to the table hotter, beverages were refilled with greater regularity, and in general more of the guest's needs were met. This service system made the concepts of self-interest, mutual support, sense of duty, and common values real and very connected to the individual's and team's success.

The manager has the ability to build this same team model in the operation. Building the team begins with the manager communicating the connection between the team members' self-interest and the vision of both the company and the manager.

Vision and Team Development

A vision is defined as the ability to perceive something not actually visible, or to see the future, or what could be the desired goal. A vision also

---

Primary Reasons for Team Commitment

* Self-interest: The person believes he or she will gain a personal advantage by being a member of the team.

* Belief in a vision: The person believes he or she is helping a greater vision come to fruition.

* Belief in the leader: The person feels loyalty to the leader of the team.

* Common values: The person shares the team's set of basic beliefs about what is said and what is important.

* Mutual support: The person feels a sense of comradeship with his or her teammates.

* Sense of duty: The person is committed because he or she believes that this is part of the price to be paid for being on the team.

* Demanding tasks: The person is committed because he or she wants to achieve goals or a standard of accomplishment that requires the assistance of others.

* Feeling of accomplishment: The person is committed to the team because working together, the members participate in a shared celebration of success.

* Structured socialization: New people are welcomed and are made to feel a part of the team.

FIGURE 11.1   Primary Reasons for Team Commitment.

describes the way things should be. Mission statements are very often referred to as vision statements, but a vision is not a mission statement. Mission statements are usually short, simple statements outlining what is unique about an organization or establishment, items that positively distinguish it in the minds of everybody, guests and team members.

A vision describes what the leader wants the company to become; the purpose it should serve; and the contribution it will make to the community. The single thread that runs through all success stories is the involvement of staff members in drafting a vision statement and empowering people to support this vision. The staff members, managers, owners, and leaders who effectively communicate their organization's vision report significantly higher levels of job satisfaction, commitment, pride, and loyalty. Key to creating buy-in is clarity about the organization's values when the vision is shared. Involving team members in developing a vision produces powerful results. Team members can only be empowered by a vision they have contributed to and understand. Understanding is enhanced by participation.

Establishing Team Standards

Ensuring that action follows vision requires the manager to establish the organizational and operational standards of the team. The more the team is involved in this process, the greater the "buy-in." The term buy-in is defined as the commitment of an individual to an idea or course of action. The standards include team composition, scope of team and individual responsibilities, performance expectations, performance appraisal, timelines, and resources. Determination of all of these characteristics will be based on the anticipated work to be assigned to the team.

Team composition is the combination of the skills, knowledge, and physical and mental capability of the individuals and the number of individuals needed to accomplish the work assigned to the team in an effective and efficient manner. For example, composition of the maintenance team will include individuals with the physical capacity to lift heavy items with a high degree of regularity. The team members will need to have been trained or willing to be trained in the proper operation of the equipment and use of chemical or other hazardous materials used in their jobs. The members of the maintenance team may not need to have the required level of knowledge to determine and maintain the parts inventory for the property.

The scope of team and individual responsibility is the amount of work and complexity of work assigned to the team and ultimately to the individual. For example, the banquet prep team may be responsible for the preparation of food for catering in the hotel, but they are not responsible for determining the supplies needed and making certain they are available. The scope of responsibility of the housekeeping team will probably include, but not be limited to the ongoing cleaning, sanitizing, and returning to good order of all rooms and public spaces in the hotel. The determination of appropriate inventory levels of chemicals and back-up linens and guest room amenities would probably not be part of their scope of responsibilities. An individual member's responsibilities will be based on his or her assigned work. The scullery team member assigned to dishwashing during a particular meal period would be responsible for the cleaning, sanitizing, and returning to stock of all china, flatware, and glassware used during that time as well as keeping the dishwashing area in an orderly, safe, and sanitary condition.

Performance expectations are the clear definition of what the expected outcomes are for the work assigned. For example, the banquet preparation team is assigned the preparation of canapés for 500 guests. Performance expectations will include:

- ensuring the quality (taste, appearance, accuracy of recipe duplication) of the finished canapés;
- finishing the canapés on time;
- completing the correct amount of canapés;
- providing the variety/type of canapés ordered;
- presenting the canapés in an attractive and appetizing manner; and
- protecting the safety of the canapés during preparation and storage.

Performance appraisal is the evaluation of the completed work, which must be based on clear communication of how the performance will be measured. For example, measuring the team's attainment of the communicated performance expectations may include the following actions by the manager: random product tasting; inspection of finished products; regular inspection of preparation and storage areas; and review of guest satisfaction surveys. The effectiveness of performance appraisal is directly tied to the immediacy of the feedback. Once the appraisal is complete, feedback should be provided to the team and individuals with direction for correction and improvement.

Time is both the specific time requirements that come with assigned work and the general time requirements for the team and individuals. For example, a general requirement is that team members report on time for work and that they produce an acceptable amount of product during a shift. A time requirement tied to assigned work is an order for 500 canapés by 5:30 p.m. today.

Resources consist of the number of team members, equipment, and facilities needed for the team to perform its assigned work as well as the food cost and overall expense expectations for the team and its work. For example, the team has limited members, equipment, and space to use in the preparation of the 500 canapés that have been ordered, and this order is not the only one the team has for the day. Prioritizing and using the available resources in an efficient manner will be necessary to deliver on all orders not only in a quality manner but within the team's food-cost target.

Establishing Goals and Objectives

Goals give a team something to work toward. They can be broad, and they can be achieved in a variety of ways. An example of a goal might be: "To improve the quality of room cleaning substantially." They are short, general statements of purpose and direction. On the other hand, objectives are very clear statements of what output you need to achieve such as "To reduce the number of complaints concerning room cleanliness by 75 percent by year's end." Effective objectives are more comprehensive and, as shown in Figure 11.2, should be, according to Steve Smith, "SMART."[6]

The buy-in of team members is critical to the achievement of the team's goals and objectives. Shared team goals are present when all members have participated in a process that clarifies the team's collective goals. Effective team members know and understand the team's purpose, objectives, and performance measures. All members need to believe that the team's goals are both achievable and important. If the team's expressed goals seem to be impossible to achieve, team members will become cynical and demotivated. Frustration and discouragement are the consequences of a team's failing to ensure that action follows vision.

SMART Team Objectives

* Specific: Express objectives in terms of the specific results to be achieved, not in terms of the activities needed to achieve them, i.e., outputs, not inputs. Avoid ambiguity.
* Measurable: Identify what measures will be used to judge success. Make them as quantifiable and specific as possible, e.g., time/quantity/quality/ cost. Use customer-related measures as well as internal measures.
* Agreed: The team should have the opportunity to discuss and buy into the objective rather than simply have it imposed.
* Realistic: The objectives are to be neither too easy so that talents are under used, nor too difficult so that the team may burn out. Take past performance into account in assessing realism. Be sure the objective is achievable given the resource available and the demands of other priorities.
* Timebound: The objectives should include a date by which they should be achieved. Also include interim milestones and review points if the overall timescale is long. Choose an appropriate time frame relative to the complexity of the task.

Build That Team
Steve Smith

FIGURE 11.2 SMART Team Objectives.

Team Leadership

The role of a "team facilitator" or "leader" consists of leading team discussions and group processes so that individuals learn, and team members feel that the experience is positive and worthwhile. "A team leader is the person responsible for assuring that people will want to work together to achieve a common goal or objective. The important idea here is to want to *work together*, so a leader does not need to coerce, but rather facilitates the elements necessary for the team to perform well."[7]

A manager is expected to manage and lead their team. Decision making responsibility is an integral part of managing and leading a team. There are, however, considerations required if the manager's intention is to manage and lead a true and effective team. In a "team" environment consultation and notification need to be actively engaged in by the manager. While the ultimate decision lies with the manager, seeking input from team members, providing team members with notice of the change, and allowing some time to adjust to the idea all contribute to team member buy-in. It is buy-in that contributes the most to the success of the goal, objective, and ultimately the team and operation.

The leader and team must share values and goals to succeed. When people work closely together, what one person does usually affects the others. Managers cannot deal effectively with difficult team members or difficult situations unless they understand them. A difficulty should be seen as a problem that both parties wish to solve through cooperation. Both should be on the same side of the line, attacking the problem instead of each other. Managing difficult behavior is a challenge to invent a solution that all team members support and feel committed to implementing. Therefore, working relationships are better among trusting people. People who can be counted on to keep their word are trustworthy.

Within any organization, persons with authority are tempted to force or coerce people who are being difficult to make them comply. Compliance through coercion, such as threatening dismissal, generally provides only short-term gains and long-term losses. Team members resent being coerced and this resentment eventually impacts job performance. While a final warning can be considered a coercive action, it is a last resort not a first.

Team to Team/Department to Department Dependence

In the hospitality industry, teams must constantly interact. Guests view a property as a total entity, not pieces, no matter the segment of the industry. They do not separate segments or portions of their hospitality experience; they react and evaluate the entire property, product, or service. Hospitality organizations can be likened to living organisms. The whole organism or system consists of a series of parts. Each part plays an important and vital role in the provision of a complete and high quality guest experience. If any part of the system is defective, it will damage the entire organization. If teams are not sympathetic to one another and do not work together in a complementary fashion, the product and/or service may break up and if the discord is serious, it could become irreparable. A key function in maintaining a healthy hospitality organization is for the boundaries that exist among its parts to remain open, allowing for the exchange of ideas and information. If boundaries are closed, the organism itself, the organization/company, will be seriously damaged and possibly disappear.

The process of improving team to team/department to department dependence requires a conscious effort at cross-team/cross-department communications. If team members get to know one another on a more personal basis, they may be more inclined to work together and to consider one another when making decisions. The need for personal contact becomes greater when the possibility of conflict exists.

Teams that work well together strengthen the entire hospitality organization. Each team has both internal suppliers and internal customers. As teams learn to collaborate, they overcome narrow thinking. Team to team/department to department development also serves to strengthen individual teams.

Attributes of Effective Teams

Successful teams share several attributes and demonstrate achievement in many areas. Leadership is shown by the manager who has the skills and the desire to develop a team approach and allocates time to team-building activities. Management of the hospitality team is seen as a shared function, as illustrated in Figure 11.3. Team members other than the leader are given the opportunity to exercise leadership when their skills are appropriate to the needs of the team.

Team members are committed to the aims and purposes of the team. They are willing to devote personal energy to building the team and supporting their fellow members. The team climate encourages people to feel relaxed. The members feel they can be direct and open and are prepared to take risks. The team is clear about its objectives. It sets targets of performance that require members to "stretch" mentally.

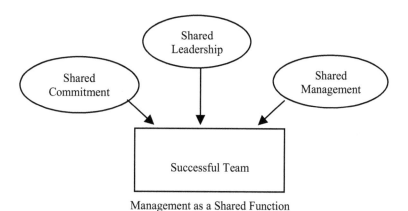

Management as a Shared Function

FIGURE 11.3   Management as a Shared Function.

Effective team structures allow for the lively and energetic solving of problems. Roles are clarified, communication is open, and administrative procedures support the team approach. The team generates creative strength and new ideas from its members; innovative risk is rewarded and good ideas are put into action.

Team and individual errors and weaknesses are examined without personal spite to enable the members to learn from experience. Dormant individual potential is often brought forward and made active through team membership. The staff members grow and become more outgoing and capable, and their professional competence is enhanced as they meet new challenges with one another's support as members of a team.

Relationships with other teams are developed systematically. It is obvious in the hospitality industry that effective and cohesive relationships between teams and departments are vital. The guest thinks of the property as a total unit and evaluates the complete hospitality experience—not sections of it.

The effective team is one that is in the improvement mode continuously and whose improvement effort is supported by the actions of the manager and the organization. The type of support that the manager and the organization must provide is shown in Figure 11.4.

Improving Team Work through Support

* Support the team effort through the culture of the company.

* Sustain the team activities through the expected plateaus.

* Provide training to maintain and advance the skills and knowledge of team members.

* Allow the team to work on problem solving, not just operational issues but also sorting through interpersonal and technical skills issues.

* Provide career paths and opportunities for team members to transfer out when necessary, so that unresolved personality clashes between key people do not persist.

* Provide members with the full picture by providing information to give them greater understanding of the overall company.

* Recognize team and individual successes.

* Have a job rotation program where members learn all the jobs and gain an appreciation for the interdependence of the jobs.

FIGURE 11.4   Improving Team Work through Support.

Eliminating Barriers

Every organization has a certain climate or culture. "That climate can be one that is positive, warm, and supportive . . . believe it or not, it can even be a climate in which people have fun and a desire to come to work."[8] To create the best possible operation work environment, a number of barriers need to be recognized and overcome. Many of the issues that create barriers are often not noticed. Some managers fail to anticipate or recognize potential barriers because of a lack of training, or perhaps even due to insensitivity and their thinking that their management style is okay because "I treat my team members in a much better way than I was treated." This type of thinking is irrelevant. The manager who adopts this type of thinking usually is one who fails to recognize the changing nature of the workplace and operation staff members. Ted Balestreri and Bert Cutino, founders of the award-winning restaurant "The Sardine Factory" in Monterey, California, state:

"We thought we had to do everything ourselves in the beginning. We realize, however, that there are people who can do things as well, if not better than we can . . . By bringing talent to the operation, giving them the tools, the authority, and the incentive, we found we have moved a lot quicker than we ever thought possible."[9]

As Jan Carlzon puts it, "Everyone wants to be treated as an individual; everyone needs to know and feel that they are needed."[10] Since the main objective of a team is internal and external customer satisfaction, removing and overcoming barriers is the first step in that process. The next action is to identify what constitutes a positive team work environment in the operation and apply it equally and fairly. A number of the barriers to building a team are shown in Figure 11.5.

Eliminating barriers is about creating a great place to work. A great place to work is characterized by loyal staff members who are proud of their work and organization and who produce high-quality products, service, and experiences that meet and satisfy customer needs. It is a place where the *team* encourages the manager, where high ethical standards are practiced, and where a shared purpose and appreciation exists among all team members. These items come first. Pay and working conditions, although they are part of "a great place to work," are not the most important factors.

As John Maxwell puts it, "I know that no amount of money, attention, privileges, and promises will motivate a staff member who really

Barriers to Building Teams

* Inappropriate leadership: Manager is unable or unwilling to use a team approach and does not encourage the use of team building activities. He or she often uses a "command" decision style rather than a "consensus" decision style. The leader does not share his or her power or leadership responsibilities.
* Unqualified membership: Team members are not qualified, (professionally or socially) to contribute to the team and as a result are unable to contribute to the successful completion of its goals.
* Insufficient team commitment: Team members are not committed to the aims and purposes of the team and are reluctant to expend personal energy on meeting the team's goals.
* A non-team building environment: The work environment/culture discourages members from feeling comfortable, from being direct and open, and from taking risks.
* Poor perception of possibility of achievement: The team may not understand its objectives; if it does, it may not believe that they are worthwhile. Targets are either uninspiring or un-achievable.
*Poor upper management support: The team may be excluded from planning. It may not understand or envision its role in the wider context of the organization.
* Ineffective work methods: Organization, training, and resources week. Equipment and resource issues are not solved in an efficient, timely, and effective manner.
* Lack of role clarity—who does what, when, where, and how: Members' roles are not clearly defined, efficient communication procedures have not been developed, and administration are not supportive of the team's efforts.
Weak critiquing program: Team weaknesses are not addressed adequately.
* Member maturity: Members have not developed the maturity and confidence needed to be assertive or to deal with other members' strong personalities.
* A lack of creativity: Members do not generate new ideas and are unwilling to take risks which may be discouraged by the organization's culture.
* Negative relations with other teams: Teams that are interdependent compete rather than collaborate. Because teams do not meet to compare their plans and agendas, priorities may conflict.

FIGURE 11.5 Barriers to Building Teams.

does not want to be on the team."[11] If a positive work environment where no intimidation or anxiety exists is created in the operation, then the motivational, training, and communication environment is also created.

Empowerment

A customer is usually defined in commercial terms: a person paying for services or products provided. On the other hand, the term "guest" means something of a higher and more personal nature. A guest is someone we entertain in our home, someone we desire to please. This last definition has an entirely different framework than that of a customer. Therefore, pleasing a guest is much different than satisfying a customer. Probably the only way to do this in a hospitality establishment is through the concept of empowerment.

According to Ken Blanchard, empowerment is the process of enabling people to do what they have been trained for and are qualified to do. People already have power through their knowledge and motivation—empowerment is letting this power out.[12] Therefore, empowerment means increasing the amount of control and discretion each team member has over his or her job. Empowerment provides involvement in decision making that supports the guests' level of quality and satisfaction. Empowering team members to take more initiative is viewed as essential to quality production and guest service.

Empowerment is also a key element in team building. There is no better way to have a shared vision and to generate commitment and loyalty than through empowerment. This results from pushing down the decision-making process to give greater latitude to each staff member and then providing training that facilitates its inception.

Empowerment also seeks to improve the hospitality organization's performance by successfully solving problems that cause dissatisfaction for internal or external customers. Open and ongoing communications with and in the team are critical to the formation and maintenance of high-performing teams. Empowerment plays a critical part in those communications. Part of being empowered is the freedom to comment on and discuss, without fear of reprisal, the policies, procedures, and decisions affecting the team. Quality standards must be established and communicated, but their execution is ultimately in the hands of the team members. The manager cannot be everywhere at the same time, so relying on team members to perform is essential.

Empowerment does not occur in a micromanagement environment. The manager who recognizes team members' need for the freedom and responsibility to make decisions about the methods for accomplishing assignments creates an environment of trust that drives quality performance. Part of establishing empowerment in a team is communicating the message that freedom to fail also exists. Team members who fear failure for whatever reason will not take the risks that are often necessary to find solutions.

Empowerment means actively seeking ideas from team members on how to improve. Empowerment comes from teaching others ways in which they can become less dependent on you. Therefore, empowered teams can do more than empowered individuals. Empowerment means encouraging innovation and allowing team members to implement their ideas. If the entire team is empowered and comes to realize that their opinions, views, and ideas are important, they will quickly take ownership of an innovation they have contributed and will seek to continuously improve it. Empowerment is not a substitute for leadership or a reduction of authority. The more the team is empowered, the greater the need for leaders who can set goals and define a vision.

The paradox of power: In order to gain power, you must give some of it away.

The outcome of empowerment linked with training includes operational improvements in areas such as problem solving, safety and sanitation, cost, production, and guest satisfaction; in other words, improvement of overall quality. These improvements are accompanied by or generated from a positive work environment where individuals and beliefs are respected and the success of the team and satisfaction of the internal and external guests are the focus.

Conclusions

The use of teams has become common in the hospitality industry. The terminology of teamwork is used constantly, such as in a title like "banquet team." The issue is whether this is just a title or it is a description. Merely calling a group a team does not make it a team. When a team has been developed, its power is greater than the sum of its parts. In a team, the individual knows that his or her personal power is amplified by that of the team. The manager who builds a successful team has created a major resource for customer satisfaction both internally and externally.

Study Questions

1. State the rationale for a team approach.
2. State the principles of building a team.
3. List and discuss the crucial elements of developing a team commitment.
4. Define the elements of establishing goals and objectives for team building.

5. Describe the key aspects of facilitating teamwork.

6. List the major criteria associated with effective teams.

7. Explain the requirements of understanding and trust in relation to team building.

8. List the steps essential to improving teamwork.

9. Explain the requirements of team to team/department to department dependence in the hospitality industry.

10. Identify and describe the elements that contribute to the creation of an organizational "vision."

Case Studies

The case studies listed below relate to the information presented in this chapter and reading, answering the case study questions and participating in discussion of a case will reinforce and expand what you have learned in this chapter. All case studies are provided in this text after the last chapter.

* Bill & Jean's Restaurant

* C&L Restaurant

* Grand Adventure Park

* L&J Cafeteria

* Prairie View Country Club

* Shady Lane Inn

* Shandong House Restaurant

* Shepherd Mountain Hotel

* Summit Resort

Notes

1. Cook, M. (1997). *Motivating people*. New York: Macmillan/Spectrum.
2. Blanchard, K., Carlos, J., & Randolph, A. (1996). *Empowerment takes more than a minute* (p. 23). San Francisco, CA: Berrett-Koehler Publishers.
3. Woods, J. (1998). *Teams and teamwork* (p. 56). New York: Macmillan.

4.   Barrie, D., Cooper, C., & Wilkinson, A. (1997). *Managing quality & human resources: A guide to continuous improvement* (p. 31). Oxford, England: Blackwell Publishers.

5.   Smith, S. (1997). *Build that team* (p. 6). London: Kogan Page Ltd.

6.   Ibid., p. 45.

7.   Woods, J. (1998). *Teams and teamwork* (p. 123). New York: Macmillan.

8.   Rinke, W. (1992). *The winning hospitality manager: Strategies for doing more with less* (2nd ed., p. 206). Rockville, MD: Achievement Publishers.

9.   Balestreri, T. (1991). *Nobody's perfect: Lessons in leadership* (p. 18). New York: Van Nostrand Reinhold.

10. Carlzon, J. (1987). *Moments of truth* (p. 5). Ballinger Publishers: Cambridge, MA.

11. Maxwell, J. (1993). *Developing the leader within you* (p. 165). Nashville, TN: Thomas Nelson.

12. Blanchard, K., Carlos, J., & Randolph, A. (1996). *Empowerment takes more than a minute*. San Francisco, CA: Berrett-Koehler Publishers.

Respect in the Workplace 12

LEARNING OBJECTIVES

When you complete reading this chapter, you should be able to:

- ▶ describe issues and elements that create fear within the work environment
- ▶ discuss providing criticism with respect for the individual
- ▶ state how to give negative criticism and achieve positive results
- ▶ recall the steps to encouraging staff members to give feedback
- ▶ explain the nature of the work environment relative to a diversified workforce
- ▶ relate the elements of a diverse workplace
- ▶ state the elements that make up sexual harassment
- ▶ relate the legal responsibilities of the manager in regard to sexual harassment
- ▶ explain the primary laws regarding equal opportunity in the workplace

Introduction

Do unto others as you would have them do unto you. This is a phrase that is often heard but also often forgotten when we deal with other people. It is the golden rule. Respect in the workplace encompasses many things, but first and foremost it must result in a comfortable work environment. A comfortable work environment is one where staff members feel they are evaluated and judged by their performance and not by their race, gender, or personal beliefs. It is a work environment that develops all staff members to their fullest potential. Staff members in a golden rule environment do not do things because they fear the consequences of not doing them. Rather, staff members do things because they want success for everyone, including themselves and the organization.

Driving Out Fear

Point 8 of Deming's 14 points addressed driving out fear, so that everyone may work effectively.[1] According to Dina Berta, "Restaurants that can successfully brand themselves as a desirable place to work stand to have an edge in attracting talent in an ever-shrinking labor pool, according to operators and personnel experts."[2] The golden rule environment is critical in branding an operation as a desirable place to work.

The use of fear as a tool of control in the work place was common in the past. The myths and legends of managers that berated, threatened, and verbally abused the staff contain all too much fact. However, industry and managers have changed in recent decades. Effective management at all levels, recognize that fear is harmful to the organization in general and to the individual staff member in particular. The use of fear as a tool of control prevents people from thinking. According to Berta, "It robs them of pride and joy in their work and kills all forms of intrinsic motivation. The thinking and creative potential of the workers are stopped cold."[3] Managers who rely on fear believe that those working under them are incapable of thinking, and regrettably this concept becomes a self-fulfilling prophecy.

Managers may not be able to eliminate all fear from the minds of all staff members, but they can eliminate the sources of fear built into the management structures.[4] Figure 12.1 shows characteristics of the manager that generates a golden rule environment, an environment free of management-generated fear.

A Golden Rule Manager

* Sensitive to issues and interests of staff members.
* Respectful of differences in people.
* Open and participative in problem solving.
* Anxious to use the power of their position to serve the teamwell.
* Fair and equitable in the distribution of work.
* Constant in their efforts to find solutions that are both technically and politically sound.
* Constant in seeking individual staff member input on decisions.
* Willing to put the welfare of the team before private interests.
* Never "better" than other staff members.
* Honest and willing to consider retaliation a sign of serious weakness.

FIGURE 12.1   A Golden Rule Manager

According to Ryan and Oestreich,[5] managers who use threatening and abusive behavior "…immediately destroy trust and end communication. They create a thick wall of antagonism and resentment." No one respects a manager who repeatedly puts others down or loses control of his or her temper. Elements of threatening or abusive actions or behaviors that demean, humiliate, isolate, insult, and threaten staff members are shown in Figure 12.2.

Threatening and Abusive Behavior

* Silence and glaring eye contact
* Snubbing or ignoring people
* Insults or put-downs
* Blaming, discrediting
* Aggressive, controlling manner
* Threats about the job
* Yelling and shouting
* Angry outburst or loss of control
* Physical threats
* Racial, ethnic, or gender slurs
* Discriminatory comments

FIGURE 12.2   Threatening and Abusive Behavior

Criticism with Respect

A primary responsibility of any manager is the quality of the team's work. Achieving quality outcomes requires evaluation of staff members' performance. Performance evaluation is fully effective only when the findings are reported to the individual being evaluated. The findings are not always positive, but the goal must be to use the knowledge of both positive and negative performance as a vehicle for improvement of performance. This can be accomplished only when "respect" is part of the workplace. Criticism is never easy for an individual to accept, but when it comes from someone that an individual respects and knows respects him or her, it is easier to accept. It is the accepting of, and ultimately acting on the criticism that brings about improved performance.

A manager who gives the staff member negative feedback in a positive manner is demonstrating respect for the individual. The following are guidelines to giving negative feedback in a positive manner.

- Limit the comments to the staff member's behavior. Do not label the person as always stubborn, difficult, or easy-going. Do not criticize the person; focus on the activity, not on the type of individual he or she is. Be specific and do not generalize about a particular behavior.
- Provide feedback as soon as possible following the problem. The problem is fresh in the mind of the staff member and the manager reducing reliance on memory.
- Listen carefully to what individual staff members have to say. Get their opinion; let them tell you what went wrong. Ask what they think the problem is. Do not prejudge an answer. Keep an open mind to what you hear.
- Be considerate. Get your point across without being loud, rude, or abrupt. Losing control will put the other person on the defensive and probably would not help you solve the problem or determine its cause.
- Do not trap or humiliate staff members. If a complaint is received from a customer, the manager should be straightforward in talking with the staff member about the complaint.
- Do not blame the entire team or department for a problem. Mistakes happen. It may be someone's fault, but as a manager, you should not generalize and accuse the entire team of acting poorly.

Verbal criticism is usually less severe than written criticism. The form the criticism takes should be balanced with the issue being addressed.

Unintended results may occur as a consequence of written criticism. Written criticism remains an issue for an extended period of time, and comments made may lack clear meaning because the tone of voice or any further explanation is not available to the reader. However, whether the criticism is verbal or written it should be communicated in private.

When providing criticism and direction the team or team member should be encouraged to give feedback. Encouraging feedback makes the process two-way and makes it clear that the goal is assist the team member in improving. This will build trust and respect. The goal is to encourage not discourage the team member. Discouragement results in lowered self-esteem and alienation from others. A discouraging manager is one who constantly criticizes and points out mistakes or one that has unrealistic expectations and does not allow for mistakes. Examples of phrases used by an encouraging manager are shown in Figure 12.3.

The difference between the best staff members and the average ones often depends on the leadership style and ability of the manager. A good manager can turn some average staff members into outstanding performers. It is what the manager does that influences performance. Sincerity is of the utmost importance. If staff members are treated with respect, then they are their own best source of motivation. Ferdinand Metz, President Emeritus of the Culinary Institute of America, recommends: "Build a team that will work towards a common objective. Lead by example. Always be willing to do what you ask others to do. They will respect you for this."[6]

Diversity

"According to the Census Bureau, the ethnic population of the United States will continue to rise. Projections show that by 2050, Hispanics will account for more than 24% of the population, Blacks will make

---

Encouraging Words

"You did a good job."

"What did you learn from that mistake?"

"Keep trying; you will succeed."

"Great improvement"

"If you need any help, let me know."

FIGURE 12.3   Encouraging Words

up over 13% and Asians will account for almost 9%."[7] According to the United States Bureau of Labor Statistics, population survey for 2013, 57.5% of individuals employed in the accommodation's category were women, 14.9% were African-American, and 25% were Hispanic.[8] The foodservices and drinking places category was similar with 51.8% women, 11.7% African-American, and 24.4% Hispanics.[9] According to Forbes in 2012 globally the hotel and catering (in the US restaurants) industry is in the top three for diversity.[10] The diverse nature of the industry workforce is changing the culture of the workplace in the hospitality industry. This diversity will continue to grow in the future.

As we move further into the twenty-first century, the hospitality industry is faced with issues of managing not only greater numbers of people, but also a more diverse workforce. Management within the operation requires a greater respect for the values and cultures of all staff members. An establishment that values diversity is one in which staff members learn to appreciate individuality and avoid prejudging people. Encouraging an awareness of diversity will facilitate the discussion of assumptions each staff member may hold regarding certain groups of people. "Understanding and accepting diversity enables us to see that each of us is needed: recognizing diversity helps us to understand the need we have for opportunity, equity, and identity in the workplace."[11]

"Now, companies are embracing diversity as a business focus and corporate value. Embracing diversity isn't just the right thing to do; there's a strong business case for it."[12] Acceptance of diversity by managers can mean getting used to different accents or languages or people who dress differently. It means feeling comfortable with staff members whose skin is a different color. Diversity in a team refers to the following physical and cultural dimensions that separate and distinguish us as individuals and groups: age, gender, physical abilities, ethnicity, race, religion, and sexual preference. Miller et al.[13] state: "Failure to understand and to respect the diversity of your employees can result in misunderstandings, tension, poor performance, poor employee morale, and higher rates of absenteeism and turnover . . . when diversity is respected, the working environment is richer."

The first step in improving respect for diversity is communication. Establish a climate that encourages a free exchange of ideas. Explore how all staff members come to the operation with a unique combination of backgrounds and influences. Start with yourself and your own background. Get to know your staff members. Do not make ethnic- or gender-oriented jokes, and more importantly do not tolerate even good-natured jokes in this area. Encourage diversity and an awareness of different cultures through events that showcase different cultures.

If individuals are having difficulty with English, be patient and encouraging. Ask them for their input. The fact that some people may not say anything does not mean they have nothing to say. Persons changing from one culture to another may experience culture shock, which may be manifested as fear. Encourage the rest of the team to understand and respect differences in people. The manager is the model. If the manager shows respect for staff members who come from different backgrounds, the team will follow the example. The self-esteem of diverse staff members remains intact if they believe their backgrounds are accepted and respected.

The following is abstracted from a job notice that appeared in an advertisement in the *Boston Globe*, October 7, 1990. It demonstrates a comprehensive understanding of valuing differences:

In every aspect of life there is diversity. Accept this and you open yourself to endless possibilities. Close your mind to diversity and you are confined in isolation. Where one may see a problem, two may find a solution.

We value and encourage the contributions of all. We recognize that while each one of us sees our own level of achievement, acceptance, and recognition, together we can attain higher goals. We can contribute to the well-being of our community by building strong bonds and implementing new ideas. This is our team—a group of people working together for the common good, while accepting the views, support, and uniqueness of each individual.

Discrimination

Harassment

In recent times, harassment in the workplace has become mostly synonymous with sexual harassment but harassment in the larger context is any act that makes an individual feel uncomfortable or unsafe. There are many forms of harassment in the hospitality industry and this encompasses harassment based on gender, sexual orientation, race or ethnicity, and physical or mental impairment.

Federal laws, executive orders, court cases, and state and local statutes provide a broad legal framework that protects these categories of employees.

The Equal Employment Opportunity Commission (EEOC) issued guidelines on sexual harassment in 1980, indicating that it is a form of discrimination under Title VII of the 1964 Civil Rights Act. The EEOC states that sexual harassment consists of "unwelcome advances, requests for sexual favors, and other verbal or physical conduct of a sexual nature." The conduct is illegal when it interferes with an employee's work performance or creates an "intimidating, hostile, or offensive working environment." The EEOC's *Uniform Guidelines* holds employers strictly accountable for preventing the sexual harassment of female or male employees. The EEOC also considers an employer guilty of sexual harassment when the employer knew about or should have known about the unlawful conduct and failed to remedy it. Employers are also guilty of sexual harassment when they allow nonemployees (guests or salespersons) to sexually harass employees. Where sexual complaints or charges have been proved, the EEOC has imposed severe penalties that include back pay, reinstatement, payment of lost benefits, interest charges, and attorney's fees. Sexual harassment can result in criminal charges if it involves physical contact. Damages are assessed against both the offender and the employer. The number of charges of sexual harassment received by the EEOC has declined from 15,889 in 1997 to 11,364 in 2011.[14] The percent of charges of sexual harassment received by the EEOC from males has increased from 11.6% in 1997 to 16.3% in 2011.[15]

Hospitality organizations should be proactive in the area of sexual harassment. There is a fine line between harassment, teamwork, and camaraderie. The majority of sexual harassment situations involve harassing women; but the occurrence of women harassing men is also on the increase. In both instances, not acting to prevent sexual harassment is the same as condoning it. Managers have a responsibility to recognize and prevent sexual harassment in the operation. Every organization must have a clearly defined policy on sexual harassment. It should be clearly communicated to every staff member. The best cure for workplace sexual harassment is a policy and an educational program designed to prevent it. Policy statements should be in writing and should stress that harassment will not be tolerated. Figure 12.4 shows the fundamental elements of an effective sexual harassment policy.

Sexual Harassment Policy and Procedures

* A system-wide comprehensive policy on sexual harassment should be developed. Experts in the area of sexual harassment should be involved in its preparation. This policy should be part of all new employee induction and orientation training programs. Current employees should be made aware what the policy is, and a strong organizational statement condemning sexual harassment should be issued by management.

* All staff should receive training in how to prevent sexual harassment.

* Procedures for dealing with complaints in this area should be established.

* Action should be taken immediately to investigate complaints of harassment.

* Offenders should be disciplined and, in serious cases, dismissed instantly.

* The policy should be equally and fairly applied to all staff members.

FIGURE 12.4   Sexual Harassment Policy and Procedures

Equal Opportunity Employment

The Equal Pay Act of 1963 is considered by many to be the starting point of the equal employment opportunity movement in the United States. This law was passed as an amendment to the 1938 Fair Labor Standards Act. The amendment requires that men and women in an organization who perform basically equal work receive equal pay. Although this law was passed in 1963, equal pay is still the subject of numerous lawsuits today.

The Title VII of the Civil Rights Act of 1964 continued to emphasize equality in personnel policies. The law applies to all employers with 15 or more employees. Title VII prohibits employment discrimination based on race, color, sex, religion, and national origin. Employers that have fewer than 15 employees may be still subject to state or local antidiscrimination regulations. There are two exemptions to Title VII. The first one is when a business owner can prove that the discriminatory qualification is a bona fide occupational qualification (BFOQ). Common examples of a BFOQ are women working in a women's locker room and specific ethnic performers for ethnic performances.

The other exemption is discrimination based on a business necessity. This is very narrowly defined and the employer must show that the practice is essential to its business. An example of a business necessity exemption would be the reassigning of pregnant female security guards to a desk position during pregnancy. The role of the guard position is to provide protection, and the pregnant guard's ability to carry out that duty is diminished. Note that in the case of both BFOQs and business necessity justifications for discrimination, the burden of proof rests with the employer.

Discrimination may be direct and indirect. The terms currently used are disparate treatment and disparate impact. Disparate treatment is when individuals who are being considered for employment or are employed by a company are treated differently based on race, gender, religion, national origin, sexual preference or some other protected characteristic. Disparate impact is when a policy has greater impact on one group than on another.

In the hospitality industry, policies that have the potential to create disparate impact include uniform requirements, education requirements, and grooming requirements. The question that must be asked whenever a policy is being considered is: "Is the action the policy requires actually necessary for a staff member to do the job?" For example: Does a head covering required by a woman's religion actually prevent her from doing her job or reduce the restaurant's business by ruining the perceived ambience? Today's manager, and all of management, must address this type of issue with an open mind.

The Age Discrimination in Employment Act was passed in 1967. This law prohibits employers from discriminating against applicants 40 years old or older on the basis of age. This law impacts all employers of 20 or more employees and all unions with 25 or more members. Common abuses of this law are firing older workers to hire younger replacements or promoting young workers over older workers.

The Vocational Rehabilitation Act was enacted in 1973 and bars discrimination against otherwise qualified people with disabilities. The Pregnancy Discrimination Act was enacted in 1978 and prohibits discrimination against pregnant women. The Immigration Reform and Control Act was enacted in 1983 and prohibits the recruiting and hiring of aliens who are not eligible to work in the United States.

The American with Disabilities Act (ADA) was enacted in 1990. Although this act was similar to the Vocational Rehabilitation Act of 1963, the terminology used is somewhat different. The ADA also has broader application. The ADA applies to most employers, and the Vocational Rehabilitation Act applied only to federal contractors and subcontractors. Specifically, the ADA prohibits workplace discrimination against people with disabilities. The ADA also requires the workplace to make reasonable accommodation to create an accessible workplace for all qualified employees. The Family and Medical Leave Act was passed in 1993. This act provides opportunity for employees to take up to 12 weeks unpaid leave for birth or adoption. Additionally, the act allows the use of the leave for care of an elderly or ill parent, spouse, or child, or to undergo treatment.

Conclusions

The manager is a critical element in any operation's success in creating and maintaining an atmosphere of respect in the workplace. The manager who models respect and makes it clear that all employees are valued will achieve that atmosphere of respect. The result will be a golden rule culture that encourages growth, embraces risk taking, and supports advancement. The outcome of such a golden rule culture will be success for both the operation and the employees with pride in achievement spanning all.

Study Questions

1. List issues and elements that create fear within the work environment.
2. Discuss providing criticism with respect for the individual.
3. State how to give negative criticism and achieve positive results.
4. List phrases that encourage staff members to give feedback.
5. Explain the nature of the work environment relative to a diversified workforce.
6. Relate the elements of a diverse workplace.
7. State the elements that make up sexual harassment.
8. Relate the legal responsibilities of the manager in regard to sexual harassment.
9. What are the primary laws regarding equal opportunity in the workplace and what do they say?

Case Studies

The case studies listed below relate to the information presented in this chapter and reading, answering the case study questions and participating in discussion of a case will reinforce and expand what you have learned in this chapter. All case studies are provided in this text after the last chapter.

Bill & Jean's Restaurant

L&J Cafeteria

Prairie View Country Club

Shady Lane Inn

Shandong House Restaurant

Shepherd Mountain Hotel

Stone Lion Hotel and Conference Center

Notes

1. The Edward Deming Institute. *The fourteen points for management*. Retrieved October 23, 2014, from https://www.deming.org/theman/theories/fourteenpoints.
2. Berta. D. Building an employment 'Brand'. *Nation's Restaurant News*, Date unknown.
3. Ibid.
4. Aruayo, R. (1991). *Dr. Deming* (p. 184). New York: Carol.
5. Ryan, K., & Oestreich, D. (1991). *Driving fear out of the workplace* (p. 75). San Francisco, CA: Jossey-Bass.
6. Metz, F. (Ed.) (1991). Success has a future perspective. In *Lessons in leadership* (p. 36). New York: Van Nostrand Reinhold.
7. Frumkin, P. (September 2005). At your service: Dining and diversity: Catering to a multicultural clientele: As the U.S. population becomes increasingly diverse, training servers to be sensitive to the distinct desires of different groups becomes more important than ever. *Nation's Restaurant News*, 39(38), 110.
8. United States Bureau of Labor Statistics. *Labor force statistics from the current population survey: Household data annual averages—18. Employed persons by detailed industry, sex, race, and Hispanic or Latino ethnicity.* Retrieved October 18, 2014, from http://www.bls.gov/cps/cpsaat18.htm.

9. Ibid.

10. Forbes. (2012). *Insights: Diversity & inclusion: Unlocking global poten-tial—Global diversity rankings by country, sector and occupation.* New York: Forbes.

11. Berta, D. (February 6, 2006). Diversity at the top: Quick-service outshines other segments with the highest percentage of women and minorities in man-agement positions: Segment study: QSR & diversity. *Nation's Restaurant News*, 40(6), 33.

12. Koonce, R. (December 2001). Redefining diversity: It's not just the right thing to do. It also makes good business sense. *Training & Development*, p. 1. Retrieved from www.findarticles.com/cf_ntrstnws/m4467/12_55`/83045836/print.jhtml.

13. Miller, J., Porter, M., & Drummond, K. (1992). *Management in the hospital-ity industry* (2nd ed., p. 92) New York: John Wiley.

14. The U.S. Equal Employment Opportunity Commission. *Sexual harassment charges EEOC & FEPAs combined: FY 1997—FY 2011.* Retrieved from http://www.eeoc.gov/eeoc/statistics/enforcement/sexual_harassment.cfm

15. Ibid.

Discipline 13

CHAPTER OUTLINE

- ▶ Introduction
- ▶ Foundations of Discipline
- ▶ Approaches to Discipline
- ▶ Administering Discipline
- ▶ Termination of a Staff Member
- ▶ Exit Interviews
- ▶ Summary

LEARNING OBJECTIVES

When you complete reading this chapter, you should be able to:

- ▶ define discipline in its broader sense as it applies to the role of the manager
- ▶ describe the discipline parameters in which the manager operates relative to unions and the Equal Employment Opportunity Commission (EEOC)
- ▶ recall the principles of the progressive approach to discipline
- ▶ relate the principles of positive discipline
- ▶ state the guidelines for administering discipline in a fair and equitable way
- ▶ state the principles of terminating a staff member
- ▶ define the strategies and rationale for conducting exit interviews.

Introduction

The words discipline and disciple share the same root, which means to mold or teach. True discipline should teach a correct action. Yet, many think of discipline merely as punishment or reprimanding a staff member for a mistake. The word disciple literally means follower. Therefore, good discipline is based on leadership, which includes the ability to guide, coach, correct, and affirm the actions of others. Discipline is also an inner force, self-discipline, which, it is hoped, develops within each staff member and causes him or her to want to follow high standards in life and the workplace. When a staff member does something such as poor job performance; too many absences; violation of an order, rule, or procedure; or some illegal act such as stealing, fighting, gambling, or involvement with illegal drugs, disciplinary action is required. The manager's goal should be effective discipline not just reprimanding or inflicting penalties. True discipline involves an entire program that teaches and guides individuals to become loyal, motivated, and responsible team players.

Discipline in a broader sense concerns the process of socialization. Staff members are given the values and rules necessary for success in organization. This process is complete when the staff member comes to accept those values and rules as legitimate. Within the team, the rules serve a purpose and each member benefits by obeying.

Discipline as punishment is overshadowed today by the concept of positive discipline. Positive discipline is the process of working to assist the staff member in changing behavior. The goal of the process is improvement of the match between the staff member's performance and the operational standards while driving the overall professional growth of the staff member. Positive discipline is about moving, when possible, past the concept of discipline as punishment only to emphasis on staff member development that encourages responsibility and self-directed behavior. It is an extension of the training and coaching process.

Foundations of Discipline

No manager enjoys the act of disciplining a staff member, but this is an unavoidable part of the job. The operation may be running smoothly, with each staff member doing his or her job well. Then a staff member is careless, an accident occurs, and the manager must take corrective action. In a golden rule environment the focus of the corrective action targets the staff member's improvement and growth not just compliance. Leadership not just management is needed to discipline and still maintain a positive environment. It is a positive, golden rule, environment that minimizes the need to be punitive. If the staff members respect the manager, then there likely is a culture of respect and it is easier to head off problems. Staff members who feel that the manager is interested in their welfare will accept criticism and direction as an opportunity to improve.

In general, staff members accept rules and directions as a condition of employment and do not set out to break rules. These same staff members observe how the manager reacts with members who do not observe the rules or perform to the declared standard. Each individual is concerned with getting fair treatment. Team morale is lowered and individual performance declines when staff members observe some individuals performing poorly without consequence or if they witness excessively harsh discipline.

Development of standards and rules must take place before the consequences of performance are determined. The standards and rules are the basis for evaluation. It is against these that performance is to be measured. The standards and rules must be clearly communicated to staff members or evaluation is meaningless and does not drive the targeted performance. These standards and rules should be an integral part of orientation and training programs. The evaluation of performance and reinforcement of the standards and rules should be ongoing.

Standards and rules should be in written form. The language used to write them should be clear. Standards and rules that are vague create confusion among staff members. It must also be clear what the penalties are if the standards or rules are not met with. Penalties must be part of the operations policies and must be fairly and equitable applied. "Knowing the consequences has its own security: people know where the boss stands, and they know what will happen if they go beyond the limits."[1] Management should be prepared to and capable of explaining why a standard or rule exists. Acceptance of a standard or rule is increased when staff members understand why they exist. In a situation where standard or rule enforcement has been lax, the standard or rule and the consequences of breaking them must be restated to the staff members before disciplinary action can be taken.

Proper disciplinary procedure requires that the individual be advised in advance of all standards and rules and the penalties for violation before evaluation begins. There are, however, some types of conduct management that can reasonably be considered being outside the bounds of acceptable conduct without having a specific rule addressing the behavior. An example of this type of conduct is a staff member that steals money or merchandise or uses illegal substances.

Effective disciplines require a foundation of well communicated and reinforced standards and rules. This foundation is enhanced by a golden rule environment that encourages a positive environment.

Approaches to Discipline

Discipline should not only be fair and consistent but also conform to legal requirements. Managers who operate in a union environment have to take extra care when disciplining staff members. Binding labor contracts set forth rules and procedures that must be followed, and they set penalties on management and workers for failing to abide by the rules. Even minor deviations from labor contract procedure can overturn an otherwise justified disciplinary action. These contracts usually contain a provision for impartial review or an arbitration process. Additionally, in union-organized establishments workers often have an increased awareness of their rights that may cause some of them to challenge the manager's disciplinary decisions. This does not mean that no form of discipline is possible under union contracts. On the contrary, it may be easier. The nature of collective bargaining requires both union and management to be rigid and specific regarding rules and procedures.

Red Hot Stove Rule

Douglas McGregor used the red hot stove rule to clarify his four points of discipline.[2] A red hot stove with its radiating heat gives a *warning* that it should not be touched. Those who touch the stove receive an immediate response, they get burned. The action is consistent; it is the same each time. The action is impersonal, it does not matter who touches the stove they get burned. McGregor was saying that disciplinary policies should be well-communicated, administered quickly, consistently, and impartially. The four principles of the red hot stove rule are shown in Figure 13.1.

```
┌─────────────────────────────────────────────┐
│              Principles of Discipline:         │
│           McGregor's Red Hot Stove Rule        │
│                                                │
│   * Warning: Burner looks hot                  │
│   * Immediate: Burns hand instantly            │
│   * Consistent: Same result every time         │
│    * Impersonal: Treats everyone the same      │
└─────────────────────────────────────────────┘
```

FIGURE 13.1   Principles of Discipline: McGregor's Red Hot Stove Rule

Progressive Discipline

Generally, discipline is imposed in a progressive manner. By definition, progressive discipline is the application of corrective measures by increasing degrees. It should motivate staff members to take corrective action on misconduct voluntarily. The goal of the progressive approach is to solve an issue when it is small and to assist the staff member in improving performance. If the issue is not solved and there is no improvement the process moves to the next level. The sequence and severity of the disciplinary action varies with the type of offense and the circumstances surrounding the misconduct. Following is a typical sequence of progressive discipline:

Step 1. Oral reprimand: When a staff member makes an unauthorized or inappropriate change in the way something is done; for the first time does not meet the standard; or breaks a minor rule, an oral reprimand may be appropriate. In general, these reprimands should be made in private, away from other staff members. The rule is to "discipline in private, praise in public." The manager should ensure that he or she makes clear and specific what should be stopped (or started). Remember, most people fear public embarrassment more than the disciplinary action itself. In the course of the reprimand, be firm and fair. Do not argue or debate side issues, but treat the individual with respect.

Sometimes, however, it is necessary to reprimand instantly without first considering an individual staff member's sensitivity. This concerns misconduct in the critical areas of safety, security, and sanitation. Because of potential hazardous risks to the public, the manager should react immediately. When this happens, it is best to soften the reprimand as much as possible. The important point is to stop the staff member from continuing the harmful action. As with all elements of discipline, actions requiring reprimands should always be documented. A record of the oral reprimand is made and placed in the individual's personnel file with a note that it is not a "written reprimand."

Step 2. Written reprimand: For the second offense, the staff member receives a written reprimand. Typically, this informs the staff member that his or her conduct is in violation of standards or rules or procedures and that further violations will result in suspension or loss of pay. The written reprimand must be signed by the manager and the staff member. The staff member's signature is an acknowledgment, not of agreement with the reprimand, but he or she has seen the notice. Normally, the staff member has the right to place a written response to the reprimand in the personnel file. Copies of this reprimand are also given to the union steward, if this is applicable. If the staff member is probationary, the letter will usually indicate that improved performance is necessary. Probation should be handled in writing so that a written record exists in the event that termination is necessary if the required improvement does not occur.

Step 3. Suspension: Violations of standards or rules and minor illegal acts often are treated with a temporary layoff or suspension. This suspension is with or without pay and consistent with the seriousness of the offense. The details are written and handled the same as the written reprimand. This written communication also indicates that another violation will call for discharge.

Step 4. Termination: If, after the third offense, it appears that there is little chance of bringing the individual's performance up to an acceptable level, termination may be the best course of action. It is presumed that the staff member has been given every opportunity to conform and improve. It is at this point that the documentation of each previous step becomes critical.

Some infractions are so serious that discharge is permitted with the first violation. Cases involving instant dismissal are rare. They usually involve illegal acts or serious misconduct that threatens the safety and security of other individuals or the organization. This category also includes requested resignations. When it appears that the organization is not meeting a staff member's interests, it may be appropriate to request him or her to seek employment elsewhere. Some of the major violations that frequently require immediate dismissal are shown in Figure 13.2.

Progressive discipline gives the staff member the opportunity to improve, and documents the specific reasons for discharge if necessary. Through the process, "The decision to discharge an employee must be based on quality and quantity of evidence, not hearsay, personal prejudices, speculation, or rumors."[3] Some of the violations requiring progressive discipline are shown in Figure 13.3.

General Grounds for Immediate Dismissal

* Possession of, drinking, smoking, or being under the influence of intoxicants or narcotics on the establishment's property

* False statements or misrepresentation of facts on employment application forms

* Sleeping on the job

* Stealing company or personal property

* Fighting on company property

* Issues that threaten the well-being of team members or guests

* Gross discourtesy to guests

* Gross negligence involving sanitation/safety

* Excessive absenteeism without prior notification

* Sexual harassment

* Refusing to follow reasonable job-related directives from the manager

(These violations are basic and are not intended to be all-inclusive or cover every situation that may arise.)

FIGURE 13.2   General Grounds for Immediate Dismissal

Example Actions
Leading to Progressive Discipline

* Tardiness

* Absence for one day without notifying supervisor

* Leaving the property without permission

* Use of abusive language

* Not performing to set standards

* Disorderly conduct during working time

* Racial slurs

* Obscene or immoral conduct

(These violations are basic and are not intended to be all-inclusive or cover every situation that may arise.)

FIGURE 13.3   Example Actions Leading to Progressive Discipline

Positive Discipline

One approach to disciplinary action is positive discipline, or discipline without punishment, an idea originally developed by John Huberman, a Canadian psychologist. Punitive and positive disciplines differ in both attitude and procedure.[4] Most of the time individuals are unaware that they are doing something they are not supposed to do. In spite of good orientation and training, rules and procedures clearly posted or contained in employee manuals, there are still things that staff members do not know. They may observe some other staff member doing something and believe it is all right for them to do it. A positive approach to discipline, therefore, is continuous education. Discipline that is applied positively is used to teach and mold. Staff members will see that it is for their welfare. Positive discipline shows staff members that performing to the standards and obeying the rules benefits them as well as the organization.

The philosophy behind positive discipline is that most people come to work wishing to do a good job. They appreciate being treated as adults. They want to learn, welcome responsibility, can be self-directed, and are capable of self-discipline. The dynamics of positive discipline are a team effort where the staff members and the manager engage in joint discussion and problem solving to resolve incidents of rule infractions.

Positive discipline focuses on the early correction of staff member's misconduct. While positive discipline seems similar to progressive discipline, its emphasis is on giving staff members reminders rather than reprimands.

We now discuss the sequence of different steps in enforcing positive discipline.

Step 1. This is an oral reminder. In a private discussion with the manager, the staff member is encouraged to explain the reason for the misconduct. In a friendly way, the rules and procedures are restated along with the reasons for having them. The manager refrains from reprimanding or threatening the staff member with further disciplinary action. This meeting may be documented, but a written record is not placed in the staff member's file unless the misconduct occurs again. During this meeting, the staff member agrees not to repeat the misconduct.

Step 2. If improvement is not made following step 1, a second meeting takes place with the offending staff member. During this private meeting, the manager adopts the role of counselor. At this stage, a written reminder is given to the staff member that summarizes the discussion and the concluding agreement. Both the staff member and manager then sign it.

Step 3. When steps 1 and 2 fail to produce the desired results, the staff member is placed on a one-day "decision making" leave with pay.

The purpose of this paid leave is to allow the offending staff member time to decide whether to remain part of the team; whether to return and abide by the rules and conditions, or to leave. If the staff member returns, it is on the basis of an agreement to conform to the organization's rules and that further infractions will be followed by termination. The organization pays for this specified leave in order to demonstrate its desire to retain the staff member. Paying for the leave eliminates any negative effects that suspension without pay has on individuals.

Step 4. If the agreed improvements do not take place, then the staff member has broken the agreement. There is then a clear reason for termination.

Positive discipline works. Organizations that have used it report success. Many people who use it report that the majority of the time employees decide to come back and follow the rules.[5]

Administering Discipline

Discipline should be administered as soon as possible after the infraction has taken place or has been noticed. For the discipline to be most effective, it must be put in motion immediately without involving emotional or irrational decisions. Notation of rule infractions in a staff member's record does not constitute advance warning and is not sufficient to support disciplinary action. A staff member must be advised of the infraction for it to be considered a warning. Noting that the staff member was warned about the infraction and having him or her sign a form acknowledging the warning is good practice. Failure to warn a staff member of the consequences of continuous rule violation is one reason often cited for overturning a disciplinary action.

The manager must recognize that each act of discipline is different and that each staff member must be handled differently. The better the manager knows all staff members and how they react, the better he or she can handle disciplinary actions. Sometimes, negative reactions are experienced. For example, rather than being motivated to improve performance, a staff member may be motivated to retaliate or "get even." The following guidelines will help ensure a positive reaction.

Discipline and the offense: Match the discipline to the offense. A trivial rule infraction does not require harsh or unreasonable discipline. A staff member's previous record must be considered.

Determining the appropriateness of the discipline action involves serious consideration of the following.

- The circumstances surrounding the incident.
- The seriousness of the incident.
- The previous record of the staff member.
- The disciplinary action taken in similar situations.
- The existing rules and disciplinary policies.
  The provisions in the labor contract (if applicable).
- The manager must take the correct steps and stay calm to effectively match the discipline with the offense. The manager should do the following.
  - Know the facts: Investigate thoroughly. Determine who was involved in the incident, what happened, where it happened, and what the staff member's involvement was.
  - Interview: Discuss the discipline problem with the staff member in private. Keep it as informal as possible to allow the discussion to proceed calmly.
  - Listen: First, the manager should ask the staff member to tell his or her side of the story. Ask questions to get further details; try not to interrupt until the individual has finished. Listen with an open mind. Do not prejudge the situation.
  - Stay calm: Control feelings and emotions. Do not argue. Do not engage in any type of name-calling. The manager may win the argument, but will lose the loyalty and contribution of an important staff member.
  - Avoid entrapment: Do not set out to "get" a staff member. Do not get involved unless something is wrong.
  - Be firm but fair: Being firm does not suggest getting tough. Being firm but fair involves explaining to a staff member why behavior is unacceptable. Do not humiliate the staff member in any way.
  - Document: Make notes on what happened and what the resulting action was. Records of disciplinary action are important for the purpose of demonstrating later that there was a fair and equitable resolution of the incident.
  - Inform others: Be sure to inform the staff member of the intended course of action. Remember, the manager is not the final voice in matters of discipline. The organization and the union (if applicable) should be informed. Matters of serious discipline are much too important for one person to decide. It is always a good idea for the manager to discuss intended disciplinary actions with other members of the

establishment's management or with members of the human resources department. These are the people who have to support the manager's actions. This will help to establish a better perspective for the action.

Terminating a Staff member

Before a decision is reached to terminate a staff member, the following questions should be answered:

- Was the staff member forewarned of the possible disciplinary consequences of his or her actions?
- Were the work standards required of the individual reasonable in relation to the safe, orderly, and efficient conduct of the organization?
- Were all reasonable efforts expended to fully and fairly determine the facts?
- Was the staff member given ample opportunity for improvement?
- Were all other options of disciplinary action considered?
- Was the staff member afforded "due process" and a fair hearing?
- Are there any unusual or mitigating circumstances surrounding the case?
- Is this action discriminatory?

For most managers, dismissing a staff member can be a painful experience. Often, it gives managers a feeling that they have failed the individual in some way. The assurance that all of the questions have been addressed is important to be fair to the staff member and the manager. Regardless of the reasons for dismissal, it should be accomplished with consideration of the individual. Every effort should be made to ease the trauma that a dismissal can create. Figure 13.4 shows guidelines that can help reduce the trauma associated with dismissal. Being dismissed can be a terrible blow to a staff member. It is important to allow the staff member to leave with self-esteem intact.

Exit Interviews

Staff members who leave voluntarily often provide feedback on their experience with the organization that can be useful in averting further employee turnover. Exit interviews enable managers to compile

Reducing Trauma Associated with Dismissal
* Make the discussion private, brief, and businesslike.
* Be tactful, honest, and straightforward.
* Give any information regarding severance pay or other benefits information.
* Outline the period the staff member has before he or she must leave the organization.
* Avoid any personality differences between the manager and the staff member.

FIGURE 13.4 Reducing Trauma Associated with Dismissal

data about the work environment as well as establish the effectiveness of orientation and training programs. They are used to establish the primary reasons people leave.[6]

Exit interview data can help determine whether there is a trend for voluntary departures. To get the most accurate data from departing employees, the interview is best conducted by a manager other than the staff member's direct manager. Another approach is to turn the whole procedure over to the human resources department. Some of the questions appropriate for the exit interview are as listed hereunder:

- What did you like most about working here?
- What did you like least?
- If you were a consultant to our organization, what changes/ improvement would you recommend?
- What was it like working for manager John Doe? If the answer is vague or answered weakly the manager may want to ask: What would have made manager John Doe a better manager, in your opinion?

To get as much information as possible from the interview, the interviewer needs to probe for specific details from each answer. No staff member should leave the organization without being interviewed. Staff members who leave voluntarily have to be replaced. This process is expensive not only in terms of dollars and time, but also often in terms of team morale.

Summary

Discipline should not be interpreted only as punishment. It is also about molding and teaching staff members to become loyal, motivated, and responsible workers. Self-discipline is an inner force that develops within staff members and causes them to want to follow high standards in life and the workplace. The manager's goal should be effective discipline not just reprimanding or inflicting penalties. True discipline involves an entire program that teaches and guides individuals to become loyal, motivated, and responsible team players.

Managers should ensure that each staff member understands the standards and rules of the organization. Disciplinary actions must be in accordance with EEOC legislation and other antidiscrimination laws. Managers should know and understand all union labor contract procedures and agreements relative to employee discipline.

Discipline should be administered in a consistent, fair, and equitable way. Progressive discipline involves the steps of oral reprimand, written reprimand, suspension, and termination. Administering discipline requires the manager to gather the facts, provide due process, and know the advance steps before termination.

Positive discipline approaches require the manager to act in a way that invests in the staff member by shifting responsibility to the individual. Its philosophy is that most people are self-disciplined, and with counseling and guidance, staff members who break rules can become productive. An important element of the process is the third step, which provides offending staff members with a paid period to decide their future with the organization, thus placing the responsibility on them for the next steps.

Exit interviews with staff members who voluntarily leave provide the organization with information that can assist in preventing future turnover and make the operation a better place to work.

Study Questions

1. Define discipline in its broader sense as it applies to the role of the manager.

2. Describe the discipline parameters in which the manager operates relative to unions and the EEOC.

3. Recall the principles of the progressive approach to discipline.

4. Relate the principles of positive discipline.

5. List the guidelines for reducing the trauma of termination for the staff member.

6. State the guidelines for administering discipline in a fair and equitable way.

7. State the principles of terminating a staff member.

8. Define the strategies and rationale for conducting exit interviews.

Case Studies

The case studies listed below relate to the information presented in this chapter and reading, answering the case study questions and participating in discussion of a case will reinforce and expand what you have learned in this chapter. All case studies are provided in this text after the last chapter.

L&J Cafeteria

Stone Lion Hotel and Conference Center

Summit Resort

Notes

1. Miller, J., Porter, M., & Drummond, K. (1992). *Supervision in the hospitality industry* (2nd ed., p. 257) New York: John Wiley.
2. What is Human Resource. *Red hot stove rule*. Retrieved October 26, 2014 from http://www.whatishumanresource.com/hot-stove-rule
3. Eade, V. (1993). *Human resources management in the hospitality industry* (p. 204). Scottsdale, AZ: Garsuch Sciarisbrick Publisher.
4. Frunzi, G., & Halloran, J. (1991). *Supervision: The art of management* (3rd ed., p. 380) Englewood Cliffs, NJ: Prentice-Hall.
5. Miller, J., Porter, M., & Drummond, K. (1992). *Supervision in the hospitality industry* (2nd ed., p. 259) New York: John Wiley.
6. Pope, B. (1992). *Workforce management* (p. 89). Chicago, IL: Business One Review.

Human Resource Management in a Union Environment 14

CHAPTER OUTLINE

- ▶ Introduction
- ▶ Union Contract
- ▶ Contract Negotiation
- ▶ Policy and Contract
- ▶ Recordkeeping and Contract
- ▶ Hiring and Contract
- ▶ Performance Evaluation and Contract
- ▶ Discipline and Contract
- ▶ Grievance Resolution
- ▶ Summary

LEARNING OBJECTIVES

When you complete reading this chapter, you should be able to:
- ▶ describe the key aspects of a union and the union contract
- ▶ relate the principles of hiring in the union environment
- ▶ recall the elements of policy development in the union environment
- ▶ relate the factors of performance evaluation in the union environment
- ▶ describe the relationship of recordkeeping and effective human resource management in the union environment
- ▶ relate the principles of discipline in the union environment
- ▶ describe the key aspects of contract negotiation

Introduction

BusinessDictionary.com defines a union as "A group of workers joined together in a specific type of organization for the purpose of improving their working conditions as well as to help in promoting the common interests of the group."[1] This definition is referring to a "trade" union which is defined by *The Free Dictionary* as "(industrial relations and human resource terms) an association of employees formed to improve their incomes and working conditions by collective bargaining with the employer or employer organizations."[2] It also refers to "labor" unions which is defined by *The Free Dictionary* as "an organization of wage earners or salaried employees for mutual aid and protection and for dealing collectively with employers; trade union."[3] In today's business world the commonly used term is simply union and union is the term that we use in this chapter.

The right of the employees to form unions was reaffirmed in 1935 by the National Labor Relations Act (NLRA) (Wagner Act). The NLRA was created to establish a national policy of encouraging collective bargaining, guaranteeing certain employee rights, and detailing specific employer unfair labor practices. The act established the National Labor Relations Board (NLRB) to enforce these provisions. The NLRB has the power to investigate, dismiss charges, or hold hearings; issue "cease and desist" orders; or pursue cases via the Circuit Courts of Appeals or the U.S. Supreme Court. The NLRA applies to private employers, their employees, and unions.

In 1947 the provisions of the NLRA were expanded in the Labor-Management Relations Act (LMRA) (Taft–Hartley Act). The act established greater control of labor disputes by enlarging the NLRB and providing that the union or the employer must, before terminating a collective-bargaining agreement, serve notice on the other party and on a government mediation service. The government was empowered to obtain an 80-day injunction against any strike that it deemed a peril to national health or safety. The act also prohibited jurisdictional strikes. A jurisdictional strike is based on a dispute between two unions over which of the unions should act as the bargaining agent for the employees. In addition the act prohibited secondary boycotts. A secondary boycott is a boycott against an already organized company doing business with another company that a union is trying to organize. The act declared that it did not extend protection to workers on wildcat strikes, it outlawed the closed shop, and it permitted the union shop only on a vote of a majority of the employees. Most of the collective-bargaining provisions were retained, with the extra provision that a union before using the facilities of the NLRB must file with the U.S. Department of Labor financial reports and affidavits that union officers are not Communists.

In 1959 further regulation of unions and guarantees of certain rights to all union members were provided by the Labor-Management Reporting and Disclosure Act (Landrum–Griffin) (LMRDA). The rights guaranteed in the act are referred to as the union member's "Bill of Rights." These rights are as listed hereunder:

- equal rights to participate in union activities;
- freedom of speech and assembly;
- voice in setting rates of dues, fees, and assessments;
- protection of the right to sue; and
- safeguards against improper discipline.

The Office of Labor-Management Standards (OLMS) of the U.S. Department of Labor (DOL) administers and enforces most provisions of the LMRDA.

Managing human resources effectively in a union environment requires knowledge of the union contract. The focus of this chapter is on clear understanding of the impact of the union contract on the actions of the manager and the staff members. The role of the manager and human resource officer as the provider of vision, goals, objectives, resources, direction, and performance do not change when a union contract is in effect. There is an increased need for clear policy enforcement, adherence to procedure, and recordkeeping when a union contract is in effect.

Union Contract

A contract is a voluntary, considered, and legally binding agreement between two parties. Three things must be present for a contractual bond to be established: (1) an offer; (2) acceptance of the offer; and (3) a legal and valuable consideration. All parties to a contract should receive fair value from the contract but that value is not necessarily equal. A contract gives each party rights and responsibilities relative to rights and responsibilities of the other parties.

Contract Negotiation

A contract between a company, the employer, and the union, the bargaining agent for the collective of employees, is generally achieved through collective bargaining. The bargaining unit is the specific group of employees being represented by a specific union. There can be multiple unions, each representing a different group of employees in an operation. The Walt Disney Company works with the following unions in the United States: Service Trades Council Union; Unite Here; Teamsters Union; Transportation Communications International Union; United Food and Commercial Workers Union; International Association of Theatrical Stage Employees Union; Actors Equity; Security, Police and Fire Professionals of America; and International Association of Fire Fighters. The term "collective" refers to the joining together of a group of employees who agree to be represented as a unified group, the bargaining unit. The unified group, the collective, is the foundation of the union's ability to effectively negotiate on behalf of the employee. This process of negotiation is called collective bargaining.

The collective bargaining process includes the presentation of the union's desired content for the contract when no contract exists or the changes and additions to the existing contract. Management also brings to the bargaining table its content or changes and additions. The desired objective is to arrive—through negotiation—at an agreement, thereby establishing a contract for a specified length of time. It is possible that the union and management will be in immediate agreement but more often there is negotiation to arrive at a compromise that falls somewhere between the two positions but that each side can accept. Negotiation is definitely a matter of give-and-take. It requires a high level of diplomacy and is generally carried out on both sides by individuals very skilled in the process.

An important factor that a management must constantly recognize is that the union's ultimate negotiating tool is the strike. Businessdictionary.com defines strike as "Collective, organized, cessation or slowdown of work by employees, to force acceptance of their demands by the employer."[4] In most instances, for a strike to be legal, five actions as listed hereunder must take place.

1. A strike has to be voted on and approved by a majority of the union members.
2. The vote must be verified if the number of votes exceeds a certain number. That number most commonly is 50.
3. A notice of the impending strike vote must be given, in most cases, seven days in advance.
4. The employer must be provided with the results of the strike vote.
5. Notice of intent to move forward with the strike must be given to the employer, in most cases, seven days in advance.

The goal of both management and the union in any contract negotiation needs to be to avoid a strike. A strike can be economically disastrous for both the company and the union.

The manager, human resource officer, or the professional negotiator must be prepared for the negotiations. There are five basic steps in the preparation process as elaborated hereunder.

1. Review the previous negotiation process. Review minutes of the meetings and notes from previous negotiators. The review includes looking at the previous strategies used and how well they worked. Look at the issues in the last negotiation. It is likely that many of these will reappear and this allows the negotiator to be prepared to address them. Look at the personalities of the individuals involved in the previous negotiation. If these individuals are part of the current negotiation it will allow for more directed planning and strategy.

2. Review the outcomes and operational experience from the last contract. Look into the contracts impact on performance, productivity, and overall quality. Review the grievances and arbitration record under the current contract. The goal is to determine what in the contract had positive outcomes and what created operational challenges.

3. Generate the necessary data to speak to issues such as levels of salary and benefits. Examples of the information gathered include hourly wages for the last 10–15 years; average weekly hours per bargaining unit, work unit, job classification, and department; paid time for union business; and overtime worked. Additionally, look at the estimated cost of contract components and their impact on the operation of the business.

4. Look at comparable companies. Look at what is being paid and what types of benefits and concessions are being provided in the company's marketplace.

5. Develop strategies based on the information gathered. Looking at the previous contract and anticipated issues develop a draft contract offer that addresses the economic and noneconomic issues. A draft timeline for the negotiations should be prepared.[5]

The goal of this preparation is the conduct of an effective negotiation in a reasonable amount of time.

Once the union and the company have come to agreement on a contract it does not mean that the process is not finished. The contract will generally need to be voted on by the union members. Once approved by the union members the contract can be put into force.

Negotiating the contract is the single most critical responsibility for both the management and the union. The process of negotiation and the results have the potential to destroy the relationship between the management and union. It can also impact how effectively management can manage its workplace and the union's ability to represent the interests of its members. Ultimately, the contract can lead to the success or the end of the company, and the viability of membership in the union.[6]

The contract will include provisions for a wide range of personnel-related issues and actions. These can include, mentioning only a few, the following.

- pay
- benefits
- leave
- hiring, retention, and promotion
- seniority
- position property rights
- working conditions
- duties and responsibilities for positions
- position qualifications.

Once in effect, the provisions of the contract determine the majority of policies and procedures relating to personnel.

Personnel Policy Development and the Union Contract

Policy development when operating with a contract requires constant references to the contract provisions. Policies of the types listed hereunder, but not limited to these, must be aligned with the provisions of the contract.

- Leave: calling in sick, information on jury duty, time off for bereavement
- Safety procedures
- Employee assistance programs
- Work standards
- Performance evaluation
- Disciplinary action
- Promotion
- Termination
- Personnel record handling
- Employee grievance procedure.

Record Keeping and the Union Contract

In all circumstances the employer is obligated to maintain accurate records for each person employed by the company. These records will normally be a history of:

- dates of employment
- salary and tax withholding
- performance evaluation
- promotion
- assigned duties and responsibilities
- accommodations
- disciplinary actions
- vacation
- sick leave
- workplace injuries.

When a contract is enforced it is likely that the contract will have provisions related to personnel records and these provisions must be enforced. In all situations, the content of the personnel file should be limited to work-related material.

A personnel file (record) is a legal document. Access to its contents should be limited to those in the company that have a job-related responsibility that requires they have knowledge of the contents of the file. The employee's right to see the content of the file is governed first by any laws related to that access. There is no federal law providing for employee access but there a variety of state laws regarding employee access to their personnel file. The human resource officer needs to be familiar with the law in the state where they are located. Beyond the law it is likely that the contract will have a provision related to employee access.

Hiring and the Union Contract

The contract will likely have provisions that will determine many of the policies and procedures related to hiring personnel. The contract will generally provide specific criteria for the qualifications of positions represented by the union. The contract may also require the involvement of a union and/or employee representative in the hiring process. Additionally, the contract will generally include a provision calling for promotion from within and preferential treatment of existing employees represented by the union. Whether or not the individual hired must be or must become a union member to hold a position represented by the union will depend on the contract.

Performance Evaluation and the Union Contract

Performance evaluation will generally be covered by the contract. Examples of items the provisions will generally specify in regard to performance evaluation are listed hereunder:

- number of performance reviews during a year;
- evaluation process;
- evaluation criteria;
- consequence of a negative evaluation; and
- role of evaluation in pay increases and promotion.

The performance evaluation should be documented. A negative evaluation may lead to a grievance by the employee. Well-documented evaluation with documentation that supports the evaluation is critical.

Discipline and the Union Contract

Discipline is always a sensitive action requiring due diligence on the part of the manager or human resource officer. When a union contract is enforced, this due diligence becomes paramount. The union contract will almost always have provisions specifying the steps required before disciplinary action can take place. These steps are generally what you have studied previously as progressive discipline. Documentation is the keystone to carrying out disciplinary action when operating with a union contract. Progressive discipline is the application of corrective measures by increasing degrees. The steps of progressive discipline are oral reprimand; written reprimand; suspension; and termination. Generally, unless there is irreproachable evidence, the manager or human resource officer should be prepared for the employee who is being disciplined to file a grievance. This is not an issue when the discipline is not only justified and appropriate but also the basis for the action is well documented.

Grievance Resolution

The filing of a grievance when a contract is enforced becomes the time for management and the human resource officer to be extremely diligent in their duty. Their duty in this circumstance is to fairly represent both the interest of the employee and the manager/management. This may appear to be a situation of great ambiguity but it is actually not. Carrying forward, in a prompt manner with a full investigation of the issue being grieved is in the best interest of all parties. The role of the human resource officer is to carry out an impartial investigation. The human resource officer should work to resolve the issue with either a decision in support of one party or the other or with a compromise between the two parties. While the employee is represented in this process by the human resource officer they will generally be more specifically represented by their union steward (representative) or someone appointed by the union.

When an agreement cannot be reached, then the grievance will generally be addressed via arbitration. Arbitration is when the grievance is submitted to an independent third party that has been agreed to by both the union and the management. Both parties have also agreed to abide by the decision of the arbitrator. Arbitration should be considered as a last step.

Summary

A union is a group, collective of workers joined together in an organization for the purpose of improving their working conditions as well as to help in promoting the common interests of the group. Human resource management in a union environment requires knowledge of the laws governing the relationship between unions and business. The NLRA affirmed the right of employees to form a union and this applies to private employers, their employees, and unions. The National Labor Relation Board enforces the provision of the NLRA. The LMRA established regulations for labor-management disputes. The LMRDA created the union member "Bill of Rights" and established the OLMS of the U.S. Department of Labor (DOL), which administers and enforces most provisions of the LMRDA.

A contract is a voluntary, considered, and legally binding agreement between two parties. Three things must be present for a contractual bond to be established: (1) an offer; (2) acceptance of the offer; and (3) a legal and valuable consideration. All parties to a contract should receive fair value from the contract but that value is not necessarily equal. A contract gives each party rights and responsibilities relative to rights and responsibilities of the other parties.

A contract between a company, the employer, and the union, the bargaining agent for the collective of employees, is generally achieved through collective bargaining. The bargaining unit is the specific group of employees being represented by a specific union. There can be multiple unions, each representing a different group of employees in an operation. The collective bargaining process includes the presentation of the union's desired content for the contract when no contract exists or the changes and additions to the existing contract. Management also brings to the bargaining table its content or changes and additions. The object is to arrive, through negotiation, at an agreement, thereby establishing a contract for a specified length of time. Ultimately, the contract can lead to the success or the end of the company, and the viability of membership in the union. Once in effect, the provisions of the contract determine the majority of policies and procedures relating to personnel.

Study Questions

1. Describe the key aspects of a union and the union contract.
2. Relate the principles of hiring in the union environment.
3. Recall the elements of policy development in the union environment.
4. Relate the factors of performance evaluation in the union environment.
5. Describe the relationship of recordkeeping and effective human resource management in the union environment.
6. Discuss the proper maintenance and handling of personnel files.
7. Relate the principles of discipline in the union environment.
8. Describe the key aspects of contract negotiation.

Case Studies

The case studies listed below relate to the information presented in this chapter and reading, answering the case study questions and participating in discussion of a case will reinforce and expand what you have learned in this chapter. All case studies are provided in this text after the last chapter.

Barefoot Beach Resort

Notes

1. BusinessDictionary.com. Retrieved February 16, 2014, from http://www.businessdictionary.com/definition/union.html

2. Dictionary.com. Retrieved February 16, 2014, from http://www.thefreedictionary.com/trade+union

3. Dictionary.com. Retrieved February 16, 2014, from http://www.thefreedictionary.com/labor%20union

4. BusinessDictionary.com. Retrieved February 16, 2014, from http://www.businessdictionary.com/definition/strike.html

5. Lynn, K. (July 1, 2005). *Preparing for labor negotiations: An overview.* Retrieved October 27, 2014, from http://www.hr.com/SITEFORUM?&t=/Default/gateway&i=1116423256281&application=story&active=no&ParentID=1119278060437&StoryID=1119642219296&xref=http%3A//www.google.com/url%3Fsa%3Dt%26rct%3Dj%26q%3D%26esrc%3Ds%26source%3Dweb%26cd%3D10%26ved%3D0CIABEBYwCQ%26url%3Dhttp%253A%252F%252Fwww.hr.com%252Fhr%252Fcommunities%252Flabor_relations%252Fpreparing_for_labor_negotiations__an_overview_eng.html%26ei%3Du04JU5acHsnroASwxoH4AQ%26usg%3DAFQjCNE5NMy19y5QPUTbP7Bm_QkXLOq6ng%26sig2%3DmX9a66xfnve5pXeGhtApkw%26bvm%3Dbv.61725948%2Cd.cGU

6. Canadian Professional Management Services. *Union contract negotiations.* Retrieved October 27, 2014, from https://www.cpmsnational.com/programs/program-content/union-contract-negotiations#.UwlYiIWn5V8

Case Studies

CASE STUDY 1

Barefoot Beach Resort

The Barefoot Beach Resort has just completed a new wing that includes an additional 150 guest rooms and 40,000 square feet of event space. This brings the total number of guest rooms at the resort to 650 and the event space to 80,000 square feet. The resort has been recruiting and training new staff for three weeks in anticipation of the grand opening celebrating the new facilities. They failed to reach their target number for new hires by a wide margin. In fact they only hired about half of the projected number of staff needed with the new facilities and projected increased guest count through-out the property.

The Barefoot Beach Resort has always faced a challenge in recruiting and hiring personnel because they are located on an Island that is a 51/2 hour flight from the closest continent. The labor pool on the island has always been limited but it has become even tighter in the last 18 months because all the businesses on the island are expanding. There little piece of heaven has been discovered in a big way! The staffing situation has been intensified by a push by mainland unions to unionize the hotel and restaurants on the island.

The Barefoot Beach Resort is a family owned business. The owners believe they deal fairly with their employees. The success of the union in gaining the support and ultimately being established at a number of the corporately owned hotels and restaurants has created a dilemma for the owners. The wages established in the unionized properties are considerably higher than what the Barefoot Beach Resort is currently paying. Additionally, the unionized properties are now providing both paid vacation and paid sick leave. The owners believe that raising wages and providing paid vacation and sick leave will put them out of business. Their existing clientele has proven in the past to be extremely price sensitive. When prices increased in the past there was an immediate decline in business which had to be overcome. The owners fear that the new debt service they have taken on with the expansion coupled with the anticipated decline in existing business if they increase labor cost and therefore prices will put them out of business.

Today preparation for the grand opening began and all staff were informed that they will need to work overtime and will, at times, be assigned to work outside their current job description in order to complete preparations on time because of the shortage of staff. A group of employees met this afternoon with the owners and expressed their dissatisfaction with the work and amount of work they were being asked to complete. Additionally they brought up wages and benefits. It was suggested by the employees that if something did not change there could be a work stoppage in some form, such as a mysteriously localized flu epidemic among the Barefoot Beach Resort staff. After meeting with the owners the group also met with union representatives from other hotels and restaurants to get information about establishing a union at the Barefoot Beach Resort.

Case Study Analysis Questions

- What are the factors that the owners of the Barefoot Beach Resort must consider as they work to resolve the current situation? List a minimum of five.
- Taking into consideration the factors you listed above what options for action do the owners have to resolve the current situation?
- Legally what can the owners do to stop the unionization of their property?

CASE STUDY 2

Bill & Jean's Restaurant

Mother's Day is Bill & Jean's Restaurant's busiest day of the year. The restaurant has seating for 350 guests. On a normal Sunday the restaurant will serve a total of 1200 guests. Five years ago the original owners of Bill & Jean's Restaurant, Bill and Jean, decided to try something different on Mother's Day. On Mother's Day the restaurant converted to all buffet service. The Mother's Day buffets were an instant success and have been continued every year with the number of guests served increasing every year. Bill & Jean's is well known for its elaborate Mother's Day breakfast, brunch and dinner buffet.

The Mother's Day buffet also becomes something looked forward to by all of the restaurant's staff. A tradition had been established the first year when Bill and Jean invited the immediate family members of all staff to be their guests for the breakfast buffet. A staggered schedule was even established that allowed the staff member to have 45 minutes to eat with their family.

Last year between 8am and 8pm the restaurant served 2800 guests, 50 of which were staff and their family members, up from 2550 the previous year. Bill and Jean decided to retire shortly after Mother's day last year and sold the restaurant. The goal of the new owners is to increase the number of paying guests by fifteen percent this year for a total of 3048 paying guests. They have reviewed the previous year's Mother's Day sales and profitability. It is clear to them that the impact of the free meals for the staff member's families on profitability and extra labor cost for the special scheduling has to be stopped. The cost is just too high.

The key to success on Mother's Day at Bill & Jean's has always been planning and execution of the plan grounded in a foundation of teamwork. Planning for the buffets began the week after Mother's Day. Bill and Jean had started the planning process with the Mother's Day team (better known as the MDT) of the managers and chef before leaving. After their departure the new owners, Ron and Jeff, took over the planning personally. They quickly made it known to the previous members of the MDT that there would be no "family comps or staff member eating with family" on the upcoming Mother's Day.

Ron and Jeff know that too succeed in their goal on Mother's Day the level of teamwork throughout the restaurant must be high. They are 1 month away from the big day and worried. Everything they have tried to maintain and increase the level of teamwork has failed. The staff just does not seem to have any enthusiasm for either the day-to-day business or the upcoming "big day." A number of staff members have indicated that they are not willing to work overtime to do prep for or on Mother's Day. Ron and Jeff have even heard rumors that members of the management team, including the chef, are looking at jobs with other restaurants.

Based on what you have learned from previous chapters and the content of this chapter answer the following questions.

Case Study Analysis Questions

- What is the overall reason for the challenges occurring in Bill & Jean's Restaurant?
- What are the primary fundamental causes for the challenges occurring in Bill & Jean's Restaurant?
- What specific steps could have been taken to avoid the current situation occurring in Bill & Jean's Restaurant?

CASE STUDY 3

C&L Restaurant #32

The C & L Restaurant chain has a proud history. It was started in 2004 by two brothers, Cecil and Leicle with one restaurant and has grown to 75 locations in a tri-state area. The restaurant is a fast-casual restaurant with an extensive menu of scratch, speed scratch and convenience items where guests come for breakfast, lunch, or dinner. C&L restaurants pride themselves on a consistently high level of customer satisfaction and repeat customers.

Miguel Ortiz, the general manager of store #32 is concerned. He has received increasing numbers of guest complaints in the past twelve months. The restaurant has been in business in this location for ten years. There has been very little change in the original menu offerings that have been the corner stone of their success. The staff of the restaurant, both front and back-of-the-house, has been relatively stable during that time. The customer base for the restaurant has not changed and they still seem to be drawing their regular crowd. The customers are complaining about both the quality of the food and the service. Miguel is concerned that if the level and severity of complaints continue the business will be impacted.

Miguel has brought his concern to the attention of the kitchen manager and the dining room manager. He has directed them to motivate the staff to reduce the number of complaints. The response of both department heads has been to increase supervision of production and service. Additionally each has meet privately with Miguel to explain that the poor performance in the other department head's area is undermining their individual efforts to reduce the number of complaints.

The kitchen and service staff is comprised primarily of individuals with 5 or more years with the restaurant in the same positions. They were well trained when originally hired and have been doing the same job for a number of years. They are generally unconcerned about the guest complaints because when a guest complains they respond quickly to correct the problem.

Case Study Questions

- Is the primary challenge facing Miguel as General Manager one of supervision, management, or leadership?
- What are the primary causes for the challenges occurring at C&L Restaurant #32?
- What role did supervision/management play in the decline at C&L Restaurant #32?
- What role did leadership play in the decline at C&L Restaurant #32?
- What types of supervision/management actions need to take place to stop the decline at C&L Restaurant #32?
- What types of leadership actions need to take place to stop the decline at C&L Restaurant #32?

CASE STUDY 4

Good Night Inn

The Good Night Inn is located on downtown St. Clair. It is operated by the Paul Bryant Group which has a number of other downtown hotels. The company has over 100 full-time employees.

Camilla worked full-time at the Good Night Inn for 18 months as a front desk clerk. She became pregnant and requested from her supervisor a 12-week leave of absence beginning 4 weeks before her due date. The supervisor granted the leave. Camilla left her job as agreed 4 weeks before her due date. The delivery went well and she had a healthy baby girl. Two weeks before her leave was to end she contacted the supervisor and informed him she would be returning to work as agreed. The supervisor informed her that she could come back to work but the only position he had open was a dishwasher position in the hotel's restaurant at a lower wage. Camilla thanked him and hung up.

The Paul Bryant Group received a notice from John Liu, an attorney, that Camilla was filling a lawsuit against the company.

Case Study Analysis Questions

- What basis might Camilla have for a lawsuit against the Paul Bryant Group?
- What specific steps could have been taken to avoid the current situation?
- What, specifically, can be done to overcome the challenges and generate motion in a positive direction for the Paul Bryant Group?

CASE STUDY 5

Grand Adventure Park

The Grand Adventure Park is considered by most employees to be an excellent place to work.

Competition for open positions at the park is fierce. The Grand Adventure Park has extremely stringent selection criteria for all positions but their reputation as one of the best places to work insures that they always have a large pool of applicants for any opening. It is considered to be the finest theme park in the tristate area.

The Grand Adventure Park has 165 staff members and 12 managers. All Grand Adventure Park employees are fulltime. The Grand Adventure Park is open 365 days per year, seven days per week. Staff works a 5–6 day week with a total of forty hours and managers work a 6 day week with a total of 48 hours. Staff members receive one-week paid vacation per year after one year of service and two-week paid vacation per year after five years of service. Managers receive a two-week paid vacation per year after one year of service and three-week paid vacation per year after five years of service.

Additionally, managers receive two personal holidays per year. Employees also earn sick-leave at the rate of ½ day per month after one year of service.

The Grand Adventure Park management believes that outstanding performance should be recognized and rewarded. Employees earn performance recognition points toward involvement in an annual cultural experience trip and participation in the trip does count toward the staff member or managers regular vacation time. Last year's trip was to Peru and the six staff members and five managers who went on the trip became a developmental team for a new Peru themed attraction for the next year. Performance recognition points also apply to other performance recognition rewards such as gift cards to local attractions and movie tickets which are awarded annually.

Performance recognition points are awarded by managers and department heads for outstanding performance based on criteria developed by each department head. Managers are automatically included in a trip every other year. Managers do not participate in the other performance recognition awards. Managers receive a quarterly cash bonus if financial targets are achieved.

The Grand Adventure Park has an established method for the scheduling of vacation days. The minimum vacation time that can be used at one time is one week and the maximum is two weeks. Vacation scheduling is managed within each department. The calendar clearly shows the number of employees that may be on vacation at the same time during each week of the year. Grand Adventure Park treats holidays such as Christmas, Thanksgiving, Rosh Hashanah, and July 4th the same as any other day in the year.

The Maintenance Division which has three departments, grounds, attractions, facilities, has always based vacation scheduling on seniority. Beginning the first week in September a vacation calendar is circulated in each department according to seniority. The attractions department in the Maintenance Division has fourteen full-time attraction engineers. Five of the full-time attraction engineers have been with the park for more than seven years each. For the past three years the five attraction engineers with the greatest seniority have selected vacation dates that included the major holidays. The other staff in the attractions department had no opportunity to select holiday dates as part of their vacation dates and resentment has steadily grown in the past few years over the scheduling of vacations.

Leslie, an attraction engineer, has been with Grand Adventure Park for eighteen months. Leslie was recognized for her outstanding performance and was one of the six staff members that were selected to travel to Peru this year. Leslie mentioned the vacation scheduling to James, one of the five managers, during the trip to Peru. She stated that she was considering leaving Grand Adventure Park because she considered the scheduling of vacations in the Attractions Department to be unfair and inequitable. She also indicated that there were other team members in the Attractions Department looking for positions elsewhere because of the vacation scheduling for the department.

James asked each of the other five staff members on the trip, 1 from the Attractions, 2 from the Guest Service Department and 2 from the Sales Department, how they felt about the scheduling of vacations in their department. All of the staff members indicated that seniority was the basis for scheduling and they felt it created inequities and discontent. All of the staff members stated that they felt the system was designed to reward longevity not performance.

James organized an open discussion of the issue with the other four managers and all of the staff members during the trip. The five managers returned from the trip convinced that the general manager, who was not present on the trip, needed to address the issue of vacation scheduling to avoid losing valuable staff members.

Case Study Analysis Questions

As the human resource manager of the Grand Adventure Park you are tasked by the general manager to look into this issue and report the following:

- What is/are the primary and secondary issue/s?
  - Primary:
  - Secondary:
- Should something be done short-term to address the issue/s.
- What should and can be done long-term to address the issue/s.
- As the companies human resource professional you have always been a major supporter of the "performance recognition" program. The general manager, in light of the recent issues, has asked if you think the program should continue. What is your recommendation and why?

CASE STUDY 6

L&J Cafeteria

Leon had been the dishwasher for the L&J Cafeteria since before it had been the L&J Cafeteria. The L&J had originally had been a "Wilderness Café." Leon was the first dishwasher hired at the "Wilderness Café." When the L&J Company bought the property, he was asked to stay on. No one seemed to know exactly how old Leon was, but he was thought to be about 60. His original application was lost in the buyout, and a new one had never been completed since his payroll records were in good order. If he had any family, the management or staff did not know them. Leon could barely read and write. He could, however, wash pots and pans at an amazing rate.

Leon had always been a minimum wage hourly employee. The only raises that Leon had received in his long history with L&J and Wilderness were the increases in minimum wage. Leon's schedule had always been to work a split-shift from 11:00 A.M. to 2:00 P.M. and 6:00 P.M. to 9:00 P.M. Monday through Saturday, 36 hours per week.

Part-time L&J employees received no benefits. A full-time employee was someone that worked 38 or more hours per week. L&J had no full-time employees other than managers. Only full-time employees were provided with a meal. All other employees paid half-price for all food. Water, coffee, and tea were free to all employees. Employees paid half-price for any other beverages. The level of pilferage and theft at the L&J Cafeteria was a constant challenge for managers. There had been four general managers in the property in the past 14 months.

When the district manager was visiting the property he caught Leon eating a piece of fried chicken in the pot and pan room. He informed the general manager that Leon had stolen the food and that he was to be fired. The general manager stated that Leon had not stolen the chicken. He stated that he had given Leon the piece of chicken, and a soft drink the district manager had not noticed, as a reward for his hard work. The district manager expressed concern about the precedent that would be set by giving free food to employees. He told the general manager he would have to pay for the items himself. The general manager paid for the items as instructed.

The general manager submitted his notice the following week.

Case Study Analysis Questions

- Why did the general manager quit and why is his quitting significant?
- Are the company's personnel policies creating a positive work environment? Justify your answer.
- What specific steps can be taken to improve management retention?
- What, specifically, can be done to generate motion in a more positive direction at the L&J Cafeteria?

CASE STUDY 7

Naples by the Sea Resort

Naples by the Sea Resort's personnel policies require that all personnel be given a formal performance evaluation each year. Lucian Salome, Front Desk Manager, feels it is best to do all performance evaluation at the same time so January 15th of each year he begins doing employee evaluation. To complete the evaluations he meets with two employees each day for three weeks. This year he has scheduled a full 15 minutes for each meeting.

Lucian completes the evaluation form provided by Human Resources for each employee prior to the meeting. Occasionally he refers to the employee's personnel file if he remembers that there has been an incident involving the employee. Generally he depends on his excellent memory to complete the form. Since the form has a graphic rating scale Lucian rarely makes written comments about the employee's performance unless he remembers something exceptional about the staff member.

Lucian feels strongly that if employees succeed in retaining their position at Naples by the Sea their work has to be satisfactory so most employees receive a satisfactory rating in each category every year. Lucian also feels that the evaluations really have little purpose other than to comply with company policy. He has been doing performance evaluations for the front desk staff every year for the six years he has been at Naples by the Sea and he has not seen any changes result from the evaluations. He does not expect the results to be any different this year. Lucian does consider the annual meeting with each employee to be an opportunity to ask how their family is doing and give them a pat on the back.

Case Study Analysis Questions

- Do you believe that the annual performance evaluation of staff at the Naples by the Sea Resort contributes to growth and improvement of the individual or the operation? Explain your answer including the following:

- What is the overall reason you believe the annual performance evaluation does or does not contribute to growth and improvement.
- List in priority order what you envision will be the long-term outcome of Mr. Salome's performance evaluation technique and state what in the technique is the primary cause of each.
- List three specific steps that Mr. Salome must take in the future to either insure the continuation of a positive result of the process or to change the process to achieve a positive result.

CASE STUDY 8

Prairie View Country Club

Prairie View Country Club is located in a city of 35,000. Metro Oil, the city's largest employer, dominates the city's economy and the economic well-being of the club. Metro Oil is one of the largest oil companies in the world and Prairie View is the home of Metro Oil's International headquarters. Metro Oil is generous in its support of the club because the "Club" is the only place in the city that they can "properly" entertain the individuals from around the world that visit the company on a daily basis. The reason for the large membership is the number of members that hold memberships by virtue of their position with Metro Oil.

The executives of Metro Oil, many of who are on the Club's Executive Board, and all of who are club members, have begun expressing their dissatisfaction with the food served at the club. These individuals, as do most of the club's members, regularly travel the nation and the world on behalf of Metro Oil. Through their travels they are exposed to many cuisines and trends in cuisine. They have well developed palates and enjoy the variety and change they experience when traveling. This has presented an ongoing challenge for the management of the club. The club has maintained a reputation for high quality food that is well prepared for many years with its long-standing menu of steaks, chops, local freshwater fish and traditional local dishes. Management's, including the chef's, efforts over the years to change the menu has been frustrated by the lack of trained personnel in the local area and the inability to attract trained culinarians to Prairie View. The club has consistently offered above average wages to attract individuals from outside the area, but the lack of a career path has still kept them from attracting trained, skilled culinarians.

The Executive Board in its last meeting informed the General Manager and Chef that they wanted changes made in the menu and they wanted it accomplished within six months or they would look at finding a new management team for the club. The General Manager and Chef immediately worked to develop a plan to make the changes that had been mandated. The first step was, with the approval and support of the Board, the General Manager and the Chef did a whirlwind tour of the major culinary pacesetting cities in the United States. In a two-week period they traveled to San Francisco, New

Orleans, Chicago, and New York. They spent two days visiting and eating at the top restaurants in each city. Additionally, they spent an extra day in Chicago, New York and San Francisco consulting with faculty from the prestigious culinary schools in those areas.

The General Manager and Chef utilized the information and experience from their trip to develop a new menu that incorporated different cuisines, new types of dishes and presentations, as well as, new ingredients, but that still contained the most popular of the club's traditional items. The challenge was to train the existing staff to provide the new items to the club members at the same quality level that had always been the hallmark of the Club's food.

The training needed to familiarize the culinary team with the cuisines and products being introduced included their storage and handling, as well as, how to prepare the dishes. An aggressive timeline was developed for the training and it was determined that the culinary team members would be paid for participation in the mandatory training.

The General Manager and Chef knew that the integration of the training into the Club's normal operation was a major challenge. The operation of the kitchen had to continue with no reduction in quality while the training was taking place. The extent of the changes that would take place had not been formally announced and the resistance of the culinary team to change was clearly evident. Many members of the team had already questioned the value of training that would not increase their wages or increase their opportunities for advancement.

Case Study Analysis Questions

As the human resource professional for the club the general manager and chef have come to you with their concerns since you are arranging for the training. They have tasked you with developing a training program that will achieve the desired results without disrupting business or impacting the current level of service and quality of food.

- What recommendations will you make to the general manager and chef?
- What are the top three things you, as the human resource officer, can do to bring a successful conclusion to the process that has been started.

- What are the top three things the general manager can do to bring a successful conclusion to the process that has been started?
- What are the top three things the chef can do to bring a successful conclusion to the process that has been started?
- Success should be measured how in this situation?

CASE STUDY 9

Shady Lane Inn

Marietta was extremely glad that she had been hired as an apprentice at the prestigious Shady Lane Inn. She felt that her successful completion of the three-year apprenticeship in the kitchen would lead to opportunities in the finest restaurants around the country. Marietta had wanted to be a manager ever since she first began to help her Mother in the kitchen. Starting at the age of 12, one of her greatest treats was to prepare food for her family and friends. She was eager to learn the "right way" to prepare food.

Marietta's first day, she reported to General Manager, Mrs. Fulani at 8am and Mrs. Fulani immediately sent her to the Human Resource office to complete paperwork. After she completed the necessary paperwork, one of the Human Resource officers quickly reviewed the benefits package. She was also given an employee handbook and instructed to read it carefully so that she would be familiar with the various company policies. After signing a form acknowledging that she had received a copy of the handbook Marietta was told to report to Chef Terrell. It was 9:30 AM.

Chef Terrell met with Marietta and explained to her that as an apprentice she would be rotated through various areas of the kitchen and would receive training from virtually all the cooks and managers.

He gave her a training manual and training journal. Chef Terrell instructed her to familiarize herself with the manual and to ask her first lead to show her how to keep a record of her training in the journal. He said that he reviewed the journal of each apprentice on a weekly basis. Chef Terrell explained that her first assignment would be the banquet kitchen because it was an excellent place to learn and refine her basic skills. He said she could expect to be in the banquet kitchen for 6–8 weeks. He also told Marietta that generally on Mondays he brought all the apprentices, there were a total of 12, together to discuss how their training was progressing and discuss any concerns they might have.

Chef Terrell escorted Marietta to the banquet kitchen where he introduced her to the banquet chef, Hank. It was 10:15 AM. When Chef Terrell left, Hank told Marietta that he was extremely busy and would meet with her later. He introduced her to two other apprentices, Jim and Gale that were prepping for that evening's banquet. Hank told the apprentices to give Marietta some work to do and told her he would speak to her when things slowed down. Marietta noticed that Jim and Gale gave each other a "Yeah right!" look as Hank walked away.

Gale told Marietta that she could start by peeling and fine dicing fifty pounds of onion. She showed Marietta where the cutting boards were located and where to work. As she walked away she told Marietta "welcome to the grunt squad." Later, when Marietta was about half finished with the onions, Jim told here that it had been decided that the onions needed to be thin sliced rather than diced and that she would need to start over.

He told her to put the diced onion in containers, label it and place in the walk-in refrigerator "because someone would use it for something." It was 11:30 AM. He also told her that before she started cutting onion again they would go get some lunch in the employee dining room. During lunch, Gale and Jim told Marietta all about being an apprentice or as they called it a "grunt" at the Shady Lane Inn. She asked how long they had been at the Inn and they each said four months. She asked why they were still in the banquet kitchen since Chef Terrell had told her she would be their only 4-8 weeks. Jim and Gale said that the training schedule in the manual was rarely followed and that Chef Terrell had never reviewed their training journals. Marietta asked if the schedule and journals were discussed in the Monday meetings and they said there had not been a Monday meeting in three months. Jim and Gale made it clear to Marietta that they were both looking to leave the Inn as soon as they could get another position because they did not feel they were learning anything. They said all they ever did was cut and chop things and sweep and mop floors.

After lunch Marietta started peeling and slicing onions. It was 12:15 PM. Marietta finished peeling and slicing the onions and then cleaned the area where she had been working. Jim then told here to sweep out the store rooms and walk-in refrigerators associated with the banquet kitchen. At 5:30 PM Hank came by and told her that she could leave for the day that he would meet with her at 7:30 AM the next day and give her a work schedule and discuss her duties with her. He asked her what she thought of being part of the team at the Shady Lane Inn and she said, "It's ok, I guess." Hank told Marietta that she better get a more enthusiastic and positive attitude or she would not last long at the Inn.

Case Study Analysis Questions

- What is the overall reason for Marietta's perceived lack of enthusiasm and positive attitude?
- What are the primary causes for Marietta's perceived lack of enthusiasm and positive attitude?
- What role did leadership and supervision/management play in Marietta's perceived lack of enthusiasm and positive attitude?
- What specific steps could have been taken to avoid Marietta's perceived lack of enthusiasm and positive attitude?
- What, specifically, can be done by the Shady Lane Inn to avoid a repeat of Marietta's perceived lack of enthusiasm and positive attitude by future apprentices?

CASE STUDY 10

Shandong House

The Du Restaurant Group began with the Supreme Seafood Restaurant in 1963. In January 1995 the company had 1191 restaurants around the world. These included five hundred and seventy-three Supreme Seafood Restaurants, four hundred and sixty Tuscan Piazza Restaurants and forty-nine Shandong House Restaurants. They were the largest, most successful and most stable restaurant company in the world. On April 10, 1998 Du Restaurant Group shocked Wall Street and the restaurant industry when, without any type of prior announcement, they simultaneously closed all 49 Shandong House properties. On the afternoon of April 10, 1998 the company released the following statement:

"Du Restaurant Group has made the strategic decision to discontinue the Shandong House Restaurant concept. The company has been unable to address recurring challenges in the area of food quality and consistency, service quality and workforce stability."

Du Group had determined during the initial conceptualization of the Shandong House Restaurants that serving authentic Chinese cuisine would be one of the cornerstones of the concept. To achieve this goal Chinese were hired as general managers and the majority of the kitchen staff hired was Chinese. Managers, assistant managers, wait staff and other personnel were not necessarily Chinese.

The management and operation of the Shandong House Restaurants was built on the model that had been used so successfully for the Supreme Seafood and Italian Palace Restaurants. This model recognized the importance of the general manager and other members of the management team but with close control from the corporate office. An operations manual was developed that effectively addressed every eventuality. Managers did not have to guess how to handle most issues; they simply had to refer to the manual. All sales, purchasing and payroll information was forwarded to the corporate office on a daily basis. This information was analyzed and guidance was provided to the management from the corporate office daily regarding the operation. All menu and recipe development was done at the corporate level and then distributed to the properties. Stringent guidelines were in place for the preparation of the food and sanitation in the facility. This tightly controlled model had been very successful for the company for many years. Their experience with 1,000+ restaurants had yielded a wealth of knowledge and insight into the management and operation of restaurants. The model worked well in the first few units that were created close to the corporate offices and initially opened by a team of Chinese and Chinese speaking managers from other Du properties.

Based on the strength of the model and the success of the initial success of the first few properties, the company rapidly expanded the Shandong House Restaurants, building 51 in less than five years. The model did not continue to work. Expansion only compounded the problems that began to appear when the company had to hire individuals from outside the company to be general managers. The new general managers all hand strong management backgrounds in the operation of similar type single-unit restaurants. Since there had never been a chain of this type before, almost none had experience in operation of a chain restaurant. To assist them in the transition to the concept they were put through a well-designed three-month training program to teach them the Du way and culture. This program was used as the starting point for all Du management personnel. Additionally the managers were given one week of intensive training in the operation and systems specific to the Shandong House Restaurants. The training program did not achieve the desired results.

The general managers did not submit their information in a timely fashion, and did not pay attention to the input provided by the corporate office. Shoppers reported major differences in the menu items from one property to another. The sanitation levels in the properties were far below that of the other Du restaurants. Customer traffic at the properties began strongly but slowly crept downward. Guests complained of slow service and the properties food cost percentage were consistently out of line. The regional managers consistently referred to the managers as too entrepreneurial when asked why they could not get control of the properties. One district manager stated, "They act like they own the business and can run it any way they want." The district managers also reported a disruptive level of friction between the front and back of the house. The district managers freely admitted that they had little ability to directly address problems in the back of the house because the majority of the cooks did not have a good command of English and they did not speak any Chinese dialect. All communication was through the general managers in the properties. The communications problem was compounded in the properties that had non-Chinese members in the management teams. These management team members, hired by the corporation and assigned to the property, complained of being excluded from the actual operation of the restaurant by the managers who spoke Chinese. They also reported that they were unable to communicate with the kitchen staff.

The President of Shandong House characterized the speed of service issue as the application of western restaurant management principles to an oriental restaurant operation. He stated that speed of service in the restaurant was directly related to the number of woks in the kitchen. "One wok, one cook, one dish!" A Du Restaurant Group Vice President stated "going from three or four units to 50 was the kiss of death."

Case Study Analysis Questions

- Why did the Shandong House concept fail?
- Narrow your answer above to two major, primary, overriding reasons for the failure?
- Discuss why these reasons. What is so important about them that they could take down a Du concept?
- In your opinion could Du have saved the concept? Justify your answer.

CASE STUDY 11

Shepherd Mountain Hotel

The Rockyhill family has owned the Shepherd Mountain Hotel for over three (3) decades. The Shepherd Mountain Hotel (SMH) is located near the famous Shepherd of the Hills area on a lake in the heart of the Ozarks, located – as mentioned in their website - in the heart of Missouri. The Lake of the Ozarks is the Midwest's premier lake resort destination, offering world-class boating, golfing, shopping and fishing, and a wide variety of lodging, restaurants, state parks, and other recreational activities. According to the website, Lake of the Ozarks vacations are defined by the Lake and its many waterfront accommodations, restaurants, recreational and entertainment venues.

For over 30 years, the Rockyhill family has managed The Shepherd Mountain Hotel, employing family members in management positions headed by the patriarch of the family – John Rockyhill Sr. in the hotel and overall management of SMH, Inc., his wife, Mavis Rockyhill in the kitchen, and John Rockyhill Jr. in front of the house and bar. The Rockyhill Family had established a statewide reputation for clean rooms, along with good food and generous drinks all at a reasonable price.

SMH Business Summary:

- A full service hotel with 90 rooms
- A 120-seat restaurant & bar
- Open for Breakfast, Lunch & Dinner – 7 days a week
- The physical plant is a traditional double loaded slab constructed on the water. Note: The hotel and restaurant are over 50 years old and are in need of a major renovation.

The Present

Two years ago, the Rockyhill Family decided to sell the business as John Jr. (the Rockyhill family's sole heir) had a problem with alcohol and did not want the responsibility of running the family business. Because the hotel and restaurant/bar had an excellent reputation initially there was a lot of buyer interest when the family announced that the SMH was for sale after three decades of family management. Unfortunately, the local economy was still struggling after the last recession, gas prices continued to soar, and revenues and occupancy were trending downward at an alarming rate. Adding to the increasingly desperate situation, Mavis Rockyhill- who had always masterfully managed the back of the house operations for the restaurant - developed health problems of her own and retired from day to day operations leaving her son John, Jr. in charge

Desperate to sell, John Jr. took over all responsibility for the restaurant and bar. He thought he could reverse the downward trend by hiring a group of new, pretty, young college woman, putting them in new skimpy cocktail uniforms, paying them at below the state minimum wage (but augmenting their wages with a bar surcharge on the guest bill which was to be shared equally between the servers and the house.) All bar employees would be hired/recruited from the local community college in order to lower labor costs and also to attract a younger crowd to the operation.

Unfortunately, over the last six months restaurant revenues continued a steep decline. The restaurant also experienced a further drop in their regular customer base and saw their beverage cost in the bar operation soar with a 20% increase in costs over a year ago.

There was a good deal of disagreement among the members of the family management team (father and son) about the direction of the operation and what to do about continued reports of theft and complaints of sexual harassment by the new staff regarding John Jr. that began to surface. In addition, MHV was on the receiving end of a threatened law suit by a 25 year old male student, who was experienced and qualified to serve drinks, but who was not hired because the new uniforms were intended for women exclusively.

John Sr. when confronted with these reports, stated that John Jr. was an alcoholic, but "didn't mean anything" by the occasional 'hug, grab, and squeeze' because he couldn't help himself – after all alcoholism is a disease. After all, they were the ones that choose to go to work wearing a sexy outfit every day. What did they expect? John Sr. was also of the belief that servers were most likely using this issue as a distraction to 'steal them blind' because of John Jr.'s 'good heart but lack of supervisory skills' and wanted to hire "secret shoppers" to find out how and when the theft was occurring.

Case Study Analysis Questions

- Answer the following questions regarding the new wage system introduced by SMH for servers in the bar and restaurant.
  - Were the servers being fairly compensated?
  - Was there a violation of law regarding hourly wage rates?
  - Did the new system act as an incentive to motivate the staff? If not, what would you change?
- How should John Sr. address the issue of allegations of sexual harassment by his son?
- What is the responsibility, if any, of the SMH to John Jr. regarding his purported alcoholism?
- Does the threatened law suit by the 25 year old male student have any merit? If so, what is the basis for his law suit? Are there ways that SMH could shield itself from possible liability?
- What evidentiary weight does testimony from a "secret shopper" have when dealing with allegations of employee theft?

CASE STUDY 12

Stone Lion Hotel and Conference Center

Janet Marsh joined the management team at the Stone Lion Hotel and Conference Center three months ago as executive housekeeper. Brian Small has continued as assistant executive housekeeper. Brian has been working at Stone Lion for six years, working his way up from room attendant. Ms. Marsh believes in empowering her staff. She believes in delegating duties and authority. Ms. Marsh does not believe in micro-managing staff once responsibilities have been delegated. One of Ms. Marsh's first actions as executive housekeeper was to delegate the authority to hire and fire personnel to the assistant executive house-keeper Brian. Her belief was that as assistant executive housekeeper, Brian had a better understanding of the staff's performance and could make more considered judgments regarding their performance.

Today the Stone Lion Human Resource Officer (HRO) informed Ms. Marsh that the number of dismissals and new hires in the house-keeping department has been consistently increasing over the past two months. Additionally, one of the employees recently dismissed has filed a wrongful dismissal charge with the state Labor Board. While preparing to respond to the charge, the HRO met with Brian. The HRO asked Brian why he had fired the individual in question. Brian stated, "The guy's work was sloppy, and he was slow." The HRO asked to see the documentation of the employee's performance, and Brian stated, "The guy was not in the new position long enough to document any-thing. I needed to get rid of him, so I got rid of him."

The HRO informed Ms. Marsh that the employee had been with the Stone Lion for 3 years with no previous history of performance problems. The employee had been placed in the new position by the assistant executive housekeeper two weeks before he was dismissed. The HRO stated it was clear the Stone Lion could not defend the dis-missal. Either the former employee would be reinstated or a settlement amount would be negotiated to avoid further "fallout." The HRO also indicated that after speaking with the assistant executive housekeeper it was clear this was not the only incidence of improper dismissal. Ms. Marsh assured the HRO that he would meet immediately with Brian and "straighten things out."

Case Study Questions

- List the issues must be addressed at the Stone Lion Hotel and Conference Center.
- What is the one overriding factor that has led to the Stone Lion Hotel and Conference Center facing a lawsuit from a dismissed staff member?
- What specific steps could have been taken to avoid the situation that has arisen at the Stone Lion Hotel and Conference Center?
- What role did leadership and supervision/management play in the situation that has arisen at the Stone Lion Hotel and Conference Center?
- What, specifically, can be done to avoid a repeat of the situation that has arisen at the Stone Lion Hotel and Conference Center?

CASE STUDY 13

Summit Resort

The Summit Resort is a boutique Relais & Châteaux property, one of the few in the United States. Summit holds the prestigious designation for both the hotel and the restaurant. The chef, Sandia Chiang, holds the honor of designation as a Relais & Châteaux Grand Chef. Chef Chiang has been the Summit's chef for eighteen months. She gained the Grand Chef status shortly after becoming the Summit's chef. Chef Chiang has increased the quality of the food served and the amount of revenue and profit from food sales in the restaurant. As the reputation of Chef Chiang has grown the occupancy rate of the resort has increased.

The Summit's general manager is Hernando Garcia. Mr. Garcia is very pleased with what Chef Chiang has done with the restaurant and the fact that these changes are also contributing to increased occupancy in the resort. He is also concerned because the improvements in the restaurant are not reflected in the banquet kitchen. He hired Chef Chiang with the understanding that she was the executive chef for the resort not just the restaurant.

Mr. Garcia has observed that Chef Chiang directly supervises preparation of every item served in the restaurant. Chef Chiang personally develops all menus and recipes. She checks and adjusts the flavor of every food item prepared in the restaurant kitchen. Chef Chiang is known for saying, "this is my food, and the quality of every item depends on me."

Mr. Garcia has also observed that Chef Chiang has placed one of the properties two sous chefs, Chef Lee, in charge of banquet food preparation. In the eighteen months that Chef Chiang has been at the Summit Mr. Garcia has only seen her involved in banquet preparation twice, when Chef Lee was ill and when he was on vacation. In both instances she expressed full confidence in Chef Lee's culinary team and made few changes to any item prepared, instead focusing on organizational issues.

The banquet manager has begun to receive complaints from guests that the food served at their function was not what they expected. The comment often heard by the banquet manager is, "The food was good but it was not as good as what I have been served in the restaurant." The banquet manager has brought this situation to the attention of Mr. Garcia, pointing out that they will soon be up for review by Relais & Châteaux.

Case Study Analysis Questions

- What is the challenge that Mr. Garcia must address?
- What are the variables involved in the challenge?
- What should be Mr. Garcia's top three goals in addressing the challenge? List the goals in order of importance with discussion/ justification?
- Develop a plan of action for Mr. Garcia to successfully address the challenge, achieving the goals you previously listed.

Index

internal customer, 9

quality principles, 9–10

TQM. *See* Total quality management (TQM)

Trust and empowerment, 161–162

Turnover rate, 137

Two-factor theory, 155–157

U

Unemployment insurance fund, 80

Union contract

contract negotiation, 219–222

definition, 219

discipline and, 224

grievance resolution, 225

hiring and, 223–224

performance evaluation and, 224

personnel policy development and, 222

record keeping and, 223

Unstructured interviews, 58

V

Verbal criticism, 192–193

Vesting, 83–84

Vision and team development, 175–176

Vocational Rehabilitation Act, 198

Vroom, Victor, 159

W

Wellness programs, 147

Wildcat strike, 37

Workers' compensation, 79

Workplace environment

health and wellness, 144–147

job satisfaction, 136–141

safe work environment, 141–144

World Travel & Tourism Council's (WTTC), 3

Y

Youth wage employee, 38

For Product Safety Concerns and Information please contact our EU
representative GPSR@taylorandfrancis.com
Taylor & Francis Verlag GmbH, Kaufingerstraße 24, 80331 München, Germany

www.ingramcontent.com/pod-product-compliance
Ingram Content Group UK Ltd.
Pitfield, Milton Keynes, MK11 3LW, UK
UKHW011457240425
457818UK00022B/887